CONTESTED CONCEPTS
OF RELIGION

CONTESTED CONCEPTS IN THE STUDY OF RELIGION

A CRITICAL EXPLORATION

Edited by George D. Chryssides and Amy R. Whitehead

BLOOMSBURY ACADEMIC

LONDON • NEW YORK • OXFORD • NEW DELHI • SYDNEY

BLOOMSBURY ACADEMIC
Bloomsbury Publishing Plc
50 Bedford Square, London, WC1B 3DP, UK
1385 Broadway, New York, NY 10018, USA
29 Earlsfort Terrace, Dublin 2, Ireland

BLOOMSBURY, BLOOMSBURY ACADEMIC and the Diana logo are
trademarks of Bloomsbury Publishing Plc

First published in Great Britain 2023

Cover design by Rebecca Heselton

A catalogue record for this book is available from the British Library.

Library of Congress Control Number: 2022933166

ISBN: HB: 978-1-3502-4381-1
        PB: 978-1-3502-4380-4
        ePDF: 978-1-3502-4383-5
        eBook: 978-1-3502-4382-8

Typeset by Integra Software Services Pvt. Ltd.
Printed and bound in Great Britain

To find out more about our authors and books visit www.bloomsbury.com
and sign up for our newsletters.

CONTENTS

Notes on contributors   viii
Acknowledgements   xiv
List of abbreviations   xv

Introduction: What is a contested concept?
George D. Chryssides and Amy R. Whitehead   1

1   **Belief**
    Nicholas Campion   9

2   **Charisma**
    Edward A. Irons   15

3   **Conversion**
    David G. Bromley   21

4   **Cult**
    Benjamin E. Zeller   27

5   **Diaspora**
    Kim Knott   33

6   **Folk religion**
    Marion Bowman   39

7   **Fundamentalism**
    Camille Kaminski Lewis   45

8   **Guru**
    Stephen Jacobs   51

9   **Indigenous religions**
    Graham Harvey   57

10   **Magic**
    Angela Puca   63

Contents

11 **Millennialism**
    Catherine Wessinger   69

12 **Myth**
    Gregory W. Dawes   75

13 **New Age**
    Shai Feraro   81

14 **New religious movements**
    George D. Chryssides   87

15 **Pilgrimage**
    Carole M. Cusack   93

16 **Prophecy**
    George D. Chryssides   99

17 **Religion**
    David Morgan   105

18 **Secularization**
    Titus Hjelm   111

19 **Spirituality**
    Steven J. Sutcliffe   117

20 **Superstition**
    Amy R. Whitehead   123

21 **Syncretism**
    Bettina E. Schmidt   129

22 **Violence**
    Negar Partow   135

23 **World religion**
    Teemu Taira   141

24 **Worship**
    Christina Welch   147

25 Concepts in practice
George D. Chryssides and Amy R. Whitehead   153

References   159
Index   179

CONTRIBUTORS

Marion Bowman is Senior Lecturer in Religious Studies at The Open University UK, and has a background in both Religious Studies and Folklore. She has researched widely on vernacular religion, pilgrimage, Celtic spirituality and material religion, in addition to conducting long- term fieldwork in the town of Glastonbury, on which she has published extensively. She co-edited with Ülo Valk both *Vernacular Religion in Everyday Life: Expressions of Belief* (2012) and *Vernacular Knowledge: Contesting Authority, Expressing Beliefs* (2022); with Simon Coleman *Religion in Cathedrals: Pilgrimage, Place, Heritage, and the Politics of Replication* (2002); and with Dirk Johanssen and Ane Ohrvik *Reframing Pilgrimage in Northern Europe, a Special Issue of NUMEN* (67 (5–6) 2020). Having served as Vice-President, European Association for the Study of Religions, 2014–19, in 2021 she was elected an International Fellow of the American Folklore Society.

David G. Bromley is Founder/Director of the World Religions and Spirituality Project, an international scholarly consortium that collaboratively produces WRSP as an online, academic reference resource. Bromley is author or editor on over twenty books related to the study of religion. He has served in faculty and administrative positions at Virginia Commonwealth University, University of Hartford, University of Texas at Arlington and University of Virginia. He has served as editor of the *Journal for the Social Science of Religion* and president of the Association for the Sociology of Religion.

Nicholas Campion is Associate Professor in Cosmology and Culture at the University of Wales Trinity Saint David. He is Programme Director of the University's MAs in Cultural Astronomy and Astrology, and Ecology and Spirituality. His PhD in the Study of Religions Department at Bath Spa University was on the extent and nature of contemporary belief in astrology (published as *Astrology and Popular Religion in the Modern West: Prophecy, Cosmology and the New Age Movement*, 2012). His other books include *The New Age in the Modern West: Counter-Culture, Utopia and Prophecy from the Late Eighteenth Century to the Present Day* (2015). He is the general editor of the six-volume *Bloomsbury Cultural History of the Universe*.

George D. Chryssides is an Honorary Research Fellow at York St John University (UK), and formerly Head of Religious Studies at the University of Wolverhampton. He studied philosophy and theology at the University of Glasgow, and obtained his DPhil at the University of Oxford. He has written extensively, focusing on new religions, Christianity and methodological issues. His most recent publications include *Jehovah's Witnesses: A New Introduction* (2022), *Jehovah's Witnesses: Continuity and Change*

(2016), *Historical Dictionary of Jehovah's Witnesses* (2nd edn 2019), *Minority Religions in Europe and the Middle East* (2019), *The Insider-Outsider Debate* (co-edited with Stephen E. Gregg, 2019) and *The Bloomsbury Handbook to Studying Christians* (co-edited with Stephen E. Gregg, 2020). He is currently president of the International Society for the Study of New Religions.

Carole M. Cusack is Professor of Religious Studies at the University of Sydney. She trained as a medievalist and her doctorate was published as *Conversion among the Germanic Peoples* (1998). She now researches primarily in contemporary religious trends and Western esotericism. Her books include (with Katharine Buljan) *Anime, Religion and Spirituality: Profane and Sacred Worlds in Contemporary Japan* (2015) and *Invented Religions: Imagination, Fiction and Faith* (2010). She edited (with Alex Norman) *Handbook of New Religions and Cultural Production* (2012) and (with Pavol Kosnáč) *Fiction, Invention and Hyper-reality: From Popular Culture to Religion* (2017).

Gregory W. Dawes is a professor in Religious Studies at the University of Otago, New Zealand. He gained his first graduate degree at the Pontifical Biblical Institute in Rome (1988) before completing PhDs in Biblical Studies (1995) and Philosophy (2007). His earlier work examined the challenges to belief that arose from the historical study of Christian origins. This led him to the study of the relations between science and religion and, more generally, of the various 'modes of thought' found across cultures. His recent works include *Galileo and the Conflict between Religion and Science* (2016), *Religion, Philosophy and Knowledge* (2016) and *Deprovincializing Science and Religion* (2021), the last two of which are devoted to broadening the scope of the philosophical discussion of religion.

Shai Feraro is a Research Associate at the University of Haifa. He also teaches at the Open University of Israel, and serves as Secretary of the Israeli Association for the Study of Religions. Dr Feraro is the author of *Women and Gender Issues in British Paganism, 1945–1990* (2020), and has co-edited *Contemporary Alternative Spiritualities in Israel* (2016) and *Magic and Witchery in the Modern West* (2019).

Graham Harvey is Professor of Religious Studies at The Open University, UK. His research largely concerns 'the new animism', especially in the rituals and protocols through which Indigenous and other communities engage with the larger-than-human world. His recent teaching-related work has involved a focus on foodways and on defining 'religion' as sensual engagement with the world. His publications include *Food, Sex and Strangers: Understanding Religion as Everyday Life* (2013), and *Animism: Respecting the Living World* (2nd edn 2017). He is editor of the Routledge series 'Vitality of Indigenous Religions' and the Equinox series 'Religion and the Senses'.

Titus Hjelm is Professor in the Study of Religion at the University of Helsinki, Finland. Previously he was Reader in Sociology at University College London. His recent publications include *Peter L. Berger and the Sociology of Religion: 50 Years after the Sacred*

Canopy (ed., 2018) in addition to several other books and many journal articles on the sociology of religion.

Edward Irons is a leadership consultant and researcher on religion. He founded the Hong Kong Institute for Culture, Commerce and Religion. He is the editor of the *Encyclopedia of Buddhism* and author of numerous articles on Chinese new religions.

Stephen Jacobs is Senior Lecturer in Media, Religion and Culture at the University of Wolverhampton. His research primarily focuses on the Hindu traditions in the contemporary world. His latest publication is an ethnographic monograph on *The Art of Living Foundation* (2015), a Hindu-derived meditation movement which has centres around the world. He has also published articles and chapters on research ethics, sacred place and the intersection between religion and popular culture. His current research is in a very different field of interest. This research is a Leverhulme funded project on sustainability and environmental communication utilizing the Centre for Alternative Technology in Wales as a case study.

Kim Knott is Professor Emerita at Lancaster University. She was Deputy Director of the Centre for Research and Evidence on Security Threats (2015–20), and Director of the AHRC Diasporas, Migration and Identities Programme (2005–11). In addition to co-editing *Diasporas: Concepts, Intersections, Identities*, with S. McLoughlin (2010), she has published recently in *Ethnic and Racial Studies* (2021), *Behavioural Sciences of Terrorism and Political Aggression* (2021) and *Politics, Religion and Ideology* (2020). She has long-standing research interests in religion, space and place, the 'secular sacred', material religion, and religion, migration and diasporas. She is President of the European Association for the Study of Religions and Chair of the governing board of Inform (Information Network on Religious Movements).

Camille Kaminski Lewis is currently an Assistant Professor in the Department of Communication Studies at Furman University in Greenville, South Carolina. She holds a PhD from Indiana University in Rhetorical Studies with a minor in American Studies. Her book, *Romancing the Difference: Kenneth Burke, Bob Jones University, and the Rhetoric of Religious Fundamentalism* (2017), was a scholarly attempt to stretch the boundaries of both Kenneth Burke's rhetorical theory on tragedy and comedy as well as stretch conservative evangelical's separatist frames. Her second book, *White Nationalism and Faith: Statements and Counter-Statements* (2020), tracks the religious arguments for and against white nationalism in America since the Civil War. She is currently working on a manuscript entitled *Klandamentalism: Dysfunction and Violence in America's Most Romantic Religious Movements*.

David Morgan is Professor of Religious Studies at Duke University. Morgan's scholarship has focused on the history of religious material culture in the modern era. His books include *Visual Piety* (1998), *The Sacred Gaze* (2005), *The Forge of Vision: A Visual History of Modern Christianity* (2015) and *Images at Work: The Material Culture of*

Enchantment (2018). His latest book, *The Thing about Religion: An Introduction to the Material Study of Religions*, appeared in 2021. Morgan co-founded the journal *Material Religion* and served as one of the editors for nearly two decades. He is an elected member of Clare Hall, University of Cambridge.

Negar Partow is Senior Lecturer in the Centre for Defence and Security Studies in Massey University (Te kunenga ki purehuroa), New Zealand. Her research focuses on the dynamics of religion and politics and its impact on human rights and human security. She is the author of *Being an Unbeliever in an Islamic State* (2014), *The Internet, Social Media Networks and Iran's Civil Society* (2014) and *War on Terror and Islamisation of Brunei* (2021). Partow's research extends to the study of human security in international organizations. She is the co-editor of *United Nations Peace Operations in the 21st Century* (2015) and *A Seat at the Table: NZ in the United Nations Security Council, 2015–2016* (2020) and the guest editor of *Women and Security, National Security Journal*, Massey University, March 2021. She received her PhD from Victoria University of Wellington (Te Herenga Waka) and holds two Master's degrees from Iran and New Zealand.

Angela Puca is a lecturer in Philosophy and Religious Studies at Leeds Trinity University, UK, which she joined in 2016. Her research focuses on magic, witchcraft, Paganism, esotericism, shamanism and related currents. The University of Leeds awarded her a PhD in Anthropology of Religion with a thesis on *Indigenous and Trans-cultural Shamanism in Italy*. Author of several peer-reviewed publications and editor of the forthcoming *Pagan Religions in Five Minutes*, she hopes to bridge the gap between academia and the communities of magic practitioners by delivering related scholarly content on her YouTube channel 'Angela's Symposium'.

Bettina E. Schmidt is Professor in the Study of Religions and Anthropology of Religion at the University of Wales Trinity Saint David, UK. Her main areas of research interests are Latin American and Caribbean religions, identity and well-being. Her academic interests include religious experience, anthropology of religion, diaspora and medical anthropology. Among her most important publications are *Spirit and Trance in Brazil: An Anthropology of Religious Experiences* (2016), *Caribbean Diaspora in the USA: Diversity of Caribbean Religions in New York City* (2008), *Handbook of Contemporary Brazilian Religions* (edited with Steven Engler, 2016) and *Spirituality and Wellbeing: Interdisciplinary Approaches to the Study of Religious Experience and Health* (edited with Jeff Leonardi, 2020).

Steven J. Sutcliffe is Senior Lecturer in the Study of Religion at the University of Edinburgh. He studies new, alternative and 'post-Christian' forms of religion in late modernity, and the post-1960s history of the Study of Religion/s as an academic discipline. He is author of *Children of the New Age: A History of Spiritual Practices* (2003), editor of *Religion: Empirical Studies* (2004), co-editor (with Carole Cusack) of *The Problem of*

Invented Religions (2016), co-editor (with Ingvild Sælid Gilhus) of *New Age Spirituality: Rethinking Religion* (2014) and co-editor (with Marion Bowman) of *Beyond New Age: Exploring Alternative Spirituality* (2000).

Teemu Taira is Senior Lecturer in the Study of Religion, University of Helsinki. He is the author of six books, including *Media Portrayals of Religion and the Secular Sacred* (2013, co-authored with Kim Knott and Elizabeth Poole) and *Taking 'Religion' Seriously: Essays on the Discursive Study of Religion* (2022).

Christina Welch is a Reader and inter-disciplinary researcher in the study of religions at the University of Winchester, where she also leads a Masters' programme in the study of death, religion and culture by distance learning. She gained her AHRB-funded doctorate from the University of Southampton in 2005. Her research interests are largely in the intersections of religion and material/visual culture (especially in relation to death). Recently she has been involved in community heritage in the Caribbean, and she is currently decolonizing archives about the island of St Vincent. Christina is neurodiverse and registered disabled with specific learning differences.

Catherine Wessinger is the Rev. H. James Yamauchi, S. J. Professor of the History of Religions at Loyola University New Orleans. She is author of *How the Millennium Comes Violently: From Jonestown to Heaven's Gate* (2000), editor of *Millennialism, Persecution, and Violence: Historical Cases* (2000) and editor of *The Oxford Handbook of Millennialism* (2011). She is co-general editor of *Nova Religio: The Journal of Alternative and Emergent Religions*. Based on interviews, she edited autobiographies for three Branch Davidian survivors: Bonnie Haldeman, David Koresh's mother (2007), Sheila Martin (2009) and Clive Doyle (2012). Her oral history project relating to the Branch Davidian case has been continued in videos available on her YouTube channel. Her most recent publication on the Branch Davidian case, based on research in internal FBI documents, is a chapter titled 'The FBI's "Cult War" against the Branch Davidians' (2017) in the edited volume *The FBI and Religion.*

Amy R. Whitehead is Senior Lecturer in Social Anthropology at Massey University in Aotearoa, New Zealand. An Anthropologist of Religion/Religious Studies scholar, she is the author of *Religious Statues and Personhood: Testing the Role of Materiality* (2013), as well as several journal articles and chapters for edited volumes. Amy's primary areas of research concern the material and performance cultures of religions, the 'turn to things' in the study of religions, the development of new approaches to animism and 'the fetish', ritual studies and Earth Traditions (Paganisms, Goddess movements). She has also co-edited volumes, including *Indigenous Religions: Critical Concepts for Religious Studies* (2018) with Graham Harvey, and *Religion and Touch* (2021) with Christina Welch, and is the managing series editor for Bloomsbury Studies in Material Religion.

Benjamin E. Zeller is Associate Professor and Chair of Religion at Lake Forest College (Chicago). He researches religious currents that are new or alternative, including new religions, the religious engagement with science and the quasi-religious relationship people have with food. He is author of *Heaven's Gate: America's UFO Religion Prophets and Protons: New Religious Movements and Science in Late Twentieth-Century America*, editor of *Handbook of UFO Religions* and co-editor of *Religion, Food, and Eating in North America* and *The Bloomsbury Companion to New Religious Movements*. He also designed the Sacred Chicago project, a digitalization project involving Chicago's sacred spaces. He holds a PhD from the University of North Carolina and a Masters of Theological Studies from Harvard University. He is co-general editor of *Nova Religio: The Journal of Alternative and Emergent Religions*.

ACKNOWLEDGEMENTS

The editors would like to thank the many colleagues who have helped to shape the material in this volume. Special thanks to the British Association for the Study of Religions (BASR) for scheduling two sessions at the 2021 Annual Conference, in which several contributors summarized their chapters and elicited useful comment.

Amy R. Whitehead wishes to thank Massey University for allowing her a sabbatical, together with funding, which was used in part to co-edit this volume.

Both editors must express their thanks to Bloomsbury's editorial staff, who are always a pleasure to work with. We would particularly like to mention Lalle Pursglove, Stuart Hay and Lily McMahon for support and encouragement, and promptness in answering queries. Thanks also are due to Margaret Wilkins for compiling the index.

Biblical quotations in the text are from the New International Version (UK), unless otherwise stated. Copyright © 1979, 1984, 2011 Biblica. Used by permission of Hodder & Stoughton Ltd, a Hachette UK company.

ABBREVIATIONS

AAR	*American Academy of Religion*
ATRs	*African Traditional Religions*
BASR	*British Association for the Study of Religions*
BCE	*Before Common Era*
CE	*Common Era*
CESNUR	*Center for Studies on New Religions*
CCP	*Chinese Communist Party*
FAIR	*Family Action Information and Rescue*
INREL	*Indigenous Religion(s): Local Grounds, Global Networks*
INSS	*International Network for the Study of Spirituality*
ISKCON	*International Society for Krishna Consciousness*
KJV	*King James Version*
LGBTQ+	*Lesbian, Gay, Bisexual, Transgender, Queer/Questioning + Others*
NHS	*National Health Service (UK)*
NRM	*New Religious Movement*
NRSV	*New Revised Standard Version [of the Bible]*
PRINERM	*Primal New Religious Movement*
RCT	*Rational Choice Theory (of religion)*
RE	*Religious Education*
WCC	*World Council of Churches*
WICCA	*Women's Intersectional Cultural and Creative Association*
W.I.T.C.H.	*Women's International Terrorist Conspiracy from Hell*
WRP	*World Religions Paradigm*

INTRODUCTION: WHAT IS A CONTESTED CONCEPT?

George D. Chryssides and Amy R. Whitehead

The idea for this volume began in 2019, when a number of scholars attended a conference organized in Torino by CESNUR (Center for Studies in New Religions). After the proceedings had finished, we were taken on a field trip which included a small monastic community called Church Universal Soul (Anima Universale). The organization is Roman Catholic in origin, but became controversial with the Roman Catholic hierarchy on account of its claims of visions, miraculous healings and an interest in oriental religious ideas such as reincarnation. Its founder Roberto Casarin is called Swami Roberto, and although most of its furniture and artefacts are plainly Christian, one can also find symbols of other faiths, including a Buddha statue and Zen garden. In his presentation to the invited audience, however, Swami Roberto explained that his community aims to transcend denominational barriers, but at the same time he stated that they were not syncretistic.

It was this last claim that started a subsequent discussion between George Chryssides and Carole Cusack. While we agreed that the claim was puzzling, we also acknowledged that the concept of syncretism itself was problematic. Although different religious and spiritual concepts can interact, scholars often use the term 'syncretism' as if it implied that there were originally 'pure' versions of religion that somehow became mixed. For example, when it is sometimes said that Zen is a blend of Buddhism and Daoism, it is as if there once were two unadulterated versions of these so-called religions, which religious innovators like Bodhidharma wove together. But what would pure authentic Daoism be like? Is it what one finds in Lao Tzu's philosophical writings, or is it the worship of the pantheon of deities that one finds in a Chinese temple?

Our discussion continued by noting that syncretism was not the only problematic concept used by scholars of religion. The term 'religion' itself is problematic, as are concepts like folk religion, charisma, leadership, spirituality, guru and many more. By the end of the day, we had identified at least two dozen problematic concepts, and after returning home the list had grown to around fifty.

Terms can be problematic for a variety of reasons. Some can be pejorative, such as 'cult' – a word typically used by opponents of certain spiritual and other groups – and 'folk religion', which might imply that popular spiritual practice is inferior to scholarly erudition. Other terms can be vague: what exactly do we mean when we describe a spiritual leader as 'charismatic', and what precisely are we claiming when we categorize a piece of narrative as 'myth'? Vocabulary can be used unreflectively: some scholars, who should know better, continue to talk about a 'fastest-growing religion', without considering how one measures growth, or what time frame they are considering. 'Violence' – which has become a popular subject in the wake of religious 'extremism' (itself a problematic concept) – has been applied to a group such as Heaven's Gate, whose members collectively committed suicide in 1997, despite the fact that the group was actually very peaceful. Does the concept of violence encompass any form of unnatural death, or should it be confined to the deliberate infliction of physical harm? Some people speak of emotional violence, or use the term to include maltreatment of vulnerable groups, such as women and children. We even talk about interpretations of language as doing violence to an expression's meaning. Even attempts to reform our vocabulary can create their own problems: the term 'new religious movement' continues to lack clear content, and is applied to spiritual and other groups that are neither new, religious or movements.

What this book is not

At the early stages of preparing this volume, one colleague described the project as 'another keywords book'. This it most certainly is not. A 'keywords' book is one that defines basic terms for the beginner, who may be unfamiliar with terms like eschatology, phenomenology, emic and etic, soteriology, among others. This kind of book defines concepts for those who simply do not know what they mean. By contrast, our current project takes the discussion up several levels. Contesting concepts means laying down challenges that critically explore the variety of uses and misuses that certain terms invite, and why. The target reader for this book, then, is one who is already familiar with such concepts, but recognizes the problems that arise with their use. For example, most readers will have come across the term 'world religion', but perhaps have used it unreflectively, or not recognized the complexity of the problems involved with the term. In short, a 'keywords' book provides answers for a novice reader, while this anthology questions some of the answers that more experienced students and scholars may think they have.

We have also made the deliberate choice not to commission chapters on wider concepts such as 'gender' and 'race'. We recognize the necessity of debate on these areas, and there is much important scholarship that has been done on religion and feminism, on issues such as the assignation of gender to God, and black theology. However, such discussion generates issues, and not clarification of concepts, and matters of gender, sexual orientation, ethnicity and race extend considerably beyond the study of religion. Of course, concepts and issues are intertwined, and how we use concepts – religious or otherwise – will affect those wider debates that go beyond concept clarification. It is necessary to keep the focus of this volume within manageable proportions.

A keywords book would have allowed fairly swift definitions and the inclusion of a greater number of concepts. Since each of the concepts that feature in this volume merits detailed discussion, the editors decided to confine themselves to two dozen. The criteria for selection were the extent to which the concepts are used, and the extent to which they are problematic. As with any anthology of this kind, no doubt critics will not always agree with our selection; there is certainly more to be said on these topics, and on many others not included here. This book is not complete, nor does it pretend to be. We hope, however, that this volume will inspire and generate further debate beyond these pages.

Each of the contributors was given a topic related to their expertise, and invited to address five questions, as they thought appropriate. These were:

1. Why is this concept problematic?
2. What are the origins of the concept?
3. How is it used or misused, and by whom?
4. Is it still a legitimate concept in the study of religion and, if so, what are its legitimate uses?
5. Are there other concepts that are preferable when writing on religion?

The responses to these questions exceeded our expectations, the results of which have resulted in a volume that not only illuminates the perspectives of a range of international scholars, but opens up debates in a way that will help us to rethink our scholarly usages of certain contested terms.

Introducing the chapters

In many anthologies it is the editors' practice to introduce each chapter sequentially. We do not think this is necessary in this volume: each chapter speaks for itself in analysing the problematic concept in the study of religion. However, a brief example will convey the kind of problems with which the contributors are dealing, and how they impinge on how we write about religion. We have chosen to take Islam as a brief case study here, since it has received disproportionately little treatment in the chapters that follow.

Many accounts of Islam in Western literature suggest that Muhammad's teachings were influenced by the geographical position of Mecca, being the meeting point of various trade routes where Muhammad would encounter Christians, Jews and possibly Zoroastrians, and that their various conversations about their faiths became blended into Islamic teachings (Ling 1968: 211–12; Hinnells 1978: 36–8). Would it therefore be justifiable to use the word 'syncretism' in connection with Islam? Certainly the majority of Muslims would reject any such description, insisting that Muhammad was declaring a divine, not a human message, reciting precisely what he was instructed by the Angel Gabriel. Muhammad is therefore regarded as God's final prophet, yet not primarily in the sense of someone who predicts future events, although Muhammad's message included an eschatological message of resurrection and judgement (Saleh 2019).

In scholarly discussion, Islam is treated as a religion in its own right, often classified as a 'world religion'. However, both the descriptions 'religion' and 'world religion' have their problems. The World Religions Paradigm (WRP) has come under a cloud (see Chapter 23), and the descriptor 'religion' has been called into question both from inside and outside the faith. One Muslim has stated, 'We don't refer to Islam as a religion. It's a way of life' (Bowker 1983: 47). Perhaps this informant was contrasting Islam with the Christian faith, which may appear to involve little more than going to church on Sunday, with no distinctive lifestyle ensuing; if this is what he meant, then it raises the question of whether concepts like religion and worship reflect the dominant religion which has characterized Western scholarship in the past. Conversely, some opponents of Islam wish to deprive it of a religious identity on the grounds that they believe it is violent, and unduly political. Following the massacres in two mosques in Christchurch, New Zealand, on 15 March 2019, the US national security adviser Michael Flynn claimed that the Muslims themselves were real cause of the bloodshed, since Islam was a violent political movement. He stated that 'Islam is a political ideology [that] hides behind the notion of it being a religion' (Uddin 2019). Of course, the majority of Muslims would wish to point out that the very name Islam means 'peace' or 'submission', and would deplore the acts of terrorism perpetrated by the Taliban. But is violence incompatible with religion, or is religion inherently violent, as one could argue if one extended the concept of violence to include the violation of human rights on the grounds of gender, sexual orientation and ethnicity?

How a concept is handled by each scholar in this volume will inevitably reveal a certain set of biases. Biases can result from contributors' use of their fieldwork sites as examples of how certain concepts can be used, from their own cultural, educational or religious (or non-religious) background. No doubt the editors have their own biases which are reflected in their choice of topics and the religious communities with which they have become familiar. It should therefore be noted that not all religions have been given equal coverage in the chapters in this book, nor could they be. Islam is not the only religion that has been underrepresented in the book. Readers may feel that Sikhism, Shinto, Judaism, Contemporary Paganism, among others, should have received greater coverage. Our aim, however, is not to provide coverage of a wide spectrum of the world's religions, and indeed one might argue about what should constitute appropriate representation (see Chapter 23). The examples are therefore more an indication of the fields in which the contributors are working, than a deliberate omission.

The anthology aims rather to provide an incentive to scholars in the field to reflectively examine their use of the concepts under discussion, as well as other examples of problematic vocabulary, and to continue to problematize them. To illustrate how this might be achieved, we offer a further case study example in Chapter 25 that demonstrates how some of the concepts in this volume can be approached, problematized and practically used as exploratory tools in relation to a specific case study event. We hope this final chapter will be useful for students and more advanced scholars alike to assess how we might critically contest concepts in the study of religions.

Deconstruction or demolition?

The study of religion is currently undergoing a revolution, with many of its key concepts being challenged or reappraised. In some instances, however, we believe that some colleagues have equated deconstruction with demolition, and risk eroding much of the subject matter of the study of religion. While many scholars unreflectively continue to use problematic terms without sufficient reflection, there are those who seem to wish to demolish any concept that appears to raise issues. Take, for example, the term 'Abrahamic', on which some scholars have imposed a taboo (Hughes 2012), but which is surely no more than convenient shorthand for referring collectively to Judaism, Christianity and Islam. Allegedly, the term is patronizing – although it is difficult to see how, or who is supposedly patronizing whom – and one colleague has argued against the term by contending, quite erroneously, that Christianity has little to do with Abraham.

Even the term 'religion' has come under a cloud, with several scholars suggesting that the term should be discarded, for a variety of reasons. Some have pointed out the difficulty of defining the term. Indeed, James H. Leuba's *A Psychological Study of Religion* (1912) is often cited as listing fifty different ways in which the word can be defined. Other scholars have posited that there are as many definitions of religion as there are scholars who are attempting to define it. J. Z. Smith's discussion in an article entitled 'Religion, Religions, Religious' argues that the term is a term of uncertain origin, which has little or no place as emic category in the Christian religion, and inappropriately applied to other systems of ritual in other parts of the world. Smith wrote that '"Religion" is not a native term: it is a term created by scholars for their intellectual purposes and therefore is theirs to define' (Smith 1998: 281); it 'has no existence apart from the academy' (Smith 1982: xi).

This does not, however, account for the fact that religious people identify as just that: religious. In fact, the King James version of the Bible mentions the word 'religion' five times; and Smith himself tells us that the term had usage in both Roman and early Christian Latin where the 'noun forms *religio/religiones* and, most especially, the adjectival *religiosus* and the adverbial *religiose* were cultic terms referring primarily to the careful performance of ritual obligations' (Smith 1998: 269). Consequently, the term has had value as an emic category for several centuries. But Smith's point is clear: 'religion', as an academic term, reflects a problem of location, the solution for which is to frame the term as a scholarly invention and understand it as a fluid category that reflects ongoing and continually negotiated processes (instead of one universal category). For this reason, he suggests 'religions' (plural) is a better reflection of cross-cultural/religious analysis so that the word does not become unduly loaded with colonial notions of 'truth' and 'authenticity'.

Like Smith's treatment of 'religion', a number of the terms contested in this book raise questions about whether or how they can be effectively used in relation to non-Western traditions. How effectively can the word 'religion' be applied to a variety of Indian religious traditions that were further blanketed by British colonialists with the term 'Hinduism'? How is the concept of religion used in reference to Indigenous traditions? Or how does the concept of worship translate into Buddhist practice when the term worship has traditionally been associated with 'houses of God'? And what about expressions of devotion in secular buildings that were never designed as places of worship? When religious artefacts are displayed in museums, there has been an increasing tendency for some visitors to leave coins in front of divine images, or to venerate religious icons. (See Chapter 24 for further discussion of this phenomenon.)

Such questions are indicative of the current state of our field, and demonstrate the necessity of a book such as this. The possibility of religion in museums, as has been addressed by Gretchen Buggeln, Crispin Paine and Brent Plate in their recent edited volume *Religion in Museums: Global and Multidisciplinary Perspectives*, would not have been found twenty-five years ago. Currently, there are several books and articles that address the theme. The concept of 'folk religion' was used differently by (mainly Protestant) scholars of religion in 1960s Britain, when scholarship was privileging theology, metaphysics and text over religious practices that involve ritual performance and material cultures. The handling of concepts such as 'guru' and 'belief' has also changed over the past two decades. Further research might profitably attempt to chart how such concepts have changed and developed over time.

Much of the study of religion in recent times has focused on theory and method, and one might be forgiven for wondering about the value of some of the more abstruse books and articles that have been written on the topic. While scholars of religion need to employ the best possible tools of the trade, tradespeople do not spend all their time honing their tools or showing them to their customers. Relating this analogy to our discipline, the distinction is sometimes made between the study of religion (singular) and the study of religions (plural). The former addresses general conceptual issues: what religion is, what is emic and etic vocabulary, to what degree it can be value-neutral, and so on; the latter – which surely ought to be the main purpose of scholarly study – is to use these tools to examine and analyse the various forms of religion themselves.

We hope, however, that those who study religions and devise academic curricula might examine their assumptions and, where appropriate, implement appropriate changes. For example, the study of so-called 'world religions' has focused on what some have called the 'famous five' (which would be more accurately referred to as the 'sacred six' due to the inclusion of Sikhism). Yet not all of these six religions are the most popularly subscribed, the most ancient, or the most influential. Further, a neat set of a 'sacred six' is misleading and can readily result in an essentialist approach to the subject matter, implying that they share similar characteristics, and that each religion is uniform, regardless of geographical location, history and local traditions, thus overlooking the rich and nuanced expressions of religions in context.

Many of the issues discussed in this volume therefore have implications for pedagogy. If the World Religions Paradigm is seriously flawed, how are we to teach religion, or what subject matter should be taught in the name of religions? Although questioning of the WRP has become commonplace in academia, schools in the UK continue to teach the 'sacred six', and teach them as discrete systems of belief – and we use the word 'belief' deliberately here (see Chapter 1). For those who to continue to teach religion, it is not enough to 'deconstruct' the WRP; something is needed to replace it.

Christopher R. Cotter and David G. Robertson's *After World Religions: Reconstructing Religious Studies* offers various suggestions from a number of scholars, spanning the New Age as a classificatory case study, using artefacts and monuments as a basis for discussion, assessing media representations, and critiquing traditional literature. However, perhaps what is needed is a clear definition of the aim of studying religion, and what any particular programme of study sets out to achieve. One might decide to give priority to religions in one's locality, or to religions that receive coverage in the media, for example. By traditionally focusing on text and beliefs, pedagogy has tended to give relatively little attention to religion as it is lived. In teaching Buddhism, for example, there still remains a somewhat unsatisfactory blend of history, textual study, philosophy and (mainly Western) practice, with little attention to popular Eastern expressions of the religion.

Concepts, then, facilitate the creation of discourses about religions. An example is how the concept of 'superstition', while pejorative and not particularly useful as a scholarly or precise term, is one that has been used cross-culturally for centuries. It has been a way of labelling the beliefs, ideologies and practices of 'others' as 'false' or 'inauthentic', in opposition to our own, thus bolstering our perceptions of our own beliefs and practices as 'authentic' or 'true'. The practice of problematizing concepts such as superstition can therefore reveal the scope of our perception about certain types of religious phenomena, enabling us to glean hidden or overlooked nuances of religions, which, if acknowledged, can enrich our disciplinary understandings about the ways in which religions are actually lived (see Chapter 25).

The critical engagement with concepts is therefore an additional tool for our trade that is capable of complementing theory and method, and enhancing our scholarly craft. The way in which terms are used not only shapes our research, but also the way we convey the worlds of others, as well as our own, to our audiences. Many times, readers of our studies in religions will have lacked exposure to the religious groups about which we have written, and hence our scholarship generates a power relationship between the scholar, the reader and the community under study. Scholars have power over the reader, particularly if he or she is unfamiliar with the subject matter, by being the authority, although unfortunately the general public may prefer the more simplistic and sensational accounts of the media. Scholars also have the power, as well as the obligation, to the communities they have studied, to present them in a clear, balanced and accurate way, and this does not only include what one says, but how one says it. Some of the early scholars of religion described their subjects as 'savage' and 'primitive', and we have now learnt better. These two terms have all but been banned from any scholarly discussion about religions and are only used when signalling mistakes made early on (and for demonstrating the evolution of the discipline). Contemporarily, work is needed to persuade the wider public that terms like 'destructive cult', 'victim', 'brainwashing' and 'messianic leader' are inappropriate ways of discussing new religious movements. The point is that language is powerful. It has the ability to not only shape our scholarship, but also to shape how religious groups, especially new religions and diaspora communities, see themselves in relation to the dominant culture. For this reason, the concepts that have been critically contested present a challenge. The chapters are not meant to reassure scholars about what they already know (as with a 'keywords' book); they are meant to unsettle. In fact, the aim of this book centres on one main concern: that concepts in the study of religions be handled with care.

CHAPTER 1
BELIEF
Nicholas Campion

The equation of the concept of belief with religion is characteristically a Christian preoccupation. The Bible refers to Jesus' followers as 'believers' (e.g. John 4:41), and the Nicene Creed – the Christian's fundamental statement of allegiance – opens with the words, 'We believe in one God.' Candidates for baptism, the means of entry to the Christian church, must affirm their belief in God as Father, Son and Holy Spirit. Christianity has had such a concern with right belief that it has excluded those with inappropriate beliefs as heretics. Since the majority of Western scholars in the past have been either practising or cultural Christians, it has been commonplace to define other religions in terms of what they believe. By contrast, the Muslim statement of faith (*shahadah*) states, 'There is no God but Allah, and Muhammad is his messenger,' as fact rather than opinion.

Definitions of belief

The Greek root for the word in the Nicene Creed which is translated into belief in English is *pisteuein*, meaning to trust, have confidence in or have faith in; all these meanings are embodied in the twelfth century English *bileave*. This word, in turn, is related to the Old English *geleafa* and Old Saxon *gilobo*, itself the root of the modern word gullible. To translate *pisteuein* as 'to believe' is a perfectly reasonable choice, but because of the Christian requirement to express absolute belief in one God, and only one God, and all rules and regulations for living attributed to that God, the word has assumed a peculiar power.

The roots of modern debates over the nature of belief lie in the eighteenth-century Enlightenment critique of religion and its expansion into a critique of the concept of belief itself as a particular form of consciousness. Belief has come to be seen either as an evolutionary cul-de-sac, the consequence of sociological difficulties, a psychological error or a neurological disorder. It therefore becomes a problem to explain. Arguments over the nature and function of belief are, though, circumscribed by language. As Eric Schwitzgebel (2019) wrote, 'Contemporary Anglophone philosophers of mind generally use the term "belief" to refer to the attitude we have, roughly, whenever we take something to be the case or regard it as true'. Meanwhile Graham Harvey (2005) argues that the privileging of beliefs takes place in a philosophical context in which 'ideas' are privileged over 'matter'.

In the strict definition of the word, one can believe in science, or that a particular phenomenon is scientific, including astrology, as did Colin Wilson when he headlined an article in the *Daily Mail* 'Why I now believe astrology IS a science' (Wilson 2001). In Wilson's strictly grammatical use of the term, belief does not carry religious connotations. In popular discourse scientists are also regularly described as believers. For example, 'some scientists believe [that evolution] has come to a standstill' (Connor 2001: 9).

Belief as a mode of cognition

Belief falls short of knowledge: as many philosophers have contended, knowledge is 'justified true belief', although the relationship between the two concepts continues to be debated. What is false cannot be known, although it can certainly be believed. Psychologists Peter Glick and Mark Snyder (1986: 22) argue that belief and scepticism are actually alternative modes of cognition. In sceptical discourse, popular discourse, and in much of the sceptical scientific literature, a 'belief' is automatically defined as false unless, in rare cases, proved otherwise. Thus David Myers (1990: 102, 109–11, 114), concedes that a false belief may be countered by a true one, suggesting confusion over the word's exact definition. Nevertheless, in the materialist paradigm, belief must have a physical cause, just as do all thoughts. Robert Park (2000: 35), Professor of Physics at the University of Maryland, has argued that brains are 'belief engines'. According to Park, belief has physiological causes and occurs when the believer mistakenly infers a causal connection between two unconnected events. If the physiological causes of belief are not contained then it develops into a superstition: when 'the chemical messengers of emotion cause the thalamus to bypass the sensory cortex and route the information directly to the amygdala', a belief becomes a 'personal superstition'. However, science has provided us with an antidote (Park 2000: 36–7).

Belief as primitive error

Theories of cultural evolution as applied to religion were developed by anti-Christian positivists, who advanced evolutionist theories of religion, notably Edward Tylor in 1873. The evolutionary position was summarized comprehensively in 1896 by Frank Jevons, who argued that progressively, over the millennia, humanity used its reason to correct false beliefs and identify true ones so that religion, even though fundamentally false, became less so (Jevons 1896: 402–3).

Broadly, the evolutionist perspective holds that religion originates as 'primitive' totemism, animism or magic, in which natural forces are animated or anthropomorphized, and evolves through polytheism into monotheism and finally atheist materialism, in line with the law of progress (Evans-Pritchard 1967: 31–3). The evolutionist view was critiqued by Rodney Stark, who argued that it was based in an 'incorrect, extremely misleading, and often simply fabricated' notion of the 'primitive mind', which had been demolished once anthropologists began to conduct rigorous fieldwork (Stark 1999: 47).

Belief, fear and social deprivation

Related to the evolutionist primitive perspective is the theory that religion originates as a means of providing security to people who are naturally insecure, fearful and unable to deal with their environment or responsibilities without a crutch. The assumption is that this insecurity then produces, in a series of stages, fear, low-self-esteem, persuasibility and, ultimately, belief. Bart J. Bok cited a statement put out by the Society for Psychological Study of Social Issues, which posited personal inadequacy, claiming that the principal reason why people turn to superstitions is that

> they lack in their own lives the resources necessary to solve serious personal problems confronting them. Feeling blocked and bewildered they yield to the pleasant suggestion that a golden key is at hand – a simple solution – an ever present help in time of trouble.
>
> (Bok and Mayall 1941: 244)

'Deprivation theory' adds to the model, maintaining that paranormal beliefs 'provide people with the means to cope with the psychological and physical strains and disadvantaged social and economic status' and predicts that 'socially marginal people will be more likely to believe in classic [paranormal] phenomena' (Rice 2003: 95, 104). Supporters of the model vary between those who hold external factors responsible, and those who blame internal conditions. Tom Rice, for example, has argued that psychological – that is, 'innate and learned personality characteristics' – may play a greater role in paranormal belief than do social factors (Rice 2003: 105). However, alternative data contradict the marginality and insecurity hypotheses: Harvey Gollob and James Dittes (1965) questioned the supposed relationship between low self-esteem and belief and, in studies of the wider culture, Stark has argued that, far from religion appealing to the inadequate and insecure, religious people enjoyed better than average mental and physical health, while Robert Wuthnow (1976: 173) and Wade Clark Roof (1993) showed that those attracted to New Age beliefs tend to be more educated than the average.

Belief as rational choice

An alternative model for belief is as a perfectly logical means of viewing the world. As C. Daniel Batson and W. Larry Ventris (1982: 141) pointed out, 'religious commitments were carefully thought out and taken seriously as a major goal in life'. Stark and Bainbridge argued, in their exposition of 'rational choice theory', that 'Humans seek what they perceive to be rewards and try to avoid what they perceive to be costs' (1985: 5). Developing their reasoning is quite simple: human beings make rational choices because their desire for certainty is less likely to be met from irrational choices whose outcome will most likely be unpredictable, and they prefer rational gods because they are likely to offer them a greater certainty of reward than a capricious, irrational one (Stark and Bainbridge 1987: 113–14).

Measuring belief

Considerable attention is paid to the quantitative measurement of belief on the assumption that the resulting figures represent an accurate picture of religious affiliation. However, as Michael Hornsby-Smith (1991: 3) argued in the introduction to his study of modern English Catholic belief patterns, each item of dogma, from contraception to papal infallibility and each activity from church attendance to pilgrimage, may be a different indicator of belief or, to use a more socially functional word, 'commitment'. Ronald Belter and Erwin H. Brinkmann (1981: 431), meanwhile, even questioned whether the attempt to quantify belief as opposed to non-belief was so epistemologically flawed as to be pointless. They found that, when testing whether believers in God placed the locus of control in their lives externally or internally, the results obtained were inconsistent. They concluded that there was a general 'problem in conceptualizing and measuring belief in God', adding that 'it is apparent that such a belief is more complex than a simple belief-disbelief dimension' and that therefore to contrast belief with disbelief as if the two are mutually exclusive opposite positions cannot 'relate adequately to the individual's locus of control orientation', that is, reveal the true complexity of an individual's worldview or meaning system. Gillian Bennett (1987), meanwhile, found that typical respondents give different answers to questions of belief depending on their trust in the researcher. In a previous study, I found that many people regard direct 'Do you believe?' questions with suspicion and are more amenable to questions concerning specific opinions or behaviours (Campion, 2015). This signals that scholars of religion may well be better placed to pay attention to things such as religious expression, either as opposed or in addition to, religious belief, an approach that would be amenable to the increasingly popular 'lived' and 'vernacular' religion approaches.

Conclusion

The English word 'belief' means no more than to have confidence, whether in a person, a political position or a worldview. However, the history of Christianity has been based on the specific requirement to hold certain beliefs while rejecting others. The notion that some beliefs are good or true, while others are bad or false continues outside the religious sphere. Modern scientists have reified belief, redefining it no longer a description of a mental state but as a mental state in itself, one which is opposed to knowledge and science; thus the search is on to discover its causes, either in malfunctions in brain chemistry, psychological tendencies or social deprivation. However, Gilbert Ryle (1990: 128) criticized these positions:

> Epistemologists are apt to perplex themselves and their readers over the distinction between knowledge and belief. Some of them suggest that these differ only in degree of something or other, and some that they differ in the presence of some introspective ingredient in knowing which is absent from believing, or vice versa.

The attempts to identify physical, psychological or sociological causes for belief are therefore based on a false premise. Whether belief remains a useful concept in the study of religions is questionable. An alternative approach is to examine religion in terms of what we can see people doing, such as practices, rituals and other forms of behaviour (Harvey 2005). It would be therefore more productive to consider specific attitudes and visible actions in addition to questions of 'belief' which are unmeasurable.

CHAPTER 2
CHARISMA
Edward A. Irons

The concept of charisma is closely tied to religion. The term was used by the Apostle Paul in his letters to newly formed congregations, many of which experienced dissension. When Max Weber took up the concept in his study of leaders he could refer to centuries of the term's usage in theology. Today charisma is particularly associated with leaders of new religious groups, whose success is often explained as being due to charisma. Yet there is little consensus on the concept's exact meaning. Attempts to unpack the meaning of charisma often equate it with admiration, adulation, compelling charm, physical presence or drawing power. In popular usage charisma is often no more than a descriptive term referring to an impression of influence.

Charis and charisma: Spiritual power in early Christianity

Paul used 'charisma' to signify the gift of God's grace. He identified such traits as glossolalia, prophecy and healing as the charismata (plural form) (1 Corinthians 12:4–11). Paul's emphasis on the concept of charisma in his writings can be interpreted as a way to ensure group solidarity and harmony in the period before the formal organization of the Church (Potts 2009: 46). Doctrinally, the charismata were explained as gifts God gave to the entire congregation by virtue of their accepting Christ. Paul did acknowledge that each person was granted these gifts of the Spirit differently: 'We have different gifts, according to the grace given us' (Romans 12:6). At the same time there was an element of radical democracy in the idea that the entire congregation shared in the gifts. The malleability of the concept allowed Paul to transform the perception of spirit from being a quality of an individual into a force-creating community.

Charisma did not long maintain its importance in later Christianity. Paul's idea of a charismatic community was replaced by one based on hierarchy, ceremony, scripture and doctrine. While charismatic individuals and even texts were still acknowledged, the role of charisma became less and less important. The role of the apostles was superseded by the position of the overseer, or bishop. In a sense the charisma of prophets had become redundant: texts were imbued with the authority previously reserved for prophets. Augustine adopted Paul's emphasis on the divine gift of grace, but downplayed other, more supernatural charismata. Christianity by 400 CE had entered a post-charismatic age.

Yet charismatic enthusiasms never fully disappeared. They were instead relegated to the sidelines. When they did appear, for instance in the teachings of desert hermits, they were often treated with suspicion. Some charismatic individuals such as Francis of Assisi embodied mystical yearnings that were expressed through charismata. Such forces also percolated within Protestant Christianity in the form of groups like Anabaptists and Quakers who sought a direct experience of the Spirit. Clearly, the divine gifts enunciated by Paul – the charismata – are enduring concepts not subject to erasure.

Weber's concept of charisma

One of Weber's many insights was to perceive the force of bureaucratization. Weber saw the striving for efficiency in all societies and periods as leading towards bureaucracy, routinization and, eventually, the loss of individual freedoms. While he saw his trend towards rationalism as inevitable, he also proposed the countervailing force of charisma as another possible direction for social development.

Weber defined charisma, in *Economy and Society*, as: 'a certain quality of an individual personality by virtue of which he is considered extraordinary and treated as endowed with supernatural, superhuman, or at least specifically exceptional powers or qualities' (Weber 1968: 241). In his later work Weber became absorbed in the disruptive impact of these extraordinary individuals on social structures. Such individuals, he said, stood apart from ordinary people. They possessed charisma.

Weber did not create his concept of charisma by himself. Just as Paul took up the existing concept of *charis* and reconfigured it, Weber borrowed charisma from predecessors. To develop his own theory, Weber had to go beyond the then-current understanding of charisma as religious love and enthusiasm. Weber first used the term near the end of *The Protestant Ethic and the Spirit of Capitalism*, in a single reference to 'the *charisma* of the disciples' (Weber 2001: 121). He again mentioned charisma in a letter in 1910. But Weber did not fully formulate the theory of charisma until 1913, in *Economy and Society*. From that point on, until his death in 1920, he explored charisma and the charismatic widely.

Weber categorized charisma as one form of domination, along with two other types, the rational-legal and traditional. Charismatic authority is based on personal trust in the exceptional person. As such it is inherently unstable; charismatic authority will be recognized and deference given only as long as the charismatic leader can prove his (or her) extraordinary powers, or until that person departs from the scene. But when the charismatic person is present, he or she exerts a disruptive impact. In this sense the charismatic leader's rise is always revolutionary. While Weber insisted that all three forms of domination coexist in reality, he indicated that charisma over history will become increasingly diluted (Potts 2009: 124). At the same time charisma will never be completely eradicated. Political party leaders, for instance, learn to mobilize and embody charisma. Rhetoric itself creates charismatic effects.

Weber often established ideal types or bundles of traits as a way to explain a phenomenon, and the ideal type of charismatic leader was the founder of a religion (Radkau 2009). Unlike other theorists who focused primarily on leaders' personality traits, Weber consistently referred to the perception of the community as key to determining charisma. 'What is alone important,' he wrote, 'is how the individual is actually regarded by those subject to charismatic authority, by his "followers" or "disciples"' (Weber 1968: 241–2).

Any concept that becomes widely adopted will garner its share of criticisms. This became true of the theory of charisma, especially once Weber's works began appearing in English translation. The American historian Arthur Schlesinger Jr. criticized Weber's concept of charisma as ' … mystical, unstable, irrational, and … incapable of dealing with the realities of modern industrial society' (Schlesinger 1960: 12). The sociologist Peter Worsley referred to charisma as 'a sponge concept' of limited analytical value (Worsley 1970: 329). Many critics argued that Weber over-emphasized the role of the charismatic leader. The psychologist Irvine Schiffer in 1973 criticized Weber's concept for overlooking group dynamics. Sociologists such as Robert Tucker and Bryan Wilson also attempted to highlight the importance of followers in the leader-follower relationship. Pierre Bourdieu felt that Weber's charisma was simply 'a naïve representation … of a mysterious quality'. Instead he proposed that the leader embodies the aspirations of the followers in a time of crisis (Potts 2009: 132–3). For Bourdieu and his followers, charisma was socially constructed.

Within the field of sociology, Harold Wolpe divides criticisms of Weberian charisma into two overall categories (Wolpe 1968: 305). On the one hand are empirical studies of charismatic leaders. Many of these studies have found much less fervent devotion among followers than would be expected from Weber's thesis. In the second category are theorists who fault Weber for not explaining the historical context of charismatic leadership. Indeed many studies continue to find charisma to be of use in a wide variety of contexts (Friedland 1964). None of these critics argue against using the concept, however. Weber's concept of charisma continues to be widely accepted in psychology, sociology and religious studies.

Charisma in religious studies

By Weber's time, charisma had become a term reserved for theological discussions. Since it was obscure to most scholars, it was available for Weber to apply in a new context, as a way to explain one form of dominance. Ironically, Weber's idea of charismatic leadership was eventually applied to the beginnings of Christianity, a period which, as we have discussed, had a very different understanding of charisma. Yet Pauline charisma still exists within the practice of Christianity. The term 'charismatic' made a major comeback in a religious context beginning in the 1960s when it was applied to the renewal movement of charismatic Christianity. John Potts explains the use of 'charismatic' as an attempt to distinguish these new forms of worship from Pentecostalism, which had grown wildly since the early 1900s. Both forms of worship involved a renewed interest in such Pauline charismata as healing, glossolalia and ecstatic possession, as well as a hunger for intense emotional experience (Potts 2009: 155–7), but unlike Penecostalism the charismatic Christian movement developed within mainstream congregations. Fully in alignment with Paul's concept of a divine gift from God, the new charisma was seen as a gift given to the body of parishioners as a group but expressed through individuals. While the sense of charisma invoked in charismatic Christianity is clearly Pauline, many Pentecostal and other Christian leaders continue to be described in the Weberian sense as being charismatic leaders. Thus both senses of the term charisma are in current use with reference to Christianity.

Charisma is particularly prominent in the study of new religious movements. Salient examples of new religions with charismatic leaders include Sun Myung Moon, founder of the Unification Church, Kelsang Gyatso of New Kadampa Buddhism and Charles Taze Russell of the Watch Tower Society. New religions often develop in the present day, and so allow observation of the action of leaders and followers. In particular, researchers in new religion studies can observe individuals described as having charisma. It is in theory possible to observe the formation and use of charisma. Why such processes come together in new religions is still an open question. There are a number of possible explanations for the importance of charisma in new religious studies, each with deficiencies.

Psychologically oriented explanations based on the leader fulfilling a lack in the follower only partially explain the diversity of charismatic connections in the real world. Yet psychological research has yielded many new insights into charismatic leaders. The psychologist Len Oakes (1997) studied a number of founders of new religions and emphasized their possession of unique and unconventional qualities. His use of the term charisma is similar to Paul's in that it focuses on unusual abilities. Such leaders as Madame Blavatsky, Joseph Smith and Rajneesh (aka Osho) have personalities 'radically different in essence' from average people, noted Oakes. He listed such qualities as self-confidence, high energy, inspiring rhetoric and empathy. Coincidentally, these qualities are consistent with narcissistic personality types.

Most scholars of new religions would agree that the exercise of charisma is conditioned by the socio-historical moment. Sociological theories, building on Weber, emphasize the qualities of leaders as well as the need for corresponding support for the charismatic claims on the part of followers. David Bromley notes how crisis moments open opportunities for individuals perceived as being charismatic because existing cultural narratives no longer suffice (Bromley 2014: 106). Eileen Barker suggests that the process of charismatization is a learned behaviour that allows the follower to perceive an 'aura' around the leader, and by so doing to verify the efficacy of the charismatic claims to authority. Usually without being aware of the process, the charismatic leader conforms to the expectations of followers and in turn is considered to be worthy of devotion (Barker 1993). Paul Joose focuses on the role of a 'charismatic aristocracy' of trusted followers who show unwavering faith in the early stages of charismatization (Joosse 2017: 339). George Chryssides argues that while personal magnetism plays a central part in a new religion's inception, it is less important than such other factors as the ambient culture, organizational skills and financing (Chryssides 2021). While these scholars come to different conclusions concerning charisma, they agree that the perceptions of followers as well as social conditions play a larger role than individual character traits in the development of charisma.

In many cases there will be a challenge to the organization when the leader passes from the scene. In theory charisma can be transferred to another. While an office-bearer such as the Pope may possess charisma, Weber was careful to distinguish between this form of charisma from original charisma springing from a person's natural endowment. New religions scholar Erin Prophet, who grew up in a family that led a new religion, shows the constant negotiation of authority required to maintain charismatic authority and manage succession. In the case of her mother Elizabeth Clare Prophet, there was an active effort to resist the routinization of charisma (Prophet 2016: 39).

Contemporary uses of charisma

The 1990s saw the publication of a slew of self-help books based around the concept of charisma. Most of these attempt to explain how charisma can be developed and mastered, and make charisma a quality interchangeable with such descriptors as confidence and presence. In some writers, charisma has simply become a convenient label for a bundle of effective communication skills. Potts describes in some detail how charisma has evolved from Weber's restricted sense to mean a quality broadly attributed to a range of situations. While Weber carefully limited his application of the term to leaders, charisma can now be applied to any person who has the elusive 'it' factor. The indiscriminate use of charisma raises the prospect that it will end up as simply a synonym for 'successful'.

Despite these difficulties, the use of the term thrives. Potts concludes this is because charisma fulfils an important role in contemporary society. We need charisma to distinguish the authentic from the artificial, and to discuss a kind of authentic personal magnetism. One further indication of its importance is its spread into a range of other languages, from Chinese to Turkic to Polish. Most other cultures import the term as a loan word, indicating that there is no suitable pre-existing term in the original language (Potts 2009: 182).

This survey has focused largely on two thought innovators, Saint Paul and Max Weber. Each took an existing idea and applied it in a new sense. Pauline charisma is a divine gift to a group of believers. Weberian charisma is a quality of an individual seen to set that person apart from others. Both versions of charisma exist today. At the same time Weberian charisma has become so popularized that it is applied to contexts beyond Weber's thoughts on charismatic authority.

What accounts for the persistence of these conceptions of charisma? Potts and others focus on the human need to explain and control the irrational. The irrational is part of the human condition. Apparently random, inexplicable forces threaten to break through the veneer of daily life at any point. Times of rapid social change create environments filled with the force of the irrational. These in turn create ideal opportunities for the rise of charismatic leaders (Barnes 1978: 4). In this sense the popular conception of charisma dovetails with Weber's: both are attempts to isolate and recognize the presence of irrationality.

Charisma points to forces within human experience that are not fully understood. Weber's insight was to apply this term as a way of understanding how humans follow and interact with leaders. As long as we have leaders we will seek explanations for their charisma.

CHAPTER 3
CONVERSION
David G. Bromley

What is termed conversion fits comfortably into a volume devoted to contested concepts in the study of religion. The contestation begins, of course, with the concept of 'religion' itself. The study of conversion is necessarily impacted by problems with the parent concept. Theory and research on emerging and alternative religions have clarified some of the issues that have needed to be addressed, but an alternative direction in the study of conversion (and religion more generally) should be developed.

Over the last several decades there has been a vigorous critique of 'religion' as an academic object of study from a variety of perspectives. For purposes of the present chapter, three important problems with the study of religion also impact the study of conversion: an understanding of religion as a naturally occurring and unique category of human behaviour, the overlapping influence of scholars and mainstream institutions (and particularly the state and established churches) in shaping what is accepted as legitimate religion and the pervasive influence of Christian religious traditions in understanding what constitutes legitimate religion. (For an extended discussion of current conceptualizations of religion, see Chapter 17.)

This chapter has three primary objectives: (1) to explore some of the problems associated with 'conversion' deriving from its present usage, (2) to indicate how the study of contemporary emergent and alternative religious movements has contributed to a more useful understanding of conversion and (3) to suggest a more useful approach to understanding conversion. As a basis for the present discussion, I simply accept the widely shared understanding that the major elements of the worlds that humans inhabit are socially constructed. This includes what is termed religion. That is to say, across times and cultures social groups have included an arena of symbolic and social organization that has envisioned and sacralized a reality beyond the everyday world that its participants inhabit. The elements used to construct this envisioned reality actually are quite diverse, but they share sufficient overlap to be gathered together analytically by scholars under the concept of 'religion.'

Problems in the traditional conceptualizations of conversion

There are a number of problems with the concept of conversion as it has conventionally been conceptualized in the study of religion. One indication of the inadequacy of conversion as a concept is that it does not anticipate a parallel separation process and therefore has no natural antonym. A number of other terms have been developed (de-conversion, exit, apostasy), but it is unclear how these separation processes relate to a traditional concept of conversion. In popular parlance, separation has sometimes been referred to as simply 'falling from the faith', which avoids articulating any theoretical position.

There is a mixing of various types of religious status change. Examples include religious status advance (cases in which individuals adopt a public religious identity of higher social rank in search of upward social mobility), wartime aftermath (cases in which defeated populations are required to profess allegiance to the victors' deities), marital accommodation (cases in which one partner adopts the religious tradition of the other) and renewal pledge (cases in which individuals ritually reaffirm commitment to their existing religious tradition). The social meaning and dynamics of these status changes are not uniform, which has undermined meaningful theory construction.

There are no clear parameters on what combination of characteristics constitutes a conversion. In the traditional conception of conversion it is largely assumed that novitiates affirm a symbolic connection to a group (belief in the doctrines, mission or leadership); novitiates have an active social connection with a group (participation, membership); the group affirms that the individual is in fact a believer or affiliate and third parties agree that the individual is legitimately connected to a group. This, of course, actually is an empirical question. If conversion is assumed to be unidirectional and permanent, it is not necessary to determine how long the connection between individual and group must persist before designating it a conversion. Similarly, it is not necessary to stipulate the social and cultural distance between origination status and destination status for individual movement to constitute conversion.

Numerous religious traditions have initiation rites (baptism, confirmation, *amrit*). Sometimes these are treated as conversion moments (being born again), but they are primarily affirmation rituals. Further, it is rare that research on conversion reports on the entire conversion career of individuals as novitiates are typically not discovered until they have begun or completed the conversion process. As a result, research reports often consist of a collage of individual experiences and retrospective accounts.

Conversion in theory and research on emerging and alternative movements

There is, of course, a long history of descriptive accounts of non-mainstream religious traditions. However, this literature was not closely connected to research on mainstream traditions. With titles like *Alternative Altars* (Ellwood 1981) and *These Also Believe* (Braden 1949), this literature approaches alternatives (to Christianity) with the studied exploratory curiosity of an anthropologist encountering a new tribal group. There is no attempt to incorporate groups discussed into a larger scholarly understanding of religion. The advent of the outpouring of theory and research on emerging and alternative religious movements beginning in the 1960s created a new subfield in the study of religion and social movements. The challenges in developing various theoretical concepts began with the necessity to develop a new category of religious organization (herein, emerging and alternative religious movements) to add to the established church-sect-cult typology. 'Conversion' was not far behind. The new area of study has addressed a number of the problems in the study of conversion, which has been the most researched topic in the area of study, and offers new insight into the process as it occurs in late twentieth-century religious movements in the West. Problems include conflating affiliation and conversion, varying levels and forms of commitment among affiliates, and not including external opposition as a factor in research on affiliation and longer-term involvement.

Research on emerging and alternative religious movements has reported that most contacts between potential converts and religious movements do not lead to group involvement, and research has shown that involvement in most cases is temporary (Barker 1988). As it became clear that involvement typically was transitory, research on the exit process intensified, which has resulted in a holistic 'career' approach to the study of conversion. It has also been reported that individuals have often been attracted to alternative religious groups on a specific basis, such as their doctrinal system, group mission, a charismatic leader or the community of adherents. The initial source of interest may or may not broaden, which is important in understanding the solidity of these movements as well as the varying types and depth of involvement that have been described as conversion. In addition, some individuals engage in sequential experimentation with a variety of groups. This has been quite common in New Age movements, as well as contemporary yoga and meditation groups, for example. In some cases individuals may experiment with several groups simultaneously.

Opposition, both legal and extra-legal, has been directed at affiliations with new groups and has had a significant impact on their functioning and survival. It is in the encounter between established institutions defending the existing social order and new movements challenging that order (with what Scott (1985) refers to as 'weapons of the weak') that power dynamics become most visible. In particular, the ritualized practice of 'deprogramming' invites comparison with other 'reversal rituals' that are intended to re-incorporate wayward individuals into mainstream society, such as exorcism, re-education and de-radicalization. The exercise of these kinds of social control mechanisms leads directly to a power-based analysis.

Two immediate conclusions follow from this brief review of findings on attachments to new groups. One, which might seem surprising, is that by a traditional definition, there actually have been relatively few 'true conversions' to emerging groups as most attachments have been short-lived and experimental. The relatively small size and brief popularity of the movements that initially triggered controversy over 'conversions' also suggest that most attachments were temporary. Second, while research on emerging religious movements constitutes an important historical case study, it also highlights the importance of broadening the study of conversion. The groups that constituted the foundation of this research generally were youth-based, were organized with a communal core and a charismatic leader, experienced high turnover and only a brief growth history, settled or declined rapidly and encountered stiff social and political opposition.

The study of emerging religious movements therefore only adds to the argument for an alternative theoretical model.

Conversion, religion and power

This brief review of the concept of conversion obviously suggests significant issues for the study of religion, matters that are beyond the mission of this chapter. However, in many respects the issues that arise in the examination of conversion coincide with those that have emerged and will emerge from an inspection of the concept of religion. The specific conclusions to be drawn from the foregoing analysis are that advancing the study of conversion (and religion more generally) involves three elements. First, there needs to be an historically based review of the concept if previous and future research on conversion are to be coordinated productively. Second, it will be crucial to connect the study of religion to broader areas of social science theory and analysis by drawing on theoretical concepts that have been fruitfully applied across a range of social groups (Bromley 2016). In the case at hand, for example, 'status transitions' is a broader category of social realignment of which conversion is one example. The prevalence, importance, ritualization and control of status transitions (in contemporary society – single/married, employed/retired, healthy/ill, alive/dead, child/adult, law abiding/deviant) – demonstrate the priority given to exercising control over moments of transition. Finally, and most importantly, the naturalistic perspective, which tends towards an assumption that the existing, established social order is inherent in the natural order of things needs to give way to a more critical, structural, power-based perspective.

There are two important implications. First, social order is continuously being constructed and reconstructed. The objective of theory and research, therefore, is not seeking a closer approximation of 'Truth' but rather mapping the social landscape in a specific social and historical context. This approach recognizes both the constructed nature of social worlds and of the scholarly concepts used to examine them. Put another way, maps are heuristic depictions and 'the map is not the territory' (Korzybski 1995). Second, religion is a source of symbolic and organizational power through envisioning a reality beyond the everyday world and for making that envisioning real. Two primary mechanisms for maintaining a religious power base are tradition transmission and conversion.

Reconceptualizing conversion begins with an understanding that contemporary societies consist of institutional power arenas, like religion, that are organized to create and sustain the existing system of social order. However, a structural, power-based approach to understanding social order recognizes that social order is always vulnerable to challenge, and all forms of social organization invite the possibility of envisioning alternatives. Religion is a dangerous social form of social order because it offers the potential for ultimate authorization and legitimation. New religions are even more dangerous because they inherently challenge established order.

In its more domesticated form, such as contemporary denominations, established religions are connected to and in alliance with other societal institutions. There are formal and informal limits on innovation and challenges to the interests of other institutions. Within that regulatory system (with variable degrees of openness), in settled times (Swidler 1986) individual movement is available and is not closely monitored; most individual realignment occurs within the legitimated set. In this circumstance there can be individual movement and realignment without systemic change. Individuals move, the system remains unchanged and the power structure remains opaque.

In unsettled times, when a substantial or important segment of the population exhibits weakened links with established institutions, alternative envisioning and accompanying organization is more likely to challenge the established order and to be regarded as a threat to that order. Conversion becomes a more engaging and consequential issue theoretically in the study of emerging and alternative movements because the display and use of power become more visible. One important element of such times is that status transitions into these groups are likely to be contested as tangible individuals and actual organization of new ways of living make alternatives to the established social order real. The possibility then exists not simply of individual status transition and realignment but of broader systemic change as well. It is these circumstances that illicit categories of organization (cults) are proposed, designations of the status transition process as illegitimate are invoked (brainwashing, radicalization) and reversal rituals (deprogramming, deradicalization) allowing or mandating a re-entry path to mainstream society are developed.

Individual status transitions and the power structure of the social order are, of course, reciprocally related as each impacts the other. The argument developed here is that, while individual realignment is significant and should be studied, power-based analysis should guide theory and research because that structure shapes the actual social status transition category of conversion/convert. Put in other terms, conversion is a socially privileged category of status transition and realignment, one that involves agreement among relevant parties that an acceptable status transition has taken place between legitimate religious entities. From this perspective, converts are not a natural category but rather the product of specific power arrangements. There is always some level of contestation between challenging and institutional power. In this struggle, conversion and its output (converts) can constitute a power resource for new movements on a number of dimensions: membership size, deployable missionaries, financial resources, conversion narratives, legitimator of doctrines and predictions, movement visibility, apparent commitment of membership, charismatic standing of leadership, organizational complexity. All of these resources ultimately are drawn from the larger society. Movement success on these dimensions threatens the established institutional order and its legitimacy, irrespective of the size of a movement. It is this dynamic that appropriately informs the status transition process designated as conversion.

CHAPTER 4
CULT
Benjamin E. Zeller

In the build-up to the 2020 American presidential elections, disgraced former White House Director of Communications Anthony Scaramucci made headlines by referring to his former boss, Donald Trump, as a cult leader, and his supporters as members of a cult. Scaramucci provides just one example of such rhetoric in the United States across the political spectrum. In both tweets and op-eds, Democrats and breakaway Republicans labelled Trumpism a cult, but Trump loyalists responded by calling the Democratic Party, the Black Lives Movement and the pursuit of social justice also cults. Clearly, if you follow American media, most people seem to belong to one or another cult.

The case of American political rhetoric raises a critical point about the concept of the 'cult.' If everyone is part of a cult, is no one part of a cult? Within contemporary usage, does the term denote any formal or informal meaning, or does it function only as a slur, a way to disparage one's opponents? Put another way: is there any legitimate usage of the term 'cult'? This chapter delves into the origin of the term and the way that sociologists, historians and psychologists have utilized it. I argue that outside of a few narrow contexts, the term today offers little utility, as it has become contentless. It has become, in a semiotic sense, a signifier that lacks a signified.

Origins

The historic usage of the term 'cult' traces to the early modern period and the formal sense of the term – borrowed from the Latin *cultus* and French *culte* – to indicate a system of religious veneration of a particular figure saint, or deity. Hence, some of the first scholars of religion spoke of ancestor veneration cults, the cult of Persephone, the cult of the Virgin Mary and so on. The term continues to be used this way by anglophone archaeologists and scholars of ancient religions, and occasionally by some scholars of and participants in contemporary Marian movements. The cognate terms also continue to be used in some other Romance languages without the pejorative sense it evokes in English. Yet in the late nineteenth and twentieth century, the term took an entirely negative meaning when applied to contemporary groups. Historian W. Michael Ashcraft explains in his historiographic treatment of the field of new religious movement studies, 'modern usage of the word cult is generally pejorative. No consensus exists among NRM scholars about how, when, or why this shift occurred' (2018: 2). This transition seemed to have occurred in the nineteenth century, for while Ashcraft points to some limited cases of earlier texts that disparagingly referred to pagan cults, such examples critiqued paganism itself rather than the term or concept of the cult.

Yet the nineteenth century, with its burgeoning of new forms of Christianity in the anglophone world, marked a transition in how English-speaking Christian writers who imagined themselves speaking on behalf of the normative Protestant tradition applied the English word 'cult' to these upstart sects. Faced with the rise of Millerism, Adventism, Mormonism, Jehovah's Witnesses, the revival of Shakerism and the emergence of non-Christian movements such as Theosophy and Spiritualism, the term 'cult' came to function as a powerful rhetorical tool to distinguish the various normative Protestant denominations from their competitors. This combined with anti-Catholicism to allow the creation of hierarchal taxonomies that divided the religious world into either legitimate Protestant denominations on the one hand, or on the other hand illegitimate religions like cults, Roman Catholicism and foreign religions (Smith 1988: 271–7). Ashcraft concurs: 'Whatever the origins of the negative use of cult, by the nineteenth century in the United States, the term was commonly applied to any religious group that mainstream culture found objectionable (e.g. the Mormons, Jehovah's Witnesses)' (Ashcraft 2018: 3).

The English word 'cult' therefore came to signify a religious movement that the trans-Atlantic Protestant anglophone majority considered abhorrent. In addition to the aforementioned groups, late nineteenth- and early twentieth-century authors wrote of Voodoo, Hinduism, Buddhism and other religious groups as cults. Such authors generally wrote either from Christian polemical perspectives, seeking out and labelling heretical groups as cults, or as historians implicitly delineating normative from deviant religious movements (Chryssides and Zeller 2014: 2–6). This set the tone for the twentieth and now twenty-first-century usage of the term. By the 1960s, such popular books as Vittorio Lanternari's *The Religions of the Oppressed: A Study of Messianic Cults* (1960/1965) and Marcus Bach's *Strange Cults and Curious Sects* (1961) could assume a readership familiar with the notion of cults as deviant or unusual religious groups. Lanternari and Bach covered groups including the Mormons, Hutterites, Shakers, Father Divine's International Peace Mission movement, Hindu Shaivism, the Lakota Ghost Dance and other Native American revitalization movements and Melanesian Cargo movements. Cult had come to mean simply a non-normative (deviant) religious group, regardless of origin, size, organizational structure or theology.

Scholarly usage

In the 1960s and 1970s, a new array of movements arose that came to be called cults. Generally emerging from, and appealing to, a global youth counterculture, such groups included the Unification Church ("Moonies"), the International Society for Krishna Consciousness (Hare Krishna Movement), Divine Light Mission, Scientology, Children of God, Transcendental Meditation, Peoples Temple and many others. Sociologists, psychologists and ethnographers of religion turned to the study of these groups, all of which were labelled as cults in popular media treatments (McCloud 2004). Many such scholars retained the terminology of cult, reflecting the popular label of such groups, as well as the corresponding concept of a 'cult scare'.

The term had by then developed some scholarly utility, and it is still utilized by some scholars in a limited sense today as a category within typologies of religious organization, what is often called church/sect typologies. Such typologies derive from the model originated by Ernst Troeltsch (1865–1923), a German sociologist as well as theologian who categorized religious movements as either churches (*Kirchen*) that aligned with the social order, or sects (*Sekten*) that did not. Fellow sociologist Max Weber (1864–1920) employed the same logic. Later sociologists, writing in English rather than German, extended the typology and often simply conflated the terms sect (German: *Sekte*) and cult, a word that did not exist in German. For example, in their comprehensive and influential sociological model of religion, scholars Rodney Stark and Roger Finke utilize the terms 'cult', 'cultic movement' and 'new religious movement' interchangeably, all of which fall under the type of sect within the church/sect typology (2000: 250–8). At other times, they extend the typology, such as William Sims Bainbridge and Stark's frequently cited article on client cults, audience cults and cultic movements (1980), each of which occupies a niche under the broader church/sect model. For Bainbridge and Stark, audience cults are socially unstructured movements based on individualistic consumption of media, client cults involve a series of direct interpersonal relationships between adherents and the movement leaders, and cultic movements build on that by providing social structure. Scholars continue to use the concepts of audience cult, client cult and cultic movement in this technical sense (e.g. Sarno and Shoemaker 2016; Pietsch and Steckel 2018). When scholars do so, they recognize the pejorative sense of the term 'cult', but believe that the technical merits of the typology of religious movements outweigh that consideration.

Another influential usage of the term 'cult' originated during this twentieth-century countercultural period: Colin Campbell's cultic milieu (1972). Campbell extended the common sense use of the term as connoting a deviant or abnormal religion, and inserted this into the church/sect typology. He developed a model of the cultic milieu as a location of cultural and religious deviance in which spiritual seekers operate and from which new sects emerge (Campbell 1972: 119–27). The cultic milieu existed in different times and places as the context of religious deviancy, but in the case of the contemporary counterculture, it encompassed 'the worlds of the occult and the magical, of spiritualism and psychic phenomena, of mysticism and new thought, of alien intelligences and lost civilizations, of faith healing and nature cure' (Campbell 1972: 122). Scholars of religion continue to deploy this concept of a cultic milieu (e.g. Kaplan and Lööw 2002).

Despite these limited examples within typological models, most sociologists of religion and religious studies scholars broadly have come to recognize the term 'cult' as lacking nuance or theoretical utility. Eileen Barker, preeminent sociologist of religion and a founder in the academic subfield of the study of such groups, cautions that even the earlier typological approaches have fallen out of favour.

Many debates have arisen over definitions of the terms involved in the cult scene. Scholars have used the technical and non-judgemental concepts of "cult" and "sect" in opposition to "church" or "denomination" as "ideal types" for comparative purposes, but by the 1970s, "cult" and "sect" had acquired such pejorative overtones in popular parlance that scholars of religion preferred to use the more neutral label "new religious movement" or, more simply, "NRM" (2017: 10)

While the term 'new religious movement' itself presents its own problems (see Chapter 14) it offers an improvement over the use of a term which implies deviancy and illegitimacy.

Historian of religion Paul Oliver notes that there are a few exceptions, namely attempts to rehabilitate the term as an indicator of social deviance. Oliver characterizes such approaches as predicated on the notion that the 'pejorative connotations' of the term are social constructs, and that 'the very subjectivity, and value-laden nature of the term … makes it useful in discussing new religious organizations' (Oliver 2012: 10). Yet Oliver himself dismisses such an approach, adopting what he calls a more 'objective' stance in his own work (2012). As Oliver implies, the labelling of a group as a cult represents a subjective value judgement that a movement is deviant. Not only is that action itself problematic, but since deviancy is culturally relative, it raises methodological questions. If the United Methodist Church is considered deviant in Greece, yet normative in Texas, but the Church of Jesus Christ of Latter-day Saints (Mormons) are deviant in both Greece and Texas but not in Utah, which of these is a cult?

One must therefore problematize the term, since to label a group as a cult implies the movement lacks legitimacy in some fundamental qualifiable sense. Scholars are increasingly wary of making such claims. Sociologists of new religions Douglas E. Cowan and David G. Bromley caution that 'though there are occasional exceptions, "cult" has become little more than a convenient, if largely inaccurate and always pejorative, shorthand for a religious group that must be presented as odd or dangerous' and that the word 'carries unrelentingly negative connotations' (2015: 2, 4). Even when studying groups that clearly violate the nearly universally recognized bounds of ethical or moral behaviour, such as the Peoples Temple, the danger in using the term 'cult' is that one simply assumes deviancy and a pejorative approach to the movement.

Psychologists of religion have been less likely to reject the term. Marc Galanter, for example, equates cults with groups he terms 'charismatic groups,' which he characterizes as sharing certain psychological elements: shared belief systems, high levels of social cohesiveness, strong influence of behavioural norms and imputed charismatic power of the leader (1989: 5). Throughout his analysis, he equates the idea of cult with such groups. Yet his definitions are slippery: he includes secular movements such as Alcoholics Anonymous, and culturally dominant charismatic movements like Iranian cleric Ayatollah Khomeini's Islamic Revolution. It is difficult to avoid the suspicion that the term cult simply means a group whose members' commitments and beliefs the author considers extreme or deviant. It is unclear how one distinguishes 'high' levels of social cohesiveness – do political parties or armed forces count, or for that matter sororal and fraternal organizations? – or what count as 'strong' influences on behaviour – the rules of monastic groups? the moral codes of Evangelicals? – or even what counts as charisma. If political movements, armies, sororities and major forms of Christianity seem to satisfy these definitions but are not considered cults, then the approach offers no utility and exists only within the bounds of circular logic.

A similar problem presents itself within the field of 'cultic studies', whose proponents generally work outside of religious studies in the mental health and law enforcement professions and identify themselves as working to prevent the rise of cults (Ashcraft 2018: 105). Cultic studies cohere around the concept of brainwashing, a notion that sociologists of religion have rejected as similarly circular and characterize as pseudoscience (Richardson 1985; Stark and Finke 2000: 137). Cultic studies proponents offer multiple models of what defines a cult, but given their therapeutic focus, they tend to consider any group that is deemed mentally unhealthy as a cult.

One cannot help but summarize that the category and terminology of cult are not a helpful one. Even those who champion its usage, those involved in cultic studies, rely on circular logic and overly loose descriptions such that any group ranging from new religious movements to fundamentalist churches, multi-level marketing schemes, political movements or even secular humanism satisfy the definition. In popular parlance, the term simply means someone else's religion that one does not like. From an academic perspective, it is a description based on social deviance, which is both relative within particular cultural movements as well as subjective in orientation. Labelling any group with which one disagrees and considers deviant as a cult may be a common occurrence, but it is not scholarship.

CHAPTER 5
DIASPORA
Kim Knott

Origins and history of usage

'Diaspora' and 'diasporas', terms now used widely to refer to migrant minorities and globally dispersed identity groups, have their origins in Greek and are related to the verb, *diasporein*, meaning to scatter or disperse. The term was first used by ancient Greeks in the context of migration and colonialization, and then appeared in the Christian *New Testament* (John 7:35, James 1:1 and 1 Peter 1:1). It later became identified with exile and trauma, with reference to the expulsion of the Jews after the destruction of the temple in 586 BCE. Subsequently it referred to the enslavement and migration of Africans in association with the slave trade and, latterly, the forced displacement of Armenians and Palestinians from their homelands as a result of war and massacre (Cohen 1997; Baumann 2010).

In scholarly circles, until the late-twentieth century, 'diaspora' was generally reserved for discussion of the Jewish exile, identity and lived experience beyond Israel (Boyarin and Boyarin 1993). In the 1990s, the development and usage of the concept took two separate directions. The first was that of cultural theorists, such as Stuart Hall (1990), Paul Gilroy (1993) and James Clifford (1994), who challenged dominant assumptions about the centrality of nations, borders and migration, and foregrounded diasporic subjectivity, hybridity and the politics of identity. The second direction was taken by scholars of migration and ethnicity, such as Avtar Brah (1996) and Robin Cohen (1997), who explored new ways of thinking about the location and connections of migrants in relation to home and away. 'Diaspora' was used increasingly in discussions of migrant mobility, identity and belonging, across borders and in new settings. In recognition of the increasing semantic breadth of the term and its wide-ranging use for diverse minorities, the plural noun, 'diasporas', emerged as the preferred term (Tölölyan 1996; Cohen 1997). Cohen, for example, developed a typology, dividing them into victim, labour, trade, imperial and cultural diasporas in recognition of their diverse motivations and experiences.

Alongside academic debates, a further trend gathered speed: migrant and other transnational cultural minorities began to use the term themselves. It added weight to their sense of identity, their connections with 'home' and their cross-border relationships. To varying degrees, it empowered them as immigrants and settlers in dealing with local authorities, and as émigrés who wished their collective voice to be heard in their countries of origin (Tölölyan 1996). From the 1990s, then, 'diaspora' was used both by cultural theorists and migration scholars as a scientific or technical concept – an *etic* term – and by minority representatives as a vernacular or *emic* term to refer to their own group and its local and transnational interests and claims.

Despite this flowering of the term, as Seán McLoughlin (2013: 125) noted, in conformity with the broadly secular character and interests of the arts and social sciences in the late-twentieth century, many scholars ignored the question of religion in their discussion of diaspora/s, irrespective of the enduring trope of Jewish exile from the promised land.

Religion and diaspora: Contact and contest

The concept of 'diaspora' is contested within and beyond the study of religions. Potential problems arise not only in relation to the meaning and core elements of the term, but the breadth of its usage, who uses it and why. In addition, scholars of religion have asked further questions about 'religious diasporas', a term first used by Ninian Smart (1987). What, if anything, is religious about diasporas? Can 'cognate phenomena' such as universal or world religions like Christianity and Islam be said to be diasporic (Cohen 1997: 187)? Do so-called ethnic religions, which relate to a particular place or people, such as Zoroastrianism and Sikhism, become diasporas as their adherents migrate and settle in new locations?

Although the earliest Greek references to 'diaspora' bore no relation to religion, once the Hebrew scriptures were translated for Greek-speaking Jews in Alexandria in the third and second centuries BCE, the term became wedded to the dispersal of Jews from the sacred land of Israel-Palestine (Baumann 2000, 2010). At that time, it conveyed none of the traumatic associations of exile it later acquired. Nevertheless, it did carry a spiritual connotation. Having disobeyed and been cast out of their promised land, Jews were to see their life in Babylon as a time to prepare and repent before an eventual return and re-gathering. This soteriological understanding (soteriology is the theology of salvation) was at the heart of the Jewish sense of collective identity and purpose, and continued to be commemorated in Jewish liturgy and rituals (Baumann 2010: 21). It gave special significance to 'diaspora', to what it meant to be scattered beyond Israel, to the ordering of Jewish life according to God's commandments and to living in the hope and expectation of return. Although no other group would mirror the Jewish experience completely, the conjoining of ideas – around exile and dispersal, being an outsider whilst belonging to one's own group, with memories of 'home' and a myth of return – drew others to apply the concept of 'diaspora' to their own circumstances.

Early Christian commentators, for example, adopted the term to signify the seeding of new Christian communities away from the heartland of Jerusalem (Baumann 2000), and this idea was repeated many centuries later in relation to the evangelical work of missionaries among expatriates living away from home. Although 'diaspora' was linked in these cases to the idea of mission rather than displacement or otherness, in other

Christian contexts it was the latter that was foregrounded. In the post-Reformation period in Europe, the term was used of Protestant and Catholic minorities living in one another's jurisdictions, with the focus on being outsiders with a shared confessional identity that differed from those around them (Baumann 2010).

The notions of traumatic dispersal, sense of being other, commitment to homeland and collective consciousness all contributed to the evocation of an African diaspora rooted in the experience of slavery (Gilroy 1993). Although 'African diaspora' only began to be used – as a scholarly concept – from the mid-1950s, 'Africans abroad have long felt an affinity with the Jewish diaspora' (Cohen 1997: 31). At times, this affinity was expressed in religious terms, for example by African Christian migrants who drew on Biblical texts and hymns of the Exodus, Babylon and the promised land to express their own spiritual longing, and by Marcus Garvey and later Rastafari who used similar tropes and symbols to evoke a new political theology of 'return to Africa' (McLoughlin 2013).

When Smart first used the concept of 'religious diasporas', he was less interested in taking this historical view than in drawing attention to new opportunities arising in the context of migration and globalization. Religious organizations and communities were now better able to sustain community bonds and links with sacred sites, and to extend their global connections, he suggested. Twin effects of this diasporic process were, first, the focus on collective self-definition, on seeing the community as distinctive and different, though comparable in kind to other religious minorities and, second, the tendency to universalize and rationalize those religious beliefs and practices that could be understood by and shared with others.

Since the 1980s, the idea of religious diasporas has been used with reference to a wide range of migrant minorities (e.g. Sikhs in Canada, Turkish Muslims in the EU, Orthodox Christians in Australia), global sectarian movements (Sufi Orders, African independent churches, the Hindu Swaminarayan movement), even entire world religions whose theology embraces a conception of global community (e.g. Islamic *umma*) or mission (e.g. evangelical Christianity). When people migrate, whether as refugees or as economic migrants, they take their religion with them. On arrival, most connect with those with a similar background and shared language, ethnicity or religion. Religious organizations in places of settlement have often used their resources and connections to welcome and support new migrants, to help them settle and belong, and even to foster their homeland connections (Vásquez 2010; McLoughlin 2013). A key consideration has been how religious communities and organizations have continued to engage with their countries or religion of origin, by remitting funds, participating in charitable activity or political involvement. These processes have contributed to the sense that there is an intrinsic relationship between religion and diaspora.

However, as scholars are at pains to remind readers, not all religions are 'equally diasporic or diasporic in the same way' (Vásquez 2010: 129), with debates arising around whether it is so-called 'universalizing religions', like Islam and Christianity, or 'ethnic religions', like Hinduism and African-based religions like Vodou, that are best described as such (Vertovec 2004; McLoughlin 2013). Comparing world religions with various types of diaspora, Cohen (1997: 189) concluded that religions 'can provide additional cement to bind a diasporic consciousness, but they do not constitute diasporas in and of themselves'. While most scholars of religion accept this position, they are less interested in whether or not religions *are* diasporas and more interested in the 'additional cement' religions provide, whether through material support or the endorsement of their beliefs and practices.

Reversing the relationship, in his work on the African diaspora, Paul Christopher Johnson (2013: 513–15) argued that diasporas *make* religions. Living in diaspora demands the conscious selection of religious ideas, rituals and objects; it requires religious minorities to stake claims for public recognition. As they make new journeys and create new spaces, diasporas mark various sites as religious and use processions and rituals to sacralize public places. Simultaneously, they memorialize sacred places in the homeland, which may take on a renewed significance locally and globally.

Alternatives and new directions

Whether it is the 'additional cement' afforded to diasporas by religious communities and organizations or the way that diasporas make and change religions, it seems clear that there is value in exploring their interrelationship and the resulting innovations. Nevertheless, semantic precision remains important, not only for distinguishing diasporas and religions, but for understanding the processes which support them. Steve Vertovec (2004) acknowledged that religious dynamics would develop differently in accordance with their context, be that one of migration, transnationalism or diaspora, all of which he believed should be understood differently: 'Diasporas arise from some forms of migration, but not all migration involves diasporic consciousness; all transnational communities comprise diasporas, but not all diasporas develop transnationalism' (Vertovec 2004: 282).

Recognizing the history and significance of religious travel and the portability and circulation of ritual and sacred objects, Vertovec suggested that studying contemporary diasporas was important for appreciating the transformative potential of religion. Religions encouraged people to cross borders – mentally as well as physically – and to reimagine connections with sacred places and times. They helped their adherents develop a consciousness of real and imagined geographies, and a sense of belonging to both.

Vertovec's comparison of cognate concepts introduced 'transnationalism' to the discussion of religion and diaspora, thus drawing attention to the process by which people, goods and services move back and forth across borders and the ensuing social, economic and cultural connections. The term was given its fullest treatment in relation to religion by Peggy Levitt (2007), who examined the impact of migrants on the changing face of religious diversity in the United States through a transnational lens. This 'optic' took as its starting point the idea of a borderless world which recognizes that people's loyalties, interests and sense of belonging are not confined within national boundaries. This perspective resonates strongly with religious claims that 'God needs no passport': religion is 'the ultimate boundary crosser', with faith traditions reaching across commonplace boundaries of time and space (Levitt 2007: 12–13).

This idea was taken still further by Thomas Tweed (2006), who developed a theory of religion based on the linked concepts of 'crossing' and 'dwelling'. Taking initial inspiration from his in-depth study of the Cuban Catholic migrant minority in the United States, Tweed drew on the idea that, as people dwell simultaneously in new locations and imagined homelands, they are supported by religious traditions which enable and constrain them to make 'terrestrial, corporeal and cosmic crossings'. Religions help people to be both in place (emplaced) and on the move (displaced) by providing practical, emotional and ideological/ theological resources. Unlike secular institutions and processes, their remit goes beyond this world and extends to the cosmic, to ultimate horizons and ends.

This theory, that 'religions are flows, translocative and transtemporal crossings', which 'bring the gods to earth and transport the faithful to the heavens' (Tweed 2006: 158), brings us back to the concept of 'diaspora' in two ways. 'Religion', according to this view, and 'diaspora' are brought together through the idea of *crossing*. Diasporas connect across borders by foregrounding a consciousness of the ties that bind dispersed people with one another and with their place of origin. Moreover, religions offer the very resources – those translocative and transtemporal crossings – that transform this-worldly migrant journeys and transnational connections into a diasporic consciousness.

'Diaspora' remains a useful term for the study of religions. Through its focus on people's imagined connections to places and communities of origin, it bridges between the academic terrains of migration and religion. It also allows scholars to highlight the role of religion and religions for people on the move.

CHAPTER 6
FOLK RELIGION
Marion Bowman

What do we think of when we hear the term 'folk religion'? Might it involve dancing around a May Pole, people watching the midsummer sunrise at Stonehenge, saying hello to the fairies when crossing the Fairy Bridge on the Isle of Man, rolling hard boiled eggs down hills on Easter Sunday in Scotland, 'evil eye' traditions, visiting holy wells, believing in ghosts? These are all answers I have received from students in the UK over the years. Or perhaps folk religion might have connotations for us of local or culturally specific traditions associated with Christianity, Islam and other so-called 'world religions', such as Malaysian Hari Raya 'kampong' scenes (models of 'traditional' Malaysian village houses which are displayed as part of the Eid al-Fitr festivities), or Maltese Last Supper Tables (tables of varying dimensions in churches' premises and private houses featuring elaborately crafted, artistically arranged displays of 'food' made from coloured rice, dried pasta and other materials, representing the table set for the Last Supper). Or perhaps 'folk religion' signifies creating and eating special festive/festival foods (such as dishes specifically associated with Ramadan or Diwali in different parts of the world, or hand-painted eggs and special breads and cakes for Easter in various countries).

Folk religion can be a problematic concept for a range of reasons, but primarily because it means such different things to different people. To some, folk religion has the connotation of ideas, practices and material culture that are quaint but outmoded; to others, folk religion denotes misguided beliefs, 'magical' practices or possibly even dangerous ideas that are an affront both to rationalism and 'real' religion. Folk religion is attractive to some in the contemporary Western world as possibly containing traces of Indigenous, pre-Christian religiosity that might be 'revived' or repurposed for contemporary life; while for some scholars, it is a fascinating field within the study of religion, central to understanding 'religion as it is lived: as humans encounter, understand, interpret and practice it' (Primiano 1995: 44). As much depends on the context in which the term 'folk religion' is used, it is important to learn to be discerning as to who is using the term and from what standpoint.

To understand this plethora of meanings, some historical background, key concepts and methodological approaches can help to unpick the different strands in this complex web of meanings and understandings.

Folk religion and 'survivals'

In the second half of the nineteenth century, evolutionary ideas were permeating all sorts of academic disciplines. Applying the theory of unilinear evolution to religion, in 1870 John Lubbock declared that 'races in a similar state of mental development, however distinct their origins may be, and however distinct the regions they inhabit, have very similar religious concepts' (Lubbock 1870: 132). Edward Tylor introduced the influential idea of 'survivals': 'processes, customs, opinions, and so forth, which have been carried on by force of habit into a new state of society different from that in which they had their original home, and thus they remain as proofs and examples of an old condition of culture out of which the newer has been evolved' (Tylor 1871: 15). Such theories had far-reaching implications for the study of religion, folklore and anthropology.

Following the founding of the Folk-Lore (later Folklore) Society in 1878, folklorist George Lawrence Gomme declared that 'The science of Folk-Lore is the comparison and identification of the survivals of archaic beliefs, customs, and traditions in modern ages' (Gomme 1891: 2). Just as it was assumed then that the anthropological study of contemporary indigenous peoples could throw light on 'Stone Age Religion', studying folk religion became regarded as a serious endeavour in relation to the history of religion, for the beliefs and practices of 'the folk' could be seen as 'survivals' of previous levels of civilization.

These were not new ideas; from at least the seventeenth century, for example, antiquaries had been describing and characterizing ancient Britons in the light of new ethnographical material arriving from the Americas and elsewhere (see Piggott 1989). However, folklore gave such ideas a boost and a wider audience, actively promoting this evolutionary model of culture and encouraging many to engage in the hunt for survivals in disparate contexts. As George Lawrence and Alice Gomme commented in *British Folk-Lore, Folk-Songs and Singing Games*:

> … in every society there are people who do not progress either in religion or in polity with the foremost of the nation. They are left stranded amidst the progress. They live in out-of-the-way villages, or in places where general culture does not penetrate easily… These people are living depositories of ancient history – a history that has not been written down, but which has come down by tradition. Knowing the conditions of survivals in culture, the folklorist uses them in the ancient meaning, not in their modern setting, tries to find out their significance and importance in relation to their origin, and thus lays the foundation for the science of folklore.
>
> (Gomme 1916: 10)

This led to cultural traditions such as calendar customs (events that happen once a year), or certain beliefs, praxis and even children's games being observed not as contemporary, dynamic, context-specific phenomena, but for what they had been in some distant past, thus clearing the way for numerous 'reconstructions' of the 'originals' which were considered to have 'degenerated' over time among the folk.

Academic folklorists abandoned the theory of survivals as the basis of the 'science' of folklore and evolutionary theories became increasingly less important within the study of religion. However, such attitudes and assumptions left definite legacies. The popular view of folklore and folk religion, and to some extent evolutionary ideas of religious development, in some contexts atrophied in its nineteenth-century roots, and the hunt for survivals which characterized so much early British folklore continues in non-academic, popular works on folk religion and sections of the media. Such attitudes undoubtedly informed the twentieth-century British folk revival (see Boyes 1993), and continue to influence certain strands of contemporary Paganism and aspects of contemporary Celtic spirituality. For instance, there are assumed to be crossovers between some contemporary indigenous religious practices and early British 'indigenous religion' (hence contemporary Druidic sweat lodges), with loosely defined and sometimes romanticized Celts being regarded as 'living depositories of ancient history' (see Bowman 2000).

For people to use folk religion as a jumping-off point to speculate about religion in the past, and to seek inspiration from contemporary Indigenous praxis and pre-Christian cultures to negotiate the present are understandable. But it is useful to discern between those who, on observing a 'folk religious' practice such as tying ribbons on trees around what are known as healing or 'cloutie' wells, would regard this as a 'survival' and try to reconstruct an ancient system of belief from it, and those who might be more interested in how it fitted into the worldview, identity and lived praxis of those doing it now.

Another sense in which folk religion has been connected with survivals has been in contexts where it has been associated with syncretism (a concept problematized elsewhere in this volume) in the sense of a newer – often missionizing – religion suspecting that previous religious and cultural traditions and worldviews are being perpetrated through 'folk religious' ideas and practices (e.g. in relation to the treatment of and communication with the dead, ghostlore and so on).

The academic study of folk religion

A frequent criticism of Religious Studies as it developed in some Anglophone and European cultures has been the extent to which it has been rather Protestant-influenced, resulting in an overly text and belief-oriented focus, neglectful or dismissive of extra-institutional activity, ideas and practices, material culture, ritual, local tradition and other aspects of lived religion.

While folklore – or folkloristics (the name preferred by some for the academic study of folklore to distinguish it from the subject matter) – and ethnology did not flourish as academic disciplines in the UK, in continental Europe, North America and elsewhere, it did. Within this, the study of folk religion has been a major strand, influenced by fieldwork-based methodological approaches that engage with religion in everyday life, within and well beyond texts and institutional settings. In this context, it should be noted, the 'folk' in folklore and folk religion are no longer the rural folk 'left stranded by progress' but diverse groups sharing worldviews, beliefs, lifeworlds and identities of different sorts (e.g. gender, locality, occupation).

A number of European countries have produced rich literatures discussing the specific meanings attached to the term 'folk religion', and to the historical, social, political and intellectual factors that gave rise to these meanings (see Hakamies and Honko 2013; Kapaló 2013). Influential American folk religion scholar Don Yoder succinctly described folk religion as 'the totality of all those views and practices of religion that exist among the people apart from and alongside the strictly theological and liturgical forms of the official religion' (Yoder 1974: 13). The study of folk religion in such academic contexts has involved the study of embodied praxis (pilgrimage, calendar custom, relationships with the environment) and oral forms (from local legend to personal experience narratives, songs, healing formulae, jokes, etc.), attention to material culture (including foodways, home altars, costume, ex votos, the uses made of objects regarded as sacred, special or 'powerful') and a pragmatic view of tradition not as something fixed and monolithic but as a fluid societal resource built upon vernacular knowledge and authority (see Howard 2013).

Despite this encompassing approach, among the consequences of designating certain beliefs, praxis, material culture and worldviews as folk religion has been a definitional dichotomy between 'folk religion' and 'official religion' and for some the implication that 'folk religion' is somehow different from, divorced from, beyond or inferior to, institutional formulations of religion. It is interesting to note that Yoder's definition was influenced by the German 'Religiose Volkskunde' – 'the folk-cultural dimensions of religion, or the religious dimension of folk culture' (Yoder 1974: 14), a term developed in 1901 by Paul Drews, a German Lutheran minister whose concern was to study religious folklife to better equip trainee ministers to deal with what they would encounter in parishes, 'to narrow the understanding gap between pulpit and pew' (Yoder 1974: 3). There is still plenty of evidence of such 'understanding gaps' within institutional settings. In response to the question 'What aspects of folk religion do you encounter?' as part of a survey of Anglican clergy attitudes, responses included Earth-religion, Wicca, road accident shrines, New Age healing, Tarot, Druidry, ley lines, Eastern religions, acupuncture, corn dollies and wassailing (Walker 2001).

However, a number of scholars within folkloristics/ethnology and the study of religion have long argued that for people 'doing religion' this is not a clear-cut or meaningful distinction, and that it artificially reifies 'official religion' as real religion. To understand 'religion as it is lived', it is necessary to envisage a much broader, combined 'package' of what might broadly be termed folk religion, official or institutional formulations of religion, and the individual component of religion (see Bowman 2004). The individual component comprises each person's understanding and reception of a religion or worldview (for people learn from a variety of overt and implicit sources, from family, by example and observation, and increasingly from various media) and the part it plays in their lifeworld (influenced by experiences and their own interpretations). It is in the interaction of all these aspects that lived religion is to be found. This is why an increasing number of scholars in both folkloristics/ethnology and the study of religion find vernacular religion a useful and realistic methodological approach (see Illman and Czimbalmos 2020).

Vernacular religion

Vernacular religion is closely associated with the study of folk religion but is *not* a synonym for folk religion; it is a new concept that builds upon the insights, subject matter and methodologies of the folkloristic and fieldwork-based approach to the study of religion. Leonard Primiano (whose background was in both folklore and the study of religion) proposed vernacular religion as 'an interdisciplinary approach to the study of the religious lives of individuals with special attention to the process of religious belief, the verbal, behavioral, and material expressions of religious belief, and the ultimate object of religious belief' (1995: 44). Belief is a controversial term in some contexts, but here it is understood not as assent to fixed doctrinal frameworks, but the worldviews and experiences that shape people's discourse, their actions, their relationships with others (including other than human beings) and their engagement with the material world (Bowman and Valk 2012: 5–10). Primiano was arguing that scholars need to recognize religion and spiritual seeking as lived, highly individual, polyphonic, context-sensitive, dynamic and ambiguous – not a simple binary that privileges 'official' religion over 'folk' religion, and that fails to take into account individual agency and creativity.

Vernacular religious theory understands religion as 'the continuous art of individual interpretation and negotiation of any number of influential sources' (Primiano 2012: 384), and it 'highlights the power of the individual and communities of individuals to create and re-create their own religion' (Primiano 2012: 383). It is an approach that starts 'on the ground' where people might be pragmatically contesting, expanding, reformulating in pragmatic ways institutional formulations of religion in a variety of ways and through various means, and it treats such activities and manifestations as equally worthy and necessary objects of study as institutional forms of religiosity. Vernacular religion brings aspects of religion previously designated 'folk religion' in from the margins of the study of religion to take its rightful place as an important aspect of the study of religion *per se*.

CHAPTER 7
FUNDAMENTALISM
Camille Kaminski Lewis

From the beginning of the twentieth century, fundamentalism identifies a subset of an established religious tradition, positioning itself on the borders of conventional norms. The concept of fundamentalism seems to persist in contemporary religious cultures as both inside and outside a particular religion's boundary. Maintaining this liminal position, as a result, makes fundamentalists pious in their adherence to original sacred texts, aggressive in their social interactions, and hyper-conservative in their patriotism. Martin E. Marty and R. Scott Appleby in their *Fundamentalism Project* identify the fundamentalist impulse in Islam, Judaism, Christianity, Buddhism and Hinduism. To Marty and Appleby, fundamentalism is a direct product of modernity, a reaction to a religious establishment followed by an attention-seeking action to launch its own identity (Marty and Applebee 1991).

Fundamentalism: The origin

Prior to the turn of the twentieth century, the term 'fundamentalism' was generically a noun variation of 'foundational' or 'conservative'. When Christian leaders used the term – either Catholic or Protestant – they used it synonymously with 'orthodox' (Oxford English Dictionary 2021). In 1882, liberal Protestant Henry Ward Beecher affirmed his belief in what he called 'fundamental doctrines', which are 'necessary to Christian life and character', such as belief in 'a personal God', the Trinity and the 'inspiration of the Bible' (Beecher 1882). Thus, the concept was apolitical, nonspecific and uncontroversial among Anglo-Christians.

However, after the turn of the twentieth century, a group of would-be Fundamentalists fused within the larger conservative branch of Protestantism known as Evangelicalism. Evangelicalism is another subset of Christianity which, according to D. W. Bebbington, foregrounds individual conversion, personal evangelism, a common-sensical interpretation of the Bible, and a hyper-focus on Jesus Christ's atonement and death on the cross (2004: 2–17). Among Anglo-Protestants, Evangelicalism additionally denotes groups that persist in mass revivals after the First and Second Great Awakenings.

When so-called liberal Protestants began promoting collective social reforms after the American Civil War, the more conservative and individualistic Evangelicals splintered even further. Their invention resisted what they sensed was any whiff of 'liberal' intellectualism and united cooperation – what they perceived as 'modern'. A founder of Union Oil, Lyman Stewart, and his brother Milton – both elders at Immanuel Presbyterian in Los Angeles—documented and promoted this resistant faction. They financed the publication of *The Fundamentals: A Testimony to Truth* to distinguish their brand of conservative Protestantism from the intellectual 'higher criticism'. The original publications did not name the two businessmen. They simply described themselves as 'two intelligent, consecrated Christian laymen' who will 'bear the expense because they believe that the time has come when a new statement of the fundamentals of Christianity should be made. Their earnest desire is that you will carefully read it and pass its truth on to others' (Torrey et al. 1910: 4).

Notice their justification. They declared their own individual piety or 'consecration'. They ignored their own denominational ties. They focused on individual readers. They concentrated those readers' attention on persuading others, on evangelism. All the canonical features that Bebbington describes as 'Evangelical' are here in this opening paragraph. What is hidden, however, is that naming 'the Fundamentals' comes from businessmen, not theologians. In other words, this was branding more than systemic thought. Rather than engaging in a disciplinary conversation among theological scholars, the Stewarts financed a populist argument to animate individuals in existing Protestant churches.

The Stewarts published their twelve-volume series from 1910 to 1915. The writers included conservative Evangelicals such as R. A. Torrey and A. W. Dixon. The essays surveyed traditional discussions of orthodoxy such as Christ's deity as well as the contemporary conflicts described as 'fallacies of higher criticism', Mormonism, 'Eddyism' and 'Romanism' (1910). Ironically, while *The Fundamentals* critique Charles Taze Russell, their volumes parallel his *Millennial Dawn* six-volume series (1886–1904). Both are lengthy and populist with an intellectual-ish writing style.

The Fundamentalist: The persona

In 1920 a Baptist pastor in Brooklyn, New York coined another variation of the term: 'Fundamentalist'. This word further individuated the concept into a single person who adheres to 'Fundamentalism'. Curtis Lee Laws had a national platform as the chief editor of the Baptist *Watchman-Examiner*. He argued that 'Fundamentalist' was a more neutral word than 'conservative' which then, he surmised, had a pejorative connotation (Marty 1997: 159–60). Yet the term quickly mutated away from Laws's notion of neutral resistance to pure social and political belligerence.

That contentious persona was already well-known in the American consciousness. Richard Hofstadter identified this same pugnacity when he described a fanatic who uses religious arguments in the public sphere. He called that person a 'one-hundred percenter', but his chief exemplar was the twentieth-century Fundamentalist evangelist Billy Sunday. To Hofstadter, Sunday demonstrates 'a mind totally committed to the full range of the dominant popular fatuities and determined that no one shall have the right to challenge them'. This persona is a 'recent' creation, Hofstadter argues, born out of religion, American exceptionalism and traditional morality. Thus, for this historian in the mid-twentieth century, the Fundamentalist is 100 per cent committed to inflexibility in their faith, their politics and their ethics. That persona is a political (not merely religious) actor who 'will tolerate no ambiguities, no equivocations, no reservations, and no criticism' (1963: 131, 146). In sum, Hofstadter sees this resistant Fundamentalist as wholly American.

Historian Martin Marty underlines that the Fundamentalist, in opposing modernity, creates a rampant individualism with the phrase, 'the Bible is all I need' (1997: 155–9). This individualism is ironically part of their collective identity. That is, to see oneself as a singular actor – a lone believer against an increasingly chaotic world – is essential to being part of their group (1970: 177–87). Thus, what Laws named in 1920 was already a persistent persona in the post-Civil-War American political sphere according to Hofstadter and a persona which would cement American individualism with religious devotion according to Marty.

The Fundamentalist fight

When an outsider perceives a rugged individualistic fight in a religious group, the concept of fundamentalism is at work. At the first World Congress of Fundamentalists, the infamous Bob Jones, Jr. stated the Fundamentalist *sine qua non* plainly enough: 'The *only* Fundamentalists are militant Fundamentalists' (Jones 1976: 132). Martin Marty and Scott Appleby describe Fundamentalists as people who 'fight'. They '*fight for*' their own, they '*fight with*' lexical resources, they '*fight against* others', but they always, in their view, '*fight under* God' (1994: ix–x). The verb 'fight' is continuous. Every interaction is a battle. In the American concept, Fundamentalists took their fight into the Civil Rights movement, splitting with their Evangelical siblings when white Evangelical Billy Graham included Black minister Martin Luther King, Jr. in his 1957 evangelistic Crusade (1997: 425–6; Lewis 2021). Dan Crawford contends that George Marsden's (1991) singular focus on militarism is misguided since it ignores the more moderate strain of conservative Protestants and conflates violent action with violent words and dogmatic beliefs. Dogmatism is 'defensive', he insists, but militancy is 'offensive'. If Marsden were to expand beyond the likes of Bob Jones and Carl McIntire, according to Crawford, he would see the kinder, gentler moderates like Billy Graham (Wood and Watt 2014: 36–54). However, both Crawford and Marsden fail to see the symbiotic relationship between the militarists and the moderates. Each gives the other an identity and the ground to argue for their own purity.

Fundamentalism – the concept's persistence

A survey of English language newspapers over the last three centuries reveals the events that prompted the most frequent use of the fundamentalist concept. 'Fundamentalism' and 'Fundamentalist' peaked in 1925 with the Scopes Trial in Tennessee, in 1992 with political unrest in the Middle East, and finally in 2001 after the 9/11 attacks on the World Trade Center in New York City. Thus, intense socio-political conflicts in the modern and post-modern condition direct the public's scrutiny on liminal religious groups, and that scrutiny forces a reckoning with the concept of 'fundamentalism'.

In the middle of those events by the 1990s, a lower-case 'fundamentalism' consistently signified any kind of religious resistance. In public conversations reporters identified 'fundamentalist Mormons' who had separated from the mainline Latter-day Saints and practised plural marriage (Watson 1944). There were 'fundamentalist Catholics' who refused secular dances and repudiated the ecclesiastical authority of the Pope (Sparks 1987). There was a 'Hindu fundamentalist opposition party' who militantly resisted the Indian government in power (New York Times 1992). And, of course, the most common usage of the 'fundamentalist Muslim Shiite population' after the 1990s Middle East turmoil (Combined 1990). Another recent use of the fundamentalist concept emerges in a journalist's description of a 'Buddhist fundamentalism' which is 'spreading its tentacles in Sri Lanka, Myanmar, and Thailand'. The opening metaphor indicates the journalist's conclusion of the group's manipulative, belligerent piety. This group 'attacks' other religious adherents and outsiders, forbids 'inter-faith marriage' and limits the creative language use of even the term 'Buddha' (Arora 2014). In assessing the political conditions across the globe in the Covid pandemic, scholars in counter-terrorism struggle with the people who coalesce opposite 'non-fundamentalist and tolerant Islamic traditions' identifying them as 'extreme right' and 'violent' (Ramakrishna 2021: 12). Violence, opposition, separatism and zealotry persist in fundamentalisms across the globe and into the twenty-first century.

Diversity and creativity, however, have stretched the concept of fundamentalism. For instance, in the mid-twentieth century the Buddhist sect Soka Gakkai used aggressive evangelism which resembled fundamentalist piety. However, Juliana Finucane argues that the group has adapted to 'embrace a "both/and" approach to proselytizing, in which they embrace pluralist values about religious tolerance while gently encouraging the conversion of others' (Finucane 2014). This adaptation challenges fundamentalism's longevity. If a group modifies from an aggressive originating action to a gentler appeal, how combative or 'fundamentalist' were they in the first place? Perhaps 'the fight' is necessary for a new religion and can be shed once their identity is established.

None of the religious adherents in any of these groups identify themselves as fundamentalists. Outsiders recognize the fundamentalist bent in order to explain to other outsiders the liminal status and personality of this particular piety. In 2017, musicologist Sarah Bereza surveyed those sectarians whom outsiders would typically identify as Evangelical 'Fundamentalists'. She perceived that the 9/11 attack on the World Trade Center was a watershed event for usually Fundamentalist people to shed the term. For example, faculty members at Bob Jones University – the most infamous of Fundamentalist institutions of higher education – resisted the term to describe themselves. They preferred to say that they 'believe in the fundamentalist doctrines' exactly as the liberal Henry Ward Beecher described himself 150 years earlier (2017: 406).

The term 'biblicist', while nearly 200 years old, is sometimes the new self-identifier for Fundamentalists among conservative Evangelicals in the United States. Mennonites use the term (Shelter 1967). Jerry Falwell's publication *The Fundamentalist Journal* and fundamentalist minister Kevin Bauder have used 'biblicist' to describe themselves 'between' or even 'above' Calvinist and Arminian theologies (Mitchell 1982; Bauder 2008). The word denotes a tone of superiority in their singular alignment with Holy Writ. That same superiority in self-identification is what prompted Curtis Lee Laws's coining of the term in 1920. While Protestants quibble over 'biblicism', some Muslims have adopted the concept of 'Quaranist' to identify their separatism motivated by a singular devotion to an original text (Smith and Haddad 2014: 150–6).

Overall, the lower-case term 'fundamentalism' persists as a legitimate concept for outsiders to understand combative separatists among traditional religions within the postmodern condition. In her 2017 dissertation about conservative Evangelical music practices, Sarah Bereza argues that the 'fundamentalism' concept is still useful and necessary. Those ideological descendants continue to occupy the same liminal space that their historical forebears created; however, in her study these separatists code their position as 'Bible-believing' or 'Bible-centred' (2017: 404–7). This hyphenated participle seems more ambiguous and less charged for the separatists that use it, but the concept of fundamentalism persists in identifying this faction of liminal Protestant Christians. Simon Wood, however, insists that scholars should resist using this more 'global' or generic meaning of fundamentalism since the term is a 'signifier [which] lacks a concrete signified' (2014: 125–43). In other words, only the 'historic fundamentalism' with origins in Anglo-American Protestantism can be properly called 'fundamentalism'. Wood's argument is more optimistically prescriptive than realistically descriptive. When a signifier has been identified, custom and use will strategically stretch, morph and alter its meaning however ambiguous.

While fewer people might identify themselves as part of fundamentalisms, this discrete but liminal category of adherents continues. When capitalized 'Fundamentalism' denotes that twentieth-century movement within Anglo-Protestant Evangelicalism which originated in the United States and which resisted education, deliberation and reform. Few fundamentalists of any religious group see themselves as outliers. Instead they perceive themselves as the historically true and pure subcategory against an increasingly secularized religious group. For the specific Anglo-Protestant Fundamentalists, the ideological walls that separated them from their Evangelical siblings have crumbled. Now the term 'Fundamentalist' is nearly synonymous with 'Evangelical' as it was prior to 1920.

CHAPTER 8
GURU
Stephen Jacobs

In the 1972 hit by the British band T. Rex, the lead singer and writer of the song *Metal Guru*, Mark Bolan envisages the metal guru all alone and wonders if he will bring the singer's rock 'n' roll child to him. While the lyrics to this song are not particularly meaningful, they do indicate that the concept of the guru has been widely incorporated into Western popular culture. The term 'guru' is often articulated with concepts such as fashion, health, social media and so on. The cover of *The Social Media Guru: A Practical Guide for Small Businesses* (2016) depicts a man with a beard, wearing a turban, seated cross-legged and hovering in the air. This stereotypical representation of a guru is consistent with what Jane Iwamura has termed 'the oriental monk', who is signified by 'his spiritual commitment, his calm demeanor, his Asian face and often-times his manner of dress' (Iwamura 2017: 53). While the use of the term 'guru' can signify someone with expertise who can offer valuable advice on any aspect of contemporary life, it can also be utilized in a far more negative way. The guru is often represented as a deceptive leader of a fraudulent 'cult', who 'brainwashes' his or her gullible devotees for their own ends. For example, a sensational headline from *The Sun* about the controversial figure Bhagwan Shree Rajneesh, later known as Osho, states: 'Abuse, violence and terror – inside notorious free love guru Bhagwan's sex cult' (Rollings 2019). These Western appropriations of the concept seem a far cry from the idea of the guru in the Hindu traditions. Joel D. Mlecko (1982: 33) notes that 'the individual guru as religious teacher plays an important role in the development of the Hindu religious tradition, from passing on religious knowledge to being himself a *locus* for worship'.

Guru, a Sanskrit term most commonly associated with the Hindu traditions, has now been absorbed into the English language. The use of a Sanskrit term suggests that there is no cognate term in English. Although the concept of the guru has connotations of teacher, preceptor and so on these are not synonymous terms. Furthermore, when any term is appropriated by a different language the meaning and significance of that term inevitably changes. However, it would be wrong to think that the meaning of the term 'guru' is static and homogenous in the Hindu context. Jacob Copeman and Aya Ikegame suggest that given the multiple roles that the guru performs in the South Asian context the concept of the guru is 'multifarious' and is characterized by the quality of 'uncontainability' (Copeman and Ikegame 2014: 37). In other words, because the concept of the guru has and is (and presumably will be) used in a plethora of contexts, it potentially has an inexhaustible range of meanings and significance.

The Sanskrit term 'guru' is often said to mean 'heavy'. Consequently, it is possible to suggest the term 'guru' is cognate with the Latin term *gravitas*, meaning heavy or weighty. The word gravitas in English suggests a person who is serious, important and influential. However, a guru often indicates much more than a person of consequence. The most cited understanding of the guru can be found in the *Guru Gītā*. This Hindu text relates how the goddess Pārvatī asks her consort Śiva to tell her of the glory of the Guru. In a much-cited verse Śiva states:

> The syllable *gu* indicates darkness and the syllable *ru* indicates light. Indeed, without doubt, the Guru is God, the one who destroys ignorance. (*Guru Gītā*, verse 23 in Swami Nityānanda 2020: 30)

There are two significant points in this verse: First, the *Guru Gītā*, clearly equates the guru with God. Secondly, the Guru brings liberatory knowledge to the disciple. There are references in many Hindu texts that liberation is not possible without the Guru.

The Guru in the Indian context

The earliest references to the guru seem to indicate someone who was knowledgeable about the Vedas, which are the ancient and extensive compositions in Sanskrit that many Hindus regard as foundational texts. The guru in this early Vedic period probably referred to a male *brahmin* who was particularly conversant with the performance of the complex rituals that are detailed in the Vedas. High-caste boys would spend a period of time in the guru's abode (*gurukula*) studying the Vedas and serving the guru. There is also an indication that the knowledge learnt at the feet of the guru was esoteric. The Vedas were oral compositions and were probably not written down until over 1,000 years after they were originally composed. The latter sections of the Vedas are called the *Upaniṣads*, which literally translates as 'to sit near'. This suggests that students had to sit near to the guru in order not only to hear the Vedas being recited, but also to have these explained to them. In other words, the original significance of the guru sits at the heart of Brahminical orthodoxy.

However, individuals referred to as gurus have also challenged the hegemony of the *brahmins*, the use of Sanskrit and the Vedas. Gavin Flood observes that within Hinduism 'there is a great proliferation of decentred traditions, often founded by a charismatic teacher or guru' (Flood 2005: 4). The concept of the guru is integral to a number of dissenting Hindu traditions, such as yoga and *bhakti* that suggest alternative religious paths to Vedic orthodoxy.

Yoga is both a philosophy and a practice, whose roots remain obscure. However, it is clear in many texts that a guru is a necessary prerequisite for the study of yoga. For example, an important yoga text called the *Śivasaṃhita* indicates that to succeed in yoga a guru is absolutely essential. One verse states: 'If it comes from a guru's mouth wisdom is potent. If it does not, it is barren and impotent and brings great suffering' (cited in Mallinson and Singleton 2017: 68). Another indication of the significance of the guru in yoga is the style of one of the most important yoga texts – *The Yoga Sūtras of Patañjali*. This text is aphoristic and makes little sense without extensive explanation. This suggests that a guru is required who can elucidate these otherwise enigmatic statements. Yoga is most commonly associated with the physical postures (*āsana*). Not only are the yoga texts very vague about these physical aspects of yoga, but it seems common sense that some sort of teacher is required to ensure that these postures are performed correctly.

Bhakti means 'loving devotion' and refers to the devotion to the divine. *Bhakti*, albeit manifesting in a multiplicity of ways, has become the dominant form of Hindu religiousness. One of the main forms of *bhakti* are the *Sant* traditions. The term refers to a number of medieval poet-saints called *sants*. Etymologically *sant* derives from the Sanskrit term *sat*, meaning truth. Therefore, a *sant* is a person who knows the truth. However, this truth is not derived from the Vedas, but from the personal experience of the sacred. These *sants* composed ecstatic poetry in vernacular languages of their experience and love of the divine. The *guru* in the Sant traditions tends to be an ambiguous and metaphysical concept. It is not at all clear in the Sant tradition, whether the guru is necessarily embodied in a human figure. The idea of the *satguru* – or true guru also develops in the Sant traditions. Kabir, one of the most important *sants*, states:

The grandeur of the *satguru* is infinite,
Infinite his bounty:
He opened my eyes to the Infinite
and showed me Infinity.
(cited in Vaudeville 1987: 34)

The idea of the *satguru* indicates three significant points. First, a distinction must be made between the 'true guru' who has a direct experience of the sacred and the more generic use of the term that simply indicates a teacher or preceptor. Second, true gurus must be distinguished from fake gurus, who are only concerned with exploiting the gullible. Finally, the concept of the *satguru* refers to the transcendent, rather than simply identifying a particular wise human individual.

The conceptualization of the *satguru* as transcendent can also be identified in Sikhi. There are ten historical gurus in Sikhi. However, the last human guru – Guru Gobind Singh rather than appointing a human successor like his predecessors, installed the sacred text as the guru. This collection of compositions bound in a volume is referred to as the Guru Granth Sahib. A copy of the Guru Granth Sahib is installed in all Sikh places of worship (gurdwara) and is regarded as being the guru. This indicates that the concept of the guru is not necessarily embodied in a human being.

Charisma and authority

The authority of the guru is often understood in terms of charisma, which is defined by Max Weber as 'a certain quality of an individual personality by virtue of which he is considered extraordinary'. Weber continues, 'what alone is important is how the individual is actually regarded by those subject to charismatic authority, by his "followers" or "disciples"' (Weber 1978: 241–2). This makes it clear that guru is a relational concept and not defined by some essential essence that inheres in a particular individual.

Contemporary Hindu gurus validate their authority through a number of discourses, which I term: traditional, experiential and *avatāra*. These are not mutually exclusive, but different gurus may combine these discourses in a variety of ways. Traditional authority is validated through a demonstration of knowledge and understanding of the Vedas and other important texts such as the *Bhagavad Gītā*. Many contemporary gurus like Sri Sri Ravi Shankar give discourses on these traditional texts which are recorded and published and released as DVDs (see Jacobs 2015: 161–5). Another form of traditional authority is that of a lineage (*paramparā*). A living guru often appoints his or her successor. It is a common practice for these guru lineages to be traced back to mythical time and frequently a Hindu deity, such as Śiva, is identified as the originator.

Many contemporary gurus, like Sri Sri Ravi Shankar, claim authority through having some form of personal mystical experience. These narratives of experience are represented as transformative and lead to the awakening of a latent quality that enables 'guruship'. This experience, which is regarded as the pivotal point in the narratives of a guru's life, empowers the individual to transform the lives of others. Devotees often recount how the encounter with their guru has transformed their lives.

Some gurus claim to be an *avatāra*, which more or less means 'divine descent' and refers to the idea that god descends to Earth in order to restore balance and harmony to creation. Mata Amritanandamayi, another popular contemporary guru, is described in her biography as being 'the descent of the nameless, formless and immutable Supreme Energy assuming a human form' (cited in Warrier 2005: 34).

Gurus in the contemporary world

Many recent and contemporary gurus, such as Sri Sri Ravi Shankar and Mata Amritanandamayi, have attracted a global following. The modern transnational guru is now both a celebrity and a branded commodity. In many ways the person who set the template for the global celebrity guru was Maharishi Mahesh Yogi (1918–2008) who founded Transcendental Meditation. Mahesh Yogi appeared on the cover of *New York Times Magazine* in December 1967, which suggested that he was 'The Chief Guru of the Western World'. Mahesh Yogi's exotic appearance with his white robes, long hair and beard, and his appeal to many famous names of the counterculture, such as the Beatles, 'made for eye-catching copy and reinforced long-embedded notions of a spiritual exoticized and extravagant India' (Iwamura 2011: 65).

Gurus increasingly appear in popular culture and are often vilified as charlatans. Gurus became associated with what the popular media identify as cults. For example, in the 1998 episode of *The Simpsons* 'The Joy of Sect', the Simpson family fall under the charismatic spell of the leader of a cult called the Movementarians. The narrative suggests that the followers are 'brainwashed' by continuously chanting 'The Leader is good, The Leader is great; we surrender our will as of this date' (cited in Feltmate 2012: 204). The title of the episode is derived from the famous book *The Joy of Sex*. The Leader at the end of the episode unsuccessfully tries to flee with the money he has embezzled from his followers. This clearly points to a stereotypical view that gurus are inherently hypocritical as they are more concerned with personal power, wealth and sexual gratification than with the spiritual well-being of their devotees. The representation of gurus as Svengali- like leaders of cults derives more from the discourses of the anticult movement than from reality. For example, The Family Survival Trust, an anticult organization in the UK, suggests that 'The guru and/or upper ranks of the cult are supported in a relatively comfortable lifestyle by the exploitation of lower ranking members' (Family Survival Trust 2019).

Stereotypical tropes such as brainwashing, hypocrisy and exploitation that are associated with gurus can also be identified in academic discourses. The renowned author and psychiatrist Anthony Storr published a book on gurus in 1996 called *Feet of Clay*. The title clearly reveals Storr's perspective. Storr acknowledges that there are some gurus 'whose holiness, lack of personal ambition, and integrity are beyond question' such as 'Jesus, Muhammad and the Buddha'. Nonetheless, he uncritically repeats many Western prejudices about gurus as 'unscrupulous wielders of power who exploit their followers in a variety of ways' (Storr 1996: xi). Another important question raised by Storr's book is: 'who is a guru?' It is doubtful whether Jesus, Muhammad or even the Buddha can be considered as being gurus as such. Even more problematic is Storr's inclusion of Carl Jung and Sigmund Freud as gurus. Storr observes that Freud considered himself to be a scientist and 'would have indignantly repudiated the title of guru' (Storr 1996: 109). While psychoanalysis gained a following and possibly even disciples (another contested concept), none of Freud's admirers suggested that he was a guru.

Conclusion

The term 'guru' is now widely used in a wide range of contexts and applied to diverse individuals in a range of different arenas. For example, there are books with titles such as *Invest Like a Guru*. In this book the author simply lists some people he calls 'gurus' who 'had the most impact on me and my investing philosophy' (Tian 2017: 1). The use of the term 'guru' in areas such as marketing or the identification of individuals such as Freud as gurus can be considered as a form of cultural appropriation. The concept of the guru has now extended well beyond its very specific meaning in the Vedic period and is now used to designate any individual who is regarded as having some sort of authority or expertise in almost any arena. The concept of the guru is also evaluated in radically opposed ways – from someone who is ethical and enlightened to the deceitful manipulator of the gullible. This multiplicity of uses and opinions raises a plethora of questions about the nature of the guru. Perhaps the most significant question to raise is: has the concept of the guru been so overused and attenuated that it has become almost meaningless? The globalization and proliferation of uses of the concept make it critical to investigate who is using the term 'guru', in what context and for what end.

CHAPTER 9
INDIGENOUS RELIGIONS
Graham Harvey

'Indigenous' is an adjective widely used to describe individuals and communities whose ancestral cultures preceded European colonization. It links diverse nations and language groups (e.g. Evenki, Lakota, Māori, Sámi and Yoruba) and is of increasing value in enabling collaborations between such communities, especially as they celebrate cultural vitality and affirm their sovereignty. It is also used in international forums like the United Nations and in the research and teaching of many academic disciplines. 'Indigenous' is increasingly preferred to such terms as 'native' or 'tribal' – and it is certainly preferable to colonial terms like 'primitive' or 'savage'. Such political and cultural uses of 'Indigenous' are the wider context in which the term has come to label the 'traditional' or inherited religions of Indigenous, Aboriginal or First Nations people.

Why is 'Indigenous' problematic?

While 'Indigenous religions' is preferable to previous identifications of these religions as 'tribal', 'primitive' or 'primal', it carries its own problems. Paradoxically perhaps, some of these problems can be helpful in advancing understanding of these and other religions – and of wider issues of global significance. That is to say, scholars interested in Indigenous religions make strategic use of the category and its problems as they seek to interest others in critical debates arising from their research. We can group the problems of the category under two headings: vagueness and uncertain comparisons. As we will see later, seeking solutions to these related problems is central to the positive value of the category.

Vagueness

It is not always immediately clear what 'Indigenous' is meant to tell us about the religions it labels. Something can be called 'Indigenous' because it originated in a particular place and time. But why should this be an important thing to say? And, if it is important, why only say it about some rather than all religions?

While identifying where and when something originated might offer interesting facts, it is not clear that this always tells us something that enhances understanding. For example, what difference does it make when we learn that oranges and chickens are Indigenous to South East Asia? Their place of origin is, perhaps, only interesting if we want to discuss how they have spread around the world. But this probably does not improve our appreciation of them. Similarly, the idea that particular religions began in particular places or times might also tell us very little about what those religions involve. Since all religions began in some place and at some time, it is not automatically clear that identifying places and times of origin provides any insight into their characteristics, practice or significance. It is equally unclear whether identifying some religions as 'Indigenous' tells us that they have anything particular in common. This vagueness about the 'Indigenous religions' concept may have everything to do with uncertain comparisons.

Uncertain comparisons

The 'Indigenous religions' category suggests that there are religions which could be called 'not Indigenous'. In fact, the comparison between 'Indigenous' and 'not Indigenous' religions began the other way round. Early studies of religion prioritized phenomena which have been described as 'world religions'. More recently, 'new religious movements' were added to the discipline's curriculum. It is instructive to tease out some of the consequences of these contrasts (noting that they too are contested). In comparison with 'world religions' it is implied that 'Indigenous religions' are constrained by space. Allegedly, they belong to a specific place or community rather than being globally present, universally significant or relevant to 'non-Indigenous' people. A similar implication is suggested when terms like 'ethnic' or 'tribal' are used. In comparison with 'new religious movements' it is implied that 'Indigenous religions' are constrained by time. Allegedly, they are 'ancient' or 'traditional' rather than contemporary or innovative. Both comparisons can wrongly suggest that Indigenous religions are fixed or static rather than mobile or dynamic. Both comparisons assume and increase a sense that these religions are marginal and or of little interest. Worse: when Indigenous people innovate or adapt received traditions they are often judged to be inauthentic or syncretistic (a pejorative term wrongly suggesting that religious improvization is abnormal).

In addition to comparing Indigenous religions with 'world' and 'new' religions, the category also suggests that the religions of Indigenous people can usefully be compared with each other. This seems unproblematic as long as it is not assumed that all Indigenous religions are identical. Put differently, if there are 'Indigenous religions' there is not a single 'Indigenous religion'. Comparisons between these religions need to probe commonalities *and* differences carefully. We might ask, for example, what ceremonies or ideas inherited by Māori have in common with those inherited among Lakota, Sámi or Yoruba communities. But equally we should also compare Indigenous religions with all other religions, asking what they have in common with those identified, for example, as Baha'i, Buddhist, Christian, Islamic or Pagan.

In short, the category 'Indigenous religions' can problematically lump together diverse religions without being clear what they have in common other than not being labelled as 'world' or 'new' religions. When this happens, the colonial marginalization of Indigenous people and their religions continues to infect scholarship. However, scholars interested in Indigenous religions are generally committed to decolonization. They are not only aware of the problems of the term but actively seek ways to do justice to the diverse and lively lifeways and worldviews currently labelled as 'Indigenous religions'.

Origins of the concept

As already noted, the category 'Indigenous religions' emerged as a comparative term steadily replacing labels like 'primitive' or 'tribal'. Sometimes these terms were used as a subset of the category 'ethnic' which also tended to suggest a negative comparison with so-called 'world religions'. Jacob Olupona (2004) and James Cox (2007) offer clarity about the development of categories 'from primitive to Indigenous' as scholarship evolved from primitivist, missiological and early anthropological sources towards more current debates and concerns.

In part, changing category terms followed recognition that scholars in other disciplines had been engaging with religious traditions that seemed to be marginal, at best, in the study of religions. A significant expansion of the number of religions available for study become possible but, more significantly, there was also an expansion of the range of critical issues. As we will see in a later section, matters of importance to Indigenous people – especially as they challenged the varied manifestations of colonialism – provided vital inspirations for new research and debate.

Alongside a growing interest in more dialogical anthropological approaches to religion(s), engagement with Indigenous religions has been influenced by the rise of scholarship by and among Indigenous people. This has often emphasized the value of Indigenous Knowledges – and more recently Indigenous Methodologies – as scholars seek to understand the world. Because the first purely Religious Studies department in the world was in Ibadan, Nigeria, the inclusion of African Traditional Religions (ATRs) in the curriculum provided an early example of these trends. Admittedly, some early studies of ATRs privileged theological approaches and themes. In part, this was because some scholars and practitioners wanted to demonstrate that Indigenous religions were as culturally and philosophically rich as Christianity and Islam in the region. Colleagues across Africa soon led the way in researching and teaching about the lived realities of religions in Africa (noting the adaptations made by many religions to regional emphases and experiences). Their influence in later developments is traced by Cox (2007) and continues in global forums like the American Academy of Religion (AAR).

The organization of several strands in the AAR conference programme (the largest annual international conference focused on religion) illustrates current uses of the concept of Indigenous religions. For example, there are strands focused on African and African diaspora religions. Two of the organizing units are labelled 'Indigenous Religious Traditions Unit' and 'Native Traditions in the Americas Unit'. The titles of the organizing units indicate the continuing salience of the term 'Native', particularly in relation to the Americas where 'Native American' continues to be a positive self-identification for many people. Nonetheless, 'Indigenous religions' is used by both units to indicate their shared interests. Also, both units emphasize their ambition to contribute to theoretical, methodological and conceptual debates in the study of religions and related humanities and social science disciplines. Similarly, they share commitments to 'robust conversations' about colonialism and marginalization as well as about the vitality of contemporary Indigenous traditions.

A growing number of university and academic presses have books and series devoted to aspects of Indigenous religions in their publication lists. Many of these illustrate the contributions of scholarship about Indigenous religions to debates about performance, materiality, social and environmental justice, relationality, gender, postcolonialism and other contemporary critical issues.

Abuses of 'Indigenous religions'

The hold of the 'world religions' paradigm continues to infect scholarship about religions, including those of Indigenous peoples. It remains possible to use the phrase to represent such religions as trapped in (past) time and (distant and limited) space. One example of this is when introductory books about religions begin with Indigenous religions as if they have chronological or evolutionary priority. Their contemporaneity and creativity are ignored in favour of what Olupona (2004) describes as 'primitivism'. Colonialism continues – to the extent that some Indigenous people speak of 'most-colonialism' rather than post-colonialism.

Primitivist accounts of Indigenous religions often set unachievable and inequitable expectations of authenticity and purity. Practitioners are judged for any innovation and condemned for adapting to contemporary life, especially when they evidence learning from putatively different religions or cultures. The 'Indigenous Religion(s): Local Grounds, Global Networks' (INREL) project conducted and published by Siv Ellen Kraft, Bjorn Ola Tafjord, Arkotong Longkumer, Gregory D. Alles and Greg Johnson (2020) challenges this approach by considering how the Baha'i Faith, Baptist Christianity, Hinduism and New Age inspired practices are braided with traditional practices. Another challenge is offered in Christopher Hartney and Daniel Tower's (2017) experiment of including Iranian Sufis and Assyrian Christians among those whose religions might be called 'Indigenous'.

Another abusive association of the 'Indigenous religions' concept is the expectation that Indigenous people might solve major global challenges such as climate change. This arises from the construction of Indigenous people and cultures as 'close to nature'. As deployed by colonialists this association was deemed negative and used to justify both 'civilizing' and eradication processes. In an era that positively values 'nature', allegedly close-to-nature Indigenous religious themes and practices are often romantically handed the messianic role of providing ecological wisdom.

Many of the difficulties of the term 'Indigenous religions' are associated with the vagueness of the term 'Indigenous'. But attaching 'religions' to 'Indigenous' can increase the problems. For many Indigenous people, 'religion' refers to a colonial weapon – after all, the lack of a Christian ruler in the Americas was explicitly used to justify and require conquest and enslavement according to Papal Bulls in the fifteenth century and in subsequent legal statements (Newcomb 2008). For some Indigenous people, the term 'spirituality' can be used to refer to Indigenous traditions but has its own problems. Where religion and spirituality are assumed to be concerned with transcendent and non-material concerns, they can be hard to align with the often pragmatic interests made visible when scholars of religion attend to lived and everyday religion. As Indigenous traditions are frequently concerned with improving relations between humans and the larger-than-human world (e.g. with other species), much of the terminology about religion (often inherited from Christian theologies) can be challenging. For example, the term 'ceremony' is more often used in relation to Indigenous activities than the word 'ritual' which, as with 'Indigenous', seems to suggest something static and only inappropriately improvised on.

Legitimate and provocative uses

One of the most exciting things about the proliferation of academic interest in Indigenous religions is the way in which key terms and concerns are given new life. Studies of ritual, myth, pilgrimage, gender, tradition, charisma, animism, totemism and many other defining issues in the study of religions are being revisited and re-evaluated. Similarly, debates about methodological practices, such as comparison, phenomenology, positionality ('insider-outsider' relations), are enriched. This is both a matter of having more people and more traditions to engage with, and a contribution to decolonizing academic practices as scholars seek to enact more just relationships.

Beyond the strategic expansion of the number of religions and the range of issues available for study, engagement with 'Indigenous religions' can provoke important debates about the construction and nature of Modernity. Religion has played important roles in defining Modernity just as religion has been defined distinctively within Modernity. In particular, the project of separating of religion from politics has made it appear of marginal importance, or, where it refuses to be restricted to private life, it appears dangerous. In the study of Indigenous religions, that which can be called 'religion' (e.g. ceremonies and etiquettes of relationship with other species) is rarely if ever considered to be a private matter. Even when the term 'religion' is rarely spoken among some Indigenous communities, the acts and ideas to which it might apply are aspects of the continuing sovereignty by which Indigenous people resist disappearing. Therefore, even people who are not particularly interested in Indigenous religions might be usefully provoked to re-examine the way in which 'religion' has been forced to fit the political and cultural project of constructing Modernity (see Clifford 2013; Hartney and Tower 2017).

Preferable terms

Recognizing that the concept of 'Indigenous religions' contributes to a strategy of challenging old paradigms and colonial approaches, it is possible to imagine reaching beyond it. We could stop grouping religions together under vague labels based on fictitious comparisons. We could simply talk about Lakota religion and Yoruba religion for example. However, this would also require resisting the notion that these are bounded and fixed practices. Instead, they are (and always have been) fluid and dynamic aspects of relationships, cultures or lifeways. As the study of religions increasingly focuses on lived and vernacular religion – and recognizes the braidedness of religion in many aspects of life – the idea that there is one way to do Christianity, one correct form of Buddhism, one pure form of Islam and so on, might be set aside in favour of a more dynamic engagement with what people actually do. This is a common theme in discussions of Indigenous religions and might inspire greater interest in the practices and lives to which the concept draws attention.

CHAPTER 10
MAGIC
Angela Puca

Birth of the term 'magic'

From the very inception of the term, magic has been used as a descriptor for foreign and mysterious practices. The ancient Greeks, who birthed the term from which the English 'magic' derives, already had their word for magic and yet borrowed a Persian term to make it plain that the referenced acts were indeed 'other' and not part of their religious framework. According to J. N. Bremmer, the oldest attestation of the word *magus* occurs in a passage by the philosopher Heraclitus as referenced by Clement of Alexandria in the *Protreptikos* (2.22.2). Here Heraclitus is explaining who is the object of prophecies, as Bremmer reports, in his transliteration (Bremmer 1999: 2).

> Those who wander in the night (*nyktipolois*): Magi (*magois*), bacchants (*bakchois*), maenads (*lēnais*), initiates *(mystais)*

The correlation between *magoi*, *mageia* and magic first occurs in Greek tragedies and again, mainly in reference to Persians. The term was later associated with purifiers and healers of inferior theology and cosmology. Since *mageia* was associated with Persian practitioners, who pronounced their incantations in a foreign tongue and whispered their incantations, this may have contributed to give this term a more esoteric and mystical connotation (Collins 2008: 58–62).

Conceptualization of magic in scholarship

The concept of magic, far beyond the connotations of the term we employ today in English, has gone through a significant amount of scholarly investigation, often characterized in relation or contrast to science and religion. The triad of science, magic and religion has spawned out of a post-Enlightenment conceptualization of these terms, which interpreted them as belonging to starkly separate areas of human endeavour. Despite the relatively recent origin, a dialectic opposition between magic and religion has been utilized by scholars from the nineteenth century onwards to investigate previous historical applications.

C. H. Toy states that there are three main views of the relation between magic and religion. Magic is usually seen either as a degraded form of religion, as a parent to religion or as a completely unrelated system (Toy 1899). E. B. Tylor deemed magic and religion as distinct modes of thought and ritual performance. Magic is an intellectual error of the 'rudest savage' and a hurtful superstition, a pseudoscience, still based on rational analogy (symbolic principle of magic) on a low intellectual condition. The practice of magic is also seen as impersonal and mechanical; it involves a direct and personal relationship between humans and spiritual forces, while in religious practice, such a relationship is established with a higher being. Similarly, James Frazer, a cultural product of his time, interpreted history through the framework of social evolution that interprets occurrences in history as going from worse to better, or, as they would have said at the time, from 'primitive' to progressive. Employing this theoretical framework, he saw magic as the first stage in human history, followed by religion and then science. Once again, magic is seen as belonging to a lower rank when compared to religion. Frazer identifies two core laws of magic; the first being the law of similarity, meaning that things that resemble also influence each other, followed by the law of contagion, according to which things that have been in contact retain an influential power over each other. Magic is used by humans to take control into their hands and it differs from religion in that the magician claims to use his or her own powers whereas the religious practitioner defers to supernatural entities (Wax and Wax 1963; Frazer 2001; Young 2017). Émile Durkheim offers a different angle, stating that religion fosters a sense of community and a shared morality while magic is more individualistic and hence more divisive. For Bronislaw Malinowski, magic aims at manipulating spiritual powers while religious prayer appeals to spiritual forces, as he observed in his research on the Trobriand Islanders. Lastly, Bremmer argues that a comparison between religion and magic is unfeasible for a few different reasons, the most relevant being that magic has been dialectically constructed in terms of what it was not and historically opposed to normative religious practice, rather than to religion *tout court* (Belier 1995; Bremmer 1999).

Magic as 'othering'

This scholarly debate shows that, for one reason or another, magic has been perceived as a religious other and/or as a way to 'other' religious practices from what is deemed to be the norm. The concepts we associate with magic and witchcraft have often been used to mark a practice – more or less tangent to the dominant religious system – that is somewhat impious and needs forbidding. This has often occurred with the concept of 'demon' as well, where the former gods or the gods of others get labelled as such. It is a demarcation that has mostly to do with rhetoric of 'us versus them' that appeared to be an integral part of the identity formation of a community throughout history (Lurker 2004: vi).

When 'magic' is not used as a scholarly category but as a term used within the practising religious communities, it is not only used as a way of 'othering' certain practices from the established religion and hence reinforcing the boundaries of what constitutes the 'us', but also to expose the inner other. Even when there are 'religio-magical' and folk Catholic practices that may include some form of magic, the latter label (along with the term 'witch', *strega*) is often rejected by those who identify as Roman Catholics because it is perceived as a derogatory term (Puca 2018).

This attitude is exemplified when we examine what the Hebrew Bible forbids. Although the common understanding of verses such as the famous 'Thou shall not suffer a witch to live' (Exodus 22:18, KJV) may seem to suggest that engaging with any kind of magical practice is not allowed, these verses harbour more complexity than one may expect. The matter of identity is embedded in the narratives of the Hebrew Bible, and the practice of magic (often referred to as witchcraft) is no exception to that. This collection of texts tells the story of the Israelites in search of their freedom, and land to settle and their cultural/ national identity. As a consequence, the prohibitions are often related to this yearning for a stable communitarian centralized identity, which leads to the magic and the gods of neighbouring countries being forbidden. The prohibition found in the Hebrew Bible is not an all-encompassing 'Do not practise magic' or 'Do not get involved in witchcraft' but rather 'Do not be *this kind* of magician' or 'Do not seek help from *this type* of witch'. Where 'this kind' usually refers to the type of magic practised by their neighbours, by the others (Bohak 2008: 14). The Israelites were, according to depiction given in the Bible, trying to distinguish themselves from the non-Israelites and the prohibitions are simply aimed at 'non-Israelite' or 'bad Israelite' customs, which were perceived as displeasing their God.

Magic, LGBTQ+ and non-normativity

Magic is often deemed within the practising communities as other than religious along with being other than what is normative. It denotes the practices of those who did not follow the dominant religious system before modernity and, after the Enlightenment, also those who do not comply with the rationalistic framework that suggests what is real and what is mere delusion. 'Other', then, means what does not comply with the prevailing religion, the majoritarian worldview and the belief system held by most and deemed the truth. The other can also be what is not deemed to be 'real' or possible according to the widespread positivistic paradigm (Preston Blier 1993: 147). Interestingly, contemporary Pagan practitioners have embraced and reclaimed this 'otherness' and incorporate magic in their religious system regardless or, perhaps, because of that. Both Paganism and magic stray away from the domineering religions and consciously engage in practices that are labelled as either superstitious or unreal by the post-Enlightenment rationalism. This perception of dwelling at the fringes may have led contemporary Pagans to associate magic with feminist values.

Since the 1960s, the United States of America has seen a resurgence of the witch re-interpreted as a feminist icon. This was made quite plain when the American feminist movement chose W. I. T. C. H. (Women's International Terrorist Conspiracy from

Hell) as the acronym to their name. We find an echo and a link to this association in contemporary Pop Culture as the TV show *Chilling Adventures of Sabrina* adopts the acronym WICCA for the 'Women's Intersectional Cultural and Creative Association' as well as in the new 'Charmed', which features a lesbian gender studies scholar in a leading role.

These new formulations of the 'witch' were based on the second-wave feminist sense of urgency to construct a political 'we' while creating a common identification with the historical oppression of women (Sempruch 2004: 113). Such a trend fostered the spreading of Wicca, finding a fertile environment among the women's and gay liberation movements seeking spiritual liberation from the Christian hegemony (White 2016: 2). Later on, feminist forms of witchcraft were born, to overcome what they perceived to be an existing patriarchal system that had, in world religions, devalued and denied women's religious experience (Greenwood 2013).

My fieldwork in Italy among Italian Pagans, alongside my decade-long attendance in such communities, has evidenced quite clearly that among those who identify as Pagans, Wiccans and Neopagans an overwhelming majority belongs to the LGBTQ+ community. As Susan Greenwood (2013) points out, feminist witchcraft has in common with all magical cosmologies a holistic philosophy, as the symbol of the Goddess unites the individual with the universe, being both microcosm and macrocosm. Kathryn Rountree also highlights that magic becomes an expression of a much wider trend that, 'is challenging the "dominator model" which has framed social relations concerning gender, ethnicity, age, class and other social distinctions, as well as human relationships with the rest of the natural world' (Rountree 2004: 5).

Notably, Ernesto De Martino argued that Magic represents a way to solve the 'crisis of presence' (*crisi della presenza*). This crisis occurs when the agency of the individual is threatened by a weakened subject-object dichotomy. Consequently, the subject (*soggetto*) goes from being acting (*agente*) to being acted upon (*agito*), from an intentional agency to an 'intentioned' one (*intenzionato*). The person is not the active agent anymore but rather a world's echo (De Martino 2007: 74–5). Minorities and outliers may often perceive a diminished agency over their environment and magic can give that agency back, resolving their 'crisis of presence' in the world, and re-affirm their existence as acting agents. The unseen power of magic becomes then a tool for those who are othered in society to get their visibility back. Magic then becomes therefore a social and a religious tool of empowerment. It is still perceived as both a 'religious other' and as 'other than religious'.

Due to this 'othering' connotation associated to magic, when studying such practices in lived contexts, scholars are faced with the issue of a potential discrepancy between how practitioners label their practices and what definition may more accurately describe them from an academic point of view. While Pagans feel comfortable using the term 'magic' to describe their endeavours, as their whole religious system dwells at the religious fringes, Roman Catholics will be more reticent and resistant to use such a definition, for their belief system does adhere to the dominant religion and they are unwilling to be 'othered' from it. As one of my studies showed, this incongruency is sometimes resolved by Italian Catholic practitioners by associating their rituals with shamanism, rather than with magic or witchcraft, as this label lacks a history of antagonism to Christianity as well as that 'othering' connotation described here (Puca 2018). Yet, there are numerous cases where scholars may find themselves perplexed in the midst of these emic/etic standpoints, between the insider's and the observer's perspective.

Conclusion

The specific challenge presented by magic to religious studies scholars, especially those engaged with living traditions, is that of otherness. The latter is so culturally attached to magic that will affect how and if practitioners decide to employ it when defining their practices, depending on how they position themselves more generally in their society. Even though such a challenge may lead scholars to argue for forsaking such a term from the scholarly debate on religions, I maintain that its inclusion is still of great benefit to the understanding of dominant and minority religions. This is, firstly, because the term is still part of contemporary religious discourse; there is no alternative that could satisfactorily substitute it, and we cannot dismiss its use among many practitioners. Secondly, precisely because of its complexity, the enquiry around magic will allow for a nuanced understanding of religious practices. Fuelled and challenged by an ever-evolving dialectic between the insider/outsider outlook on the matter, scholars will keep developing new and context-sensitive methodologies to tackle potential controversies in search of an increasing comprehension of religious phenomena.

CHAPTER 11
MILLENNIALISM
Catherine Wessinger

The meaning of words changes over time and there is not a 'true' definition of any word. The terms 'millennialism' and 'millenarianism' have a historical source in the last book in the Christian New Testament known as the Apocalypse of St. John the Apostle, or the book of Revelation. 'Apocalypse' is from the Greek word *apokalypsis*, 'unveiling' or 'revelation'. Revelation 20:2–3 (NRSV) reads:

> He [an angel] seized the dragon, that ancient serpent, who is the Devil and Satan, and bound him for a thousand years, and threw him into the [bottomless] pit, and locked and sealed it over him, so that he would deceive the nations no more, until the thousand years were ended. After that he must be let out for a little while.

Scholars of religions derive the terms 'millennialism' and 'millenarianism' from the word 'millennium' (a period of 1,000 years) for the kingdom of God on Earth predicted in the book of Revelation. These two terms are used by scholars not to specify a period of 1,000 years, but to refer to interrelated religious patterns in which believers expect a 'collective salvation' for a group of people. The definitions of these terms have been refined as scholars produce more case studies of millennial movements.

Defining 'Millennialism'

In 1962, historian Norman Cohn formulated a definition of millennialism. Cohn's definition accurately describes characteristics of the medieval millennial movements he was studying. According to Cohn, millennialists expect a salvation that is:

(a) collective, in the sense that it is to be enjoyed by the faithful as a group;

(b) terrestrial, in the sense that it is to be realized on this earth and not in some otherworldly heaven;

(c) imminent, in the sense that it is to come both soon and suddenly;

(d) total, in the sense that it is utterly to transform life on earth, so that the new dispensation will be no mere improvement on the present but on perfection itself;

(e) accomplished by agencies which are consciously regarded as supernatural (1962: 31).

More recent scholarly studies of new religious movements reveal characteristics that indicate that the definition of millennialism/millenarianism needs to be broadened from the definition provided by Cohn. Members of a number of new religious movements, such as the Aetherius Society, the Unarius Academy of Science and the Raelians, believe that extraterrestrials will accomplish the collective salvation of humans. Therefore, broadly, millennialism may involve belief in the intervention of either divine (supernatural) or superhuman agents. Some new religious movements – for example, members of Heaven's Gate – have believed in a collective salvation in what amounts to a heaven (Zeller 2014). Other millennial movements teach that the collective salvation will occur on Earth, or on Earth as well as in heaven. Millennial movements that expect that the collective salvation will occur on Earth and in a heavenly realm for different groupings of people include the Jehovah's Witnesses (Chryssides 2022) and the Branch Davidians of David Koresh (Doyle with Wessinger and Wittmer 2012: 83–96). As far as an expected 'total' transformation to a collective salvation, it depends on how one defines 'total'. For example, Marxist or Communist millennial movements, such as the Bolshevik revolution and the Soviet Union (Landes 2011: 318–51), the Maoist revolution and the subsequent Great Leap Forward in the People's Republic of China (Lowe 2000) and the Khmer Rouge in Cambodia (Salter 2000), expected to create a collective salvation in a Communist state. These atheistic Communist movements do not expect the elimination of the ordinary human limitations of sickness and death. Nevertheless, for the majority of believers, millennialism promises to 'save' humans from finitude – our mortality. The collective salvation is frequently understood by millennialists in general to be a condition of permanent well-being in which suffering, even death, is eliminated for a group of people.

Therefore, the expanded definition of 'millennialism' and 'millenarianism' refers to beliefs about an imminent transition to a collective salvation, which may come about either through a great cataclysm, or through transformation according to a divine or superhuman plan for progress. Fervent millennialists expect that the transition will occur imminently, therefore millennial beliefs may provide motivation to convert to a new religious movement to ensure salvation. The salvation for a group (sometimes known as the 'elect' in Christianity) that is the 'collective salvation' may be variously expected to occur on Earth, in heaven or in both of these locations for different categories of saved persons. Millennialists may expect that the collective salvation from the limitations of the human condition will be brought about by divine intervention, or by humans working according to a divine or superhuman plan (Wessinger 2011a: 720, 2011b: 3).

Although the terms 'millennialism' and 'millenarianism' have been derived from Christian scripture, scholars – primarily in anthropology and religious studies – use these terms to refer to similar movements expecting an imminent transition to a collective salvation in diverse religious movements throughout the world. Scholars of similar Jewish movements do not use the terms 'millennialism' and 'millenarianism', but instead use the term 'messianism' or 'messianic movement', derived from the Hebrew word 'messiah', which in Judaism refers to someone who is 'anointed', or designated by God, to carry out a task that will create or restore the kingdom of God.

Millennial movements without prophets or messiahs

Research shows that while many millennial movements begin with a prophet (someone believed by followers to be speaking God's words) or a messiah (someone who is believed by followers to speak God's words but who is also believed to be empowered by God or a superhuman agent to create the collective salvation), it is possible for millennial movements not to have prophets or messiahs. In such cases, there will be interpreters, usually of scriptures, who make predictions about an imminent transition to a collective salvation for those persons considered to be the elect.

Examples of millennial movements without an earthly messiah empowered to create the millennial kingdom (the 'millennium'), or a prophet receiving revelations of the will of God or a superhuman agent, include the Millerite movement in America from the 1830s through 1844, and the Family Radio movement in early twenty-first-century America (Sarno and Shoemaker 2016). In both cases, dates were set for the second coming of Christ and the judgment of humanity, but the individuals doing the interpreting of the biblical texts did not claim to be prophets, and the anticipated messiah was Jesus Christ returning to Earth from heaven. In both movements, believers were disappointed when nothing happened.

Trumpist Messianism added to white supremacist revolutionary millennialism in America

Another millennial movement that lacked a prophet or messiah during the twentieth century is the anti-government, white supremacist movement with no name that historian of religions Catherine Wessinger terms the Euro-American Nativist Millennial Movement (2000: 158–67, 172–9), which by the late twentieth century included members of militias, people who called themselves Patriots or Christian Patriots, Sovereign Citizens (or Freemen), Neo-Nazis, racist Odinists and adherents to a racist and antisemitic form of Christianity called Christian Identity. By the late 2010s this movement was widely known as the White Nationalist movement. Messianism was added to this movement when Donald Trump was elected President of the United States in 2016. The messianic fervour was increased during President Trump's term of office (2017–20), and especially during the run-up to the 2020 presidential election, by the 'QAnon' cryptic online posts (called 'drops') that alleged that Trump was the individual empowered by 'Q' to save Americans from the 'Deep State' and other entities, including Democrats, depicted as evil. During the late twentieth century, participants in the Euro-American Nativist Millennial Movement were expecting to rise up in the 'Second American Revolution' to overthrow the federal government, and some individuals attempted to spark that revolution by violent acts, for example, when Timothy McVeigh bombed a federal building in Oklahoma City, Oklahoma on 19 April 1995 killing 168 people including fifteen children. In the 2010s and early 2020s, during controversies over removing Confederate statues from public spaces, the rhetoric of participants in the Euro-American Nativist Millennial Movement shifted to anticipate the imminent 'Second Civil War' against the federal government. On 6 January 2021 people with those beliefs were encouraged by their messiah, President Trump, to storm the Capitol in Washington, DC, in an attempt to force Congress to declare Trump the winner of the 2020 presidential election, which he had lost. Some of the insurgents expressed their intention to hang Vice-President Mike Pence, who had indicated to Trump that he would carry out his ceremonial duty as Vice-President to declare Joe Biden the winner of the presidential election.

Terminology for variations of millennialism

Scholars of religions have noted a number of patterns of millennialism. Two distinctive patterns were identified in the history of Christianity and termed 'premillennialism' or 'premillenarianism', and 'postmillennialism' or 'postmillenarianism'. The prefixes 'pre' and 'post' refer to whether the Second Coming of Jesus Christ is expected to occur *before* the millennium (the earthly kingdom of God predicted in Revelation) or *after* the millennium. These two types of millennialism, which are not mutually exclusive and believers may shift from one type to the other in reaction to events, are found in religious traditions that are not necessarily Christian. Therefore, historian Richard Landes and Wessinger have proposed alternative terms that can be utilized when studying a variety of religions.

Landes uses the term 'apocalyptic' to refer to movements in which followers believe in the imminence of the transition to the collective salvation (2011: 29–30). He delineates the category of 'cataclysmic apocalyptic scenarios' in which believers view humans as being so depraved that the destruction of the present order is necessary before God's kingdom or some other collective salvation can be created. He posits 'cataclysmic apocalyptic scenario' as a term that can replace 'premillenarianism' or 'premillennialism' utilized in reference to Christian expectations (2011: 31–2). Landes describes the 'transformational apocalyptic scenario' as being a peaceful transition to the collective salvation effected by human beings experiencing a change within themselves that transforms society. He states that this category of millennialism is equivalent to the 'postmillennialism' of Christianity (2011: 33).

Wessinger proposes the category of 'catastrophic millennialism' to replace the terms premillenarianism and premillennialism in order to discern this pattern in religious movements that are not tied to orthodox Christian interpretations. She defines catastrophic millennialism as involving

> a pessimistic view of human nature and society. Humans are regarded as being so evil and corrupt that the old order has to be destroyed violently to make way for the perfect millennial kingdom. Catastrophic millennialism involves a radically dualistic worldview. Reality is seen as involving the opposition of good versus evil, and this easily translated into an 'us versus them' outlook.

> (Wessinger 2011a: 78)

Believers in catastrophic millennialism may await divine intervention, they may retreat to a refuge where they believe they will be safe from the expected destruction – if they are attacked they will fight back – and they may become revolutionary to carry out the divine or superhuman will to destroy current society to create a new one. Since the book of Revelation describes multiple cataclysms, Wessinger utilizes the term 'apocalyptic' as a synonym for 'catastrophic millennialism', which is consistent with common meanings of 'apocalyptic' and 'apocalypse' in popular culture.

> Wessinger proposes the term 'progressive millennialism' to refer to a perspective that is optimistic about human nature and the possibility of imperfect human society to improve. Progressive millennialism is the belief that the imminent transition to the collective salvation will occur through improvement in society. The belief is that humans working in harmony with a divine or superhuman plan will create the millennial kingdom. Humans can create the collective salvation if they cooperate with the guidance of the divine or superhuman agent.
>
> (2011a: 721)

Unlike Landes's description of transformational apocalyptic scenarios, case studies of progressive millennial movements – those movements in which people believe in progress and an imminent transition to a collective salvation – demonstrate that progressive millennial movements are not only movements in which believers engage in social justice and peace work to alleviate suffering, or movements that promote spiritual practices to achieve a planetary collective salvation. Progressive millennial movements consisting of believers who wish to speed progress up 'to an apocalyptic rate' (Ellwood 2000: 253) are revolutionary, killing anyone viewed as standing in the way of the expected collective salvation of the elect. Religious studies scholar Robert Ellwood (2000) and historian David Redles (2011) have described the twentieth-century German Nazi movement as a revolutionary progressive millennial movement. The Maoist Great Leap Forward economic and agricultural plan (1958–62) that caused the deaths of millions from starvation and forced labour (Lowe 2000), and the Khmer Rouge Communist rule (1975–9) that produced the 'killing fields' in Cambodia (Salter 2000) have been described by scholars as progressive millennial movements. Therefore, progressive millennial movements, or what Landes terms transformational apocalyptic scenarios, are not necessarily peaceful. Participants in progressive millennial movements that are revolutionary possess a radical dualistic perspective, which demonizes external opponents and internal enemies, that is no different from the radical dualism found in revolutionary catastrophic millennial movements. At the revolutionary end of the millennial spectrum, the distinction breaks down between the characteristics of movements whose participants believe in catastrophic transformation and movements whose participants believe in progress.

Nativist millennialism

There are other millennial patterns that will have either belief in imminent catastrophe or progress as the means of transition to a collective salvation (Wessinger 2011c). Some millennial movements attempt to avert the apocalypse by their prayers and spiritual practices (Wojcik 2011). 'Nativist millennial movements' have occurred all over the world and in many time periods (Rosenfeld 2011). A nativist millennial movement:

> consists of people who feel under attack by a foreign colonizing government that is destroying their traditional way of life and is removing them from their land. Nativists long for a return to an idealized past golden age. Many nativists have identified themselves with the oppressions and deliverance of the Israelites as described in the Christian Old Testament. Nativist millennialism can take the form of either catastrophic millennialism or progressive millennialism.
>
> (Wessinger 2011a: 720)

Nativist catastrophic millennialists may await divine intervention to remove their oppressors and create the collective salvation, as was the case in the Ghost Dance movement among Plains Native Americans in 1889–90. Nativist catastrophic millennialists may engage in electoral politics, for instance the white supremacists increasingly participating in the Republican Party, or they may become revolutionaries intent on overthrowing their oppressors. Nativist progressive millennialists may engage in social justice work or community building for their people, run for elected office or they may be revolutionaries. Hence nativist millennialists manifest the same range of behaviours found among other millennialists whose beliefs do not include nativist themes.

Is belief in imminent transition a required characteristic of a millennial movement?

While case studies of millennial movements have revealed that a sense of the imminence of the transition to the collective salvation is a prominent characteristic, a recent study of a Korean new religious movement called Kaengjŏngyudo (Rectified Confucian Way) by scholar of Asian religions Uri Kaplan reveals that Kaengjŏngyudo is a progressive millennial movement that emphasizes a gradual transition to the collective salvation for Korean people through education in Confucian moral behaviours (2021). Kaplan terms this pattern 'gradualist millennialism'.

Future case studies of millennial movements will produce additional information that scholars will utilize to refine categories and terminology descriptive of the characteristics of the variety of millennial movements and behaviours of believers.

CHAPTER 12
MYTH
Gregory W. Dawes

The concept of 'myth' is contested, for two reasons. The first is the everyday use of the term, which makes it difficult to employ in a scholarly context. The second relates to its utility. Even when its scholarly meaning is carefully distinguished from its everyday one, it is unclear whether the term 'myth' can serve a useful role in the study of religion, for it comes heavily weighted with questionable assumptions.

Popular and scholarly use

In everyday English use a 'myth' is (in the words of the *Oxford English Dictionary*) 'a widespread but untrue or erroneous story or belief; a widely held misconception'. ('The much-vaunted "caring society" is a myth', is a dictionary example of this usage.) In our everyday use of the word, to speak of a story or belief as a myth is to imply it is false. But when scholars of religion use the term 'myth', they are using it in a different sense.

The term 'myth' is commonly employed by scholars to refer to particular kind of narrative. Myths (in this sense) are sacred narratives, which tell stories of origins or transformations, shape the rituals of the communities that hold them sacred and function as patterns that are used to interpret later events. Often they tell of events that could be known only by way of the narrative in question (Cohen 1969: 337). What makes a story a 'myth' in this sense is not its truth or falsity, but the way it is regarded and its function within the community that transmits it. This scholarly sense of the word 'myth' is sometimes distinguished from the everyday one by the use of the adjective 'mythic' rather than 'mythical'.

As it happens, scholars of religion are unlikely to take the content of a mythic story at face value. Myths commonly speak of events that are supposed to have occurred in a long-vanished age, one in which gods and superhuman beings strode the Earth. Not only are such stories incapable of being corroborated, but their talk of gods and superhuman beings is problematic. Scholars of religion operate under an assumption of 'methodological naturalism', which limits their causal explanations to factors that can be observed to operate in our own time. Few scholars, for instance, would accept the literal truth of the Purāṇic myth of the battle of gods and demons that underlies the Indian festival of the Kumbh Melā, even if they recognize the value of the Purāṇas as sources of historical and geographical information (Klostermaier 2007: 52).

Even some religious believers no longer understand their mythic stories literally. The biblical story of God's act of creation in the first chapter of Genesis functions as a myth in the scholarly sense. It not only tells of the beginning of the world, but has profoundly shaped the Christian understanding of sexuality and sin. By speaking of God's rest on the seventh day, it forms the pattern for the Jewish practice of Sabbath observance. But it is not only scholars of religion who do not regard this story as (literally) true; some Jews and Christians also reinterpret it in a figurative sense.

A story can, however, function mythically without being (literally) false. It can refer to historical events – events for which we have reliable evidence – that have taken on mythic significance. The account of Jesus' death functions as a myth within Christianity, as does that of the Battle of Karbala within the Shi'ite Muslim community. Both stories are re-enacted in ritual and shape what is thought to be appropriate behaviour. Yet a scholar of religion might regard both stories as true, at least in the general pattern of the events they narrate.

So a first problem with the use of the term 'myth' is the need to distinguish its scholarly sense from its everyday one. But its scholarly usage is also problematic. Here, too, the word 'myth' comes with unwelcome associations.

Mythos versus logos

The kinds of narratives we call 'myths' are apparently as old as human society itself (Donald 1991: 213). But from the moment the term was used to refer to such narratives, their status was being contested (Brisson 2004: 29).

The word *mythos* in the most ancient Greek texts had the sense of 'authoritative pronouncement' (Fowler 2011: 52). But in classical times the sense of the word changed. Within the early philosophical tradition *mythos* (storytelling) was commonly set in opposition to *logos* (reasoned argument). Already in Plato's dialogues, we find the idea that myths are largely false, works of the poetic imagination rather than reliable accounts (Fowler 2011: 49–50). Aristotle follows Plato in this respect, contrasting 'those who spoke mythically' with 'those who use the language of proof' (Metaphysics 1000a). The Greek historians made a similar distinction. By the end of Aristotle's lifetime, 'myth' had come to be used primarily of what we still call 'the Greek myths': narratives about the gods and heroes of an archaic age. The historians of this period follow Thucydides in relegating such stories to 'the domain of fable' (to *mythōdes*) (Fowler 2011: 48, 50).

The philosophers and historians did not regard myths as entirely without value. The historians accepted that actual people and events lay behind some of the myths. But the underlying truth could be found only by stripping the stories of their mythic embellishments (Fowler 2011: 50–1). Plato also admits that while myths are 'for the most part false', they 'contain some truth' (*Republic* 377a). This leads him to employ myth in ways that support his philosophical arguments (Tofighian 2016: 35–6), even inventing a myth he thinks it would be useful for people to believe (*Republic* 414e–15c). But he also insists that myth needs to be interpreted in ways that conform to the results of reasoned argument. For Aristotle, too, myths can be valuable, for they embody the 'received opinions' (*endoxa*) that are the starting point for philosophical reflection (Johansen 1999: 285). But Aristotle also insists that myths be subject to reasoned analysis, to see which elements can be defensibly retained (Johansen 1999: 288).

Myth and 'primitive societies'

This 'demythologizing' attitude that we find in the classical Greek world is also found in the other two civilizations in which philosophy emerged, namely India and China (Witzel 2012: 20). But if we restrict ourselves to the history of the term 'myth', it is the Greek thinkers who first gave it a negative sense. This negative sense was compounded with the emergence of the anthropological tradition, within which myth was associated with societies that were described as 'primitive'.

One expression of this view regarded myth as a form of primitive science. E. B. Tylor (1832–1917), for instance, held that 'spirits are simply personified causes' (1913: 2, 108) and mythic stories constitute a 'philosophy of nature, early and crude indeed, but thoughtful, consistent, and... seriously meant' (Tylor 1913: 1, 258). A very different view was that of Lucien Lévy-Bruhl (1857–1939), for whom myth was an expression of a *mentalité*, a way of thinking, quite different from that of science. Mythic thinking, he held, was characterized by a 'participatory orientation' to reality, in which the relationships between persons and objects are governed, not by considerations of experience or logic, but by a mass of inherited associations (Lévy-Bruhl 1926: 109). These speak of mysterious realities which link people with one another and with the natural world.

Views of this kind assumed a developmental or 'evolutionary' scheme, in which human cultures move in stages from the primitive to the sophisticated. The problem here was that what counted as 'sophisticated' was assessed by reference to the history of European thought. Australian aboriginal peoples, for instance, had extraordinary complex kinship systems. But this kind of cultural sophistication was not taken into account. It was a particular model of scientific and technical advance that assigned cultures to points on a spectrum between 'primitive' and 'modern' (Adas 1989: 4).

There are more defensible accounts of cultural evolution. Robert Bellah, for instance, offers a version that does not imply 'a progression from worse to better' and which rejects the idea that cultures are pre-determined to take a particular trajectory (Bellah 2011: xii–xiii). Cultural evolution, in Bellah's view, involves the 'acquisition of new capabilities' (Bellah 2011: 66). These new capabilities build on the old, which continue to exist even when the newer forms have been developed. Bellah's preferred model is that of Merlin Donald, who speaks of a movement from mimetic to mythic to theoretic forms of culture (Bellah 2011: xviii). But however defensible this idea of cultural evolution may seem, it still 'limits our view to trends that seem to prefigure the road to [Western] modernity' (Arnason 2013: 149).

Prospects for 'myth'

Can the term 'myth' be stripped of this unhelpful baggage? Can it be freed from its associations with notions of falsehood? Can it be employed without assuming a unilinear account of human cultural evolution that culminates in people who resemble modern Europeans?

We can sense a way forward in the work of Claude Lévi-Strauss (1908–2009). Lévi-Strauss opposed the idea that mythic thinking was (as Lévy-Bruhl had suggested) 'prelogical' (Lévi-Strauss 1966: 268). On the contrary, he argued, it was a 'science of the concrete' that had a logic of its own (Lévi-Strauss 1966: 16). Myth and modern science represent 'distinct modes of scientific thought', which are 'not a function of different states of development of the human mind but rather of two strategic levels at which nature is accessible to scientific enquiry: one roughly adapted to that of perception and the imagination: the other at a remove from it' (Lévi-Strauss 1966: 15).

While locating himself on the side of modern science, Lévi-Strauss sought 'to legitimize the principles' of mythic thought 'and to re-establish it in its own place' (Lévi-Strauss 1966: 269). Taking a lead from these remarks, here are two suggestions for the rehabilitation of the term 'myth'.

A spectrum of modes of representation

A first move is to avoid making too sharp a distinction between modes of representing reality. There exist intermediate forms between *mythos* and *logos*. These include what Robert Bellah (following Eric Voegelin) calls 'mythospeculation': a form of 'reflection that pushes mythical thinking to its limit – to the verge of theoretical reflection without ever quite crossing the boundary' (Bellah 2011: 240). Mythospeculative thinking was highly developed in ancient Egypt (Bellah 2011: 241), but it can be found even in the first pre-Socratic philosophers, whose thinking is 'midway between mythospeculation and theory' (Bellah 2011: 365–6). What distinguishes mythospeculation from theoretical thought is the willingness to live with apparent contradictions (Bellah 2011: 246), a willingness that helps explain the much-vaunted 'toleration' of polytheistic societies (Bellah 2011: 276).

Even in modern Western societies, there exist ways of representing reality that have some of the characteristics of myth, even if they lack them all. Scientists, for instance, generally eschew the use of narrative and metaphor, aiming for what the founders of the Royal Society called a 'mathematical Plainness' of speech (Sprat 1734: 112–13). But models, analogies and metaphors remain important within science, even to the point of being constitutive of scientific theories (Boyd 1993: 486). Narrative, too, remains important, as a mode of explanation within the 'historical' sciences. Some scientific narratives come to function in much the same way as myths. Evolution, for instance, is not merely a well-supported scientific theory; it has come to be 'a powerful folk-tale about human origins' that functions as a myth (Midgley 1985: 1). So rather than a sharp divide between, say, mythic and theoretic ways of representing reality, we have a spectrum of modes, one merging into the next.

Ubiquitous modes of representation

The preceding remarks point to a second insight: the realization that these differing modes of representation are ubiquitous. One cannot distribute them between 'primitive' and 'modern' societies, even if one form is more pervasive than others at particular times and in particular places. No less a figure than Lucien Lévy-Bruhl eventually recognized this fact. In his posthumously published *Notebooks* (*Carnets*) he rejected a simple contrast between 'primitive' and 'modern' thought, recognizing that the 'participatory' and the 'causal' orientations to reality are to be found 'in every human mind' (Lévy-Bruhl 1975: 101).

A more cautious version of this view is to be found in the work of G. E. R. Lloyd. Lloyd rejects talk of 'mentalities', which encourages unwarranted generalizations 'about periods, groups, even whole societies' (Lloyd 1990: 144). But Lloyd recognizes that human beings do make use of differing 'modes of reasoning' which are employed in different 'contexts of communication' (Lloyd 1990: 140, 145). It is these 'modes of reasoning' to which we need to pay attention, 'not the reasoners themselves or their supposed mentalities' (Lloyd 1990: 145).

Such a view is clearly preferable to a simple contrast between *mythos* and *logos*. It enables us to recognize myth as a particular way of orienting ourselves to reality, one that all human beings employ in particular contexts. It allows us to recognize the value of 'mythic' modes of expression – stories of origin that guide behaviour – without needing to consign them to the realm of the fictitious or the primitive.

CHAPTER 13
NEW AGE
Shai Feraro

When it comes to terminology, scholars differ between 'New Age', 'New Age', 'New Age Spirituality' and so on. New Age is also increasingly set against terms such as 'alternative spirituality' (or spiritualities) or new religious movements, the latter being a contested term in in own right, and discussed separately in the present volume. Indeed, two recent edited volumes which focus on new religious movements (Sutcliffe 2013; Frisk, Gilhus and Kraft 2016) contain specific chapters on the term 'New Age' that aim to explain it.

Steven Sutcliffe – one of the main scholars who study the phenomenon – has argued that the term is unduly nebulous and subject to confusion between its emic and etic uses. In other words, Sutcliffe contends that is not typically used by its practitioners, nor is it a clearly defined term when used by scholars. Other researchers more broadly are unsure whether the movement's growth is still progressing or is experiencing a prolonged period of decline (Vincett and Woodhead 2016: 329). The term, however, continues to be used in academia to indicate alternative and eclectic approaches to spirituality in contrast with those of traditional Christianity. In 2007, for instance, a hefty *Handbook of New Age* was published by Brill as part of a series dedicated to contemporary religion. Yet, scholars are still divided on the question of the term's usefulness, as will be seen below.

The origins of New Age

Wouter Hanegraaff (1996) places the origins of New Age in the 1960s counterculture and the following decade, while Sutcliffe (2007) maintains that emic use of the term 'New Age' crystalized during the inter-war period in the context of Theosophist Alice Ann Bailey (1880–1949), whose 1930s writings envisioned an impending phase of worldwide turmoil which will lead humanity to an era of peace and prosperity, guided by benevolent supernatural beings. Bailey's teachings, influenced by Christian millennialism, charted an imminent change in the astrological forces affecting the Earth, a shift – from the 'house of Pisces' to that of 'Aquarius' – which some contemporary writers on astrology have already associated with the return of Christ, or the 'Christ Within' (Campion 2012).

Hanegraaff (1996) suggests a distinction between New Age *sensu stricto* (New Age in the restricted sense) and New Age *sensu lato* (in the wide sense). The former denotes a belief in an impending era that will be inaugurated by 'other-worldly' beings, building on Alice Bailey's earlier discourse and containing significant Theosophical and Anthroposophical undertones; Bailey expected a coming New Age which would be heralded by Christ's reappearance (Bailey 1948). By contrast, the *sensu lato* sense mostly forgoes these earlier millennialistic expectations in favour of an emphasis on life in the 'here and now' and is influenced by the American counterculture as well as the metaphysical and New Thought traditions. According to Sutcliffe and Gilhus (2013: 4), following 'the 1980s these sensu lato expressions increasingly travelled under new names altogether, such as "holistic" or "mind body spirit" or under revived subcultural rubrics such as "occult" or "esoteric."' The more recent appearance of phenomena such as 'Jew Age' – adaptation of 'New Age' practices by Jews in Israel – (Ruah-Midbar and Klin-Oron 2010), and the inclusion of Pagan identities in studies of North American New Age Spirituality, are but a few of other blurred boundaries of New Age *sensu lato* (Sutcliffe 2014: 42). Globalization, Sutcliffe and Gilhus maintain, furthers its border 'check points' to such an extent that with the exception of 'specifically millennialistic aim or object sensu stricto', the term itself has lost its utility for scholars studying these phenomena (2013: 4–5). That being said, Sutcliffe and Gilhus simultaneously maintain that there is clearly a 'lively and volatile' empirical field that has yet to be 'properly theorized' (5).

Studying New Age

Research into New Age spirituality emerged during the 1970s–1980s and tended to focus on the study of the literature produced by relevant adherents and propagators and chart the movement's history. Of these macro-level studies, termed by Sutcliffe as the 'first-wave' of scholarship on New Age spiritualities, one should note J. Gordon Melton and James R. Lewis's co-edited *Perspectives on the New Age*, which described it as a blend of several established groups and philosophies, ranging from Theosophy to the holistic health and Human Potential movements, as well as Native Religion (Melton and Lewis 1992: xi). Wouter Hanegraaff's *New Age Religion and Western Culture: Esotericism in the Mirror of Secular Thought* (1996) was another important contribution to the field, especially on account of its discussion of the definitional and boundary issues mentioned above, as well as due to the association of the roots of New Age spirituality with Western Esotericism. The year 1996 also saw the publication of Paul Heelas's *The New Age Movement*. Subtitled 'The Celebration of the Self and the Sacralization of Modernity', this volume highlighted a central characteristic of New Age spirituality, consideration of sacralization of the self, which Heelas sees as a reaction to the challenges of modernity. Sutcliffe's own *Children of the New Age* (2003) focuses on the historical development of Anglo-American New Age spirituality between the 1930s and the 1990s, with an emphasis on its gradual shift – mentioned above – from a focus on the coming of a new epoch guided by benevolent spiritual beings to a concentration on life in the 'here and now' of this world.

'Second wave' studies, to use Sutcliffe's terminology, tend to focus on micro-level case studies conducted in various regions of the world in order to analyse the ways in which New Age is being shaped in diverse geographical contexts. Marianna Ruah-Midbar and Adam Klin-Oron's previously mentioned discussion of 'Jew Age' spirituality and

Inken Prohl's (2007) study of New Age spirituality in Japan are good examples in that regard. Other studies – such as Michael York's *The Emerging Network* (1995), which focuses on the British scene – locate the New Age in relation to contemporary Paganism, while yet another group of 'second wave' studies centre on the sociology of New Age spirituality or its relation to popular culture, characterized by Adam Possamai's (2005) and Christopher Partridge's (2004; 2005) work respectively. Another important element that tends to differentiate 'first wave' studies from 'second wave' scholarship is that some the latter ones take a quantitative, rather than qualitative, approach. A key example is Paul Heelas and Linda Woodhead's study of New Age practices and adherents in Kendal, Lancashire, which resulted in their 2005 volume, titled *The Spiritual Revolution: Why Religion Is Giving Way to Spirituality* (2005).

Problematizing New Age

Sutcliffe and Gilhus lamented the lack of theories of religion that seriously engage with the subject and called for 'a model of religion that comprises New Age phenomena, either as part of the old model of religion in such a way as to expand its parameters, or as part of a fresh prototype' (Sutcliffe and Gilhus 2013: 2–3). They explained the marginality of New Age Spiritualities within the general study of religion mainly by the persistent dominance of the 'world religions' paradigm which is 'reinforced by Christianity as the prototypical religion' (Sutcliffe and Gilhus 2013: 8–9). In what Woodhead (2010) terms the 'inadequacy approach', New Age spiritualities' perceived recent appearance in Western culture and their myriad sources of authority make them appear to be a form of 'deinstitutionalized religion' (Sutcliffe and Gilhus 2013: 9), especially when set against Christianity's long history and established authority. Sociologist Steve Bruce – one of the major critics of the concept of New Age Spiritualities during the early 2000s – argued that it

> elicits only slight commitment and little agreement about detail. It thus makes a shared life unlikely. It has little social impact. [New Age] has little effect even on its adherents. It does not drive its believers to evangelize … [it] is vulnerable to being diluted and trivialized … eclectic to an unprecedented degree and … dominated by the principle that the sovereign consumer will decide what to believe … a low-salience world of pick-and-mix religion.
>
> (Bruce 2002: 91, 105)

According to Sutcliffe, 'second wave' studies run the risk of widening the gap between the study of New Age and general theories of religion, since those who study New Age spirituality have become less well-versed in the more traditional study of religion (2014: 44). He suggests four interlinked paths that can complement what he refers to as a 'centrifugalist' leaning of second-wave studies: by this Sutcliffe means that this wave of scholarship has become diffused, discussing a variety of movements and organizations that lack a common core. Instead, 'centripetal', 'third wave' research locates some kind of centre using traditional scholarly categories within the study of religion (2014: 44). First and foremost, Sutcliffe urges fellow scholars to develop 'new macro-theoretical approaches in which New Age is tackled ... in relation to ... general theories of religion', for example by relating New Age phenomena to concepts like 'vernacular religion', or the types of category that Émile Durkheim ([1915] 1971) identified as elementary forms of religious life – such as animism, totemism, commemorative rites, among others.

Second, he argues that the emphasis placed within religious studies – specifically in Anglophone contexts – on sociological approaches to the detriment of historical methods produces 'a kind of ahistorical presentism' (Sutcliffe 2013: 20–1) of New Age data. What is needed according to Sutcliffe are

> more nuanced histories of the modern networks and enclaves of 'alternative spirituality' from which New Age beliefs and practices emerged, especially in the first half of the twentieth century. A fuller set of social and cultural histories will also help differentiate the historiography of religion in modernity, especially in the European and American heartlands of New Age. This requires in the first instance a detailed mapping of the modern historical and spatial distension of the 'cultic milieu' (Campbell 1972) which has served as a matrix both for the production of new expressions of 'spirituality', and as a resource for the growth of specific new religions.
>
> (Sutcliffe 2014: 44)

Suzanne Newcombe's recent study (2019) of the proliferation of yoga in Britain during the twentieth century is a good example for what Sutcliffe has in mind; Newcombe not only analyses the origins of Western yoga, but relates it to wider categories such as charismatic gurus, its uptake by women and its role in popular culture. Another example for relevant work currently still in the making is my own forthcoming research into the role of occult and New Age spirituality bookshops in Britain as hubs and arenas for the transference of knowledge and information within these respective milieus between the late nineteenth century and the rise of the Internet during the early-to-mid 1990s.

The third avenue suggested by Sutcliffe for what 'third wave' research into New Age Spirituality could look like is a focus on the links between the New Age of the 1970s and 1980s – or New Age *sensu lato* – and the rise in the usage of the term 'spirituality' during the period in which New Age *sensu stricto* was experiencing decline. Its multiple meanings and applications during recent decades warrant us to handle it with care, as Vincett and Woodhead (2016: 324) remind us, yet Steve Bruce's recent *Secular Beats Spiritual* (2017), which analyses the development of New Age, alternative forms of spirituality in Britain since the 1970s and argues that these have become secularized in recent decades, could be seen as a valuable contribution to what Sutcliffe is calling for.

A fourth suggestion is to increase the attention dedicated to issues of class and economy in the study of New Age Spirituality, namely 'the cultural capital provided by

New Age beliefs and practices for certain social groups – especially middle and lower middle classes – within modern risk societies' (Sutcliffe 2014: 44). Such a focus can be seen more recently in Amanda J. Lucia's *White Utopias: The Religious Exoticism of the Transformational Festivals* (2020), for example.

Building on these suggestions for 'third wave' studies of New Age Spirituality, Frisk, Gilhus and Kraft present several additional paths for future research, such as the effects of Indigenous religions and the New Age, 'glocalization' (Robertson 1992) processes in New Age Spirituality, additional studies on media perspectives in New Age studies, as well as ones focusing on gender (Frisk, Gilhus and Kraft 2016: 472–7).

Whither New Age?

Can the concept of 'New Age' survive as part of the taxonomy of the study of religion? As this chapter shows, there are certainly those within academia – such as Frisk, Gilhus and Kraft (2016) and Aupers and Houtman (2010) – who think that it should, yet Sutcliffe warns against 'mobilizing the category "New Age" as an act of strategic essentialism' – in other words, treating the concept as if it had some common core. He argues that 'further positive deployment of the term', however well-intentioned, will not serve to clarify its boundaries, or define its relationship to concepts that are sometimes used almost interchangeably, such as 'alternative', 'holistic', 'spirituality' or 'esoteric'. Instead, he maintains, scholars should 'deconstruct and re-assign the data for New Age' – that is to say, they need to examine the various components associated with the concept, and determine how they might be reassigned and integrated within a new model of what 'religion' is (2013: 26–8). It remains to be seen how this campaign will affect both scholarship on New Age Spirituality and the wider study of religion in the near future.

CHAPTER 14
NEW RELIGIOUS MOVEMENTS
George D. Chryssides

What are 'cults'?

One of my earliest experiences in discovering new religious movements (NRMs) was back in 1982. I attended a meeting in which the secretary of the anticult group FAIR (Family Action Information and Rescue) presented the gathering with a document headed 'List of Cults, Sects and Fringe Groups'. The list contained a total of 107 items of remarkable diversity, including Baha'i, biorhythms, Bugbrooke Jesus Fellowship, Crystal Consciousness, Gestalt, Jehovah's Witnesses, Kirlean Aura Diagnosis, Theosophical Society and Yoga. There was no indication of which items fell into which of the three categories in the heading, or what precisely were the criteria for inclusion. Nor was it clear why certain items did not appear, for example Amway, astrology, Nation of Islam, neurolinguistic programming, the New Age, tarot and Spiritualism, among others that have at times been included in discussions of 'cults' or NRMs. Did the compilers of the list forget to include them? Did they not know about them? Or did they consider that they did not fit into these categories?

There are two problems about listing 'cults' in this way. First, the term 'cult' is pejorative, as is 'sect' and 'fringe group', although perhaps to a lesser degree, and one of the reasons for scholars' preference for the term 'new religious movement' is that it is intended to be of value-neutral, although the anticult movement describes it as a euphemism. The second problem is that it is not clear what should be included within the concept 'cult'. As Steven Sutcliffe has contended in a slightly different context, a viable piece of terminology needs 'predictable content' (Sutcliffe 2002: 20). In other words, it must be clear in advance what belongs to any meaningful category: we can readily identify what belongs to categories such as 'table' and 'chair', but it is not obvious what should fall within the category of 'cult'. The substitution of the term 'new religious movements' removes the pejorative connotations, but not the problem of what falls under its umbrella. Employing the concept 'NRM' must therefore not merely remove the pejorative connotations, but must introduce clear criteria for inclusion.

'New Religious Movement' as preferable vocabulary?

There is some uncertainty about the precise origin of the term 'NRM'. Ulrich Berner (2000: 267) claims that it originated from missiologist Harold W. Turner, who coined the term PRINERM (primal new religious movement) to designate religious groups that emerged as a synthesis of Christianity and 'primal' religions. Gordon Melton suggests that the term may have arisen from Japanese scholars who used the term *shinshūkyō* ('newly arisen religion') to characterize new forms of spirituality that arose after 1880. Jacob Needleman titled his 1973 book *The New Religions*, although the volume predates the public interest in the Unification Church, Scientology and the Hare Krishna Movement. Others attribute the term to Eileen Barker.

The term 'new religious movements' has the obvious advantage of neutrality, but is not without its problems. The adjective 'new' is of course problematic: 'new' is a relative concept, and the new eventually becomes old. One convenient historical benchmark is the Second World War, causing Peter Clark to identify 'those new religions that have emerged in Britain since 1945' (Clarke 1987: 5). This focus is far too narrow, however: referring to Britain, Europe or the United States fails to acknowledge that NRMs are a worldwide phenomenon, as Turner's research demonstrated. Eileen Barker has suggested a slightly later date, describing NRMs as 'a disparate collection of organisations, most of which have emerged in their present form since the 1950s … ' (Barker 1989: 9). Several other scholars, such as Melton and Moore, James Beckford and Geoffrey Nelson have offered similar criteria, noting that the proliferation of NRMs occurred in the 1960s and 1970s (Melton and Moore 1982; Beckford 1986; Nelson 1987).

Problems with 'N', 'R' and 'M'

The 1960s and 1970s were certainly the period in which many so-called NRMs attracted widespread media attention, but historically many of these organizations can be dated substantially earlier. Vipassana was 'rediscovered' in 1914; Opus Dei originated in 1928; the Soka Gakkai began in 1930 and Brahma Kumaris was founded in 1938. Defining NRMs as belonging to the post-war period therefore does not accurately demarcate the scope of NRM studies. Such considerations cause Robert S. Ellwood and Harry B. Partin to define a broader time period, suggesting that an organization might count as an NRM if it took its rise in the past 150 years (Ellwood and Partin [1973] 1988: 6). Ellwood and Partin's first edition appeared in 1973, thus making 1823 the watershed, if we were to take them literally, and allowing the inclusion of Theosophy, Spiritualism and New Thought, among others.

The concept of novelty presents other problems. The International Society for Krishna Consciousness (ISKCON), for instance, is typically regarded as an NRM, but yet claims to be an ancient tradition, possibly the world's oldest religion, if, as its devotees suggest, it originated with Krishna, whom they believe to have lived around 3000 BCE. Unitarians sometimes trace their origins to the radical edge of the Protestant Reformation, although they frequently feature in countercult literature. This problem can be partly resolved by defining the age of a movement in terms of its institutional origins. Thus, the organization ISKCON was established in 1969, while the first Unitarian body in Britain can be dated as 1813, which places them slightly outside Ellwood and Partin's threshold. Unitarian Universalists, however, often feature in Christian countercult literature and, since they came into existence in 1961 in the United States and Canada through a merger of Unitarians and Universalists, could qualify as an NRM – provided one allows mergers. However, if mergers enable an organization to qualify as an NRM, why do we not count the United Reformed Church in England, formed by a merger of the Congregational Church in England and Wales, and the Presbyterian Church of England?

With scholarly attention being focused on the new religions of the 1960s and 1970s, slightly older non-traditional religions tended to get passed over, with the exception of Mormonism, largely due to the fact that the Latter-day Saints has its own university and established its own scholarship. Until recently, however, there has been little academic writing on Christian Science and Jehovah's Witnesses, and the Christadelphians continue to be largely ignored. Whether these should be regarded as new religious movements is questionable, although they need to be accommodated somewhere within the study of religion. Some scholars have employed the term 'old new religions' to identify them, while in Japan the term 'new new religions' (*shin-shinshūkyō*) is typically used to distinguish the post-1970s religious innovations from the *shinshūkyō* of previous eras.

The term 'movement' is problematic because most of the examples that are typically discussed as 'cults' or NRMs are not really movements. A movement is a somewhat indeterminate current of thought or practice, such as the Sufi movement, the 'peace movement', the 'green movement', the alternative healing movement and possibly the New Age Movement. Needleman addresses some of the earlier organizations such as Californian's Zen Center, Subud, Transcendental Meditation and Tibetan Buddhism, but also includes sections on astrology, reincarnation and the counterculture's interest in drugs. Other authors have included yoga, meditation and Reiki. Some of these are best described as practices, while some practitioners have institutionalized their methods to form more clearly defined organizations, such as yoga groups, or Reiki fellowships, while others are more rigidly defined, such as ISKCON, Scientology and Unificationism. In Max Weber's terms, they have become institutionalized, and many of them are now registered as business or non-profit organizations.

The second component, 'religion' is itself highly contested (see Chapter 18), and some scholars have gone as far as to suggest that its deconstruction should involve discontinuing the term's use. However, it is not unduly question-begging to suggest that for something to qualify as a religion one would typically expect supernatural elements, some basic teachings, some kind of guidance for life and some prescribed ritual practices, particularly rites of passage. Numerous candidates for the label 'cult' or NRM do not seem to qualify on any of these counts. For example, Amway found its way into anticult literature and NRM scholarship, although it is essentially a pyramid-selling marketing company, and Reiki and reflexology are best described as alternative therapies.

Possible alternatives?

Faced with this range of problems pertaining to N, R and M, some scholars have looked for alternative terminology. Thus, Timothy Miller has titled one of his books as *America's*

Alternative Religions. The word 'alternative', however, raises the question of what these so-called 'alternative religions' are alternative to. If they are alternatives to mainstream Christianity, then all non-Christian religions – Buddhism, Hinduism, Judaism, Islam and indeed everything else – must count as 'alternative religions', and indeed Christianity itself is an alternative to the others. Other writers have used the term 'controversial', and this too is problematic: traditional religions can be controversial too.

The term 'minority religions' is sometimes suggested as a possible substitute. A minority religion should be distinguished from a religious minority, although the terms are frequently conflated. The Minority Rights Group International (2020) defines the principal minority religions in the UK as Muslims, Hindus, Sikhs, Jews and Buddhists. Yet, if we consider the global population of religions, all of these come within the top ten in terms of allegiance. Most scholars of religion are familiar with the problems of estimating membership, but however one estimates numbers of adherents, there are more Jehovah's Witnesses and Scientologists worldwide than Zoroastrians and Druze, and in the United States, Mormons and Jehovah's Witnesses outnumber Buddhists, and Hindus. Yet in any academic conference on new religions, one might expect presentations on Latter-day Saints, the Watch Tower Society, and the Church of Scientology, but certainly not on Mumbai's Parsees.

A further option might be to use the word 'marginal' to describe the phenomena that are typically discussed in the name of NRMs. However, the term also has pejorative connotations, possibly implying that the groups and movements under consideration are either on the threshold of acceptability, or lie at the boundaries of scholarly interest, and the criteria for inclusion remain unclear. Other related terms are 'heterodox' or 'outside the mainstream'. This might appear to differentiate NRMs from their parent religion: Jehovah's Witnesses and the Unification Church, for example, do not accept the principal doctrines of mainstream Trinitarian Christianity, as expressed in its traditional creeds and confessions of faith. However, the word 'mainstream' itself is problematic. In the context of Christianity, one might try to define 'mainstream' in terms of membership of ecumenical or umbrella organizations, such as the World Council of Churches (WCC), or the Evangelical Alliance. Such a criterion, however, raises difficulties: many Pentecostal denominations, while subscribing to the traditional Christian creeds, have decided not to join the World Council of Churches, while the Kimbanguists (often considered as an NRM) remained members until 2021. In any case, what would we mean by 'mainstream Hinduism' or 'mainstream Buddhism', and whose mainstream would Scientology be outside?

The term 'non-traditional' might also be suggested. Again, any distinction between traditional and non-traditional forms of religion runs into problems. Consider, for example, Western expressions of Buddhism, which frequently focus on meditation, retreats and doctrinal teachings, all of which are quite alien to the average practitioner of Buddhism in the East. Should we therefore regard organizations like the English Sangha Trust and Triratna (formerly Friends of the Western Buddhist Order) as new religious movements, or are they legitimate innovations within their tradition? All religions develop through time, often innovating and giving rise to new interest groups, and most have their roots in existing traditions.

Some scholars have used the term 'emergent religions', indeed the subtitle of the journal *Nova Religio* is *The Journal of Alternative and Emergent Religions*. The word 'emergent' suggests a phenomenon that is coming into view and is in an embryonic state awaiting completion. Again, this characterization is somewhat unsatisfactory since most of the communities that are typically discussed in the name of NRMs have now well and truly emerged. If 'emergent' means that organizational practice is still to develop further, then this is true of any religious organization, old or new, since nearly all religions continue to develop as time passes.

In the light of these problems surrounding the concept of NRM, what might scholars profitably do? Many NRM scholars are already reacting against the essentialism inherent in the anticult critique. First, new – and indeed old – religions must be distinguished from para-religions and para-religious organizations. The early list that I was given by the FAIR representative was not exclusively a list of religious, or even spiritual groups, but contained examples of pseudoscience, self-help and therapy organizations, techniques used within spiritual groups, or phenomena that more appropriately belong to the realm of parapsychology. This does not necessarily mean that they have no interest to the scholar of religion: some alternative therapies have religious or spiritual roots (e.g. Reiki and chiropractic), or have connections with religious ideas – for example, tai chi's relationship to Confucian and Daoist philosophy. Some examples form part of the New Age (dream groups, holistic healing, reflexology, Kirlean Aura Diagnosis), which has now virtually separated itself from NRM studies.

Far from being the 'cult experts' on whom the media draw, NRM scholars have now increasingly defined specific areas of specialism, such as New Christian movements, UFO-religions, invented religions, white supremacist organizations, esotericism, wiccan and many more. Many would now regard New Age to be outside the category of NRMs, although New Age itself – itself a contested concept – is multifaceted and has its own specialist scholars. Good scholarship makes distinctions rather than blurs differences, and, instead of speaking of new religious movements, NRM scholars might more justifiably identify their specific area of interest and expertise.

No doubt the concept NRM has now become too well entrenched to be abandoned, and there may be good reasons for sticking together as a somewhat disparate group of scholars. We deal with similar issues, such as methodology, media coverage, legal issues, anticult opposition, conversion and disaffiliation, and many more. There is much to be gained by consolidating, whatever term we use to characterize these fields.

CHAPTER 15
PILGRIMAGE
Carole M. Cusack

Pilgrimage is a phenomenon found within a myriad religions and spiritual traditions that are otherwise entirely distinct, being separated by history, geography, theology and praxis. Yet an unproblematic definition of pilgrimage is difficult to agree on, and the related phenomena of religious pilgrimage, sacred journeys, secular pilgrimage, spiritual tourism and tourism all have important common elements (Olsen and Timothy 2006: 3). The differences between these modes of travel usually involve the motivations and beliefs of travellers, and how these are interpreted by scholars studying journeys to sacred sites or places of significance outside of formal religions. Pilgrimage is a problematic concept in religious studies mainly for two reasons: a tendency to essentialize the phenomenon in very different traditions and contexts, and the deregulation of pilgrimage resulting from a combination of the retreat of institutional religion, curiosity about 'other' religious and spiritual traditions and the ubiquity of mass tourism since the mid-twentieth century (MacCannell 1976; Cohen 1979; Collins-Kreiner 2018).

Pilgrimage in world religions

Pilgrimages in the world religions broadly originate in: actions of prophets and leaders, sacred journeys chronicled in scriptures and sites rendered otherwise significant within particular religious traditions. The Hebrew Bible portrays the Israelites' salvation history from Yahweh's calling Abraham from Ur to Canaan (Genesis 12: 1–6), through Moses leading the Israelites out of Egypt, and Joshua's conquest of the Promised Land (Joshua 1–11), as a paradigm of human journeying to a holy place to encounter God (Vacaru 2015). The life of Siddhartha Gautama, the historical Buddha, forms a pilgrim route from his birthplace at Lumbini, to his enlightenment at Bodh Gaya, his first sermon in the Deer Park at Sarnath, ending with his death at Kushinagar (Geary and Shinde 2021). The Hajj, the fifth pillar of Islamic religious observance, is a mandated sacred journey to Mecca and the Kaaba (cube), a structure allegedly built by Abraham and incorporating the black stone, a meteorite believed to date to the era of Adam and Eve (Peters 1994). In India, pilgrimages vary from the vast Kumbha Mela, celebrated at four sites on a twelve-year cycle and one of the largest religious festivals in the world, to modest journeys to be in the presence of a particular shrine or holy person (Stoddard 1997: 49). These examples represent pilgrimage as a devotional activity in faith contexts. This is broadly accurate, though the reality is more complex, as such journeys operate differently in each religion *vis-à-vis* the others, and varying attitudes exist within each specific religion. For example, Roman Catholic and Orthodox Christianity value pilgrimage to scriptural destinations, the burial places of saints and major ecclesiastical buildings like monasteries and cathedrals highly, where Protestants dismiss it as being of no salvific value (Duffy 2017).

The anthropologist Victor Turner (1920–83) proposed a model of pilgrimage based partly on initiatory rites of passage as theorized by Arnold van Gennep (1873–1957). Pilgrims depart their home context (separation), to enter a marginal condition in which they experience *communitas*, a spontaneous bond with their fellow pilgrims while travelling (limen). Arrival at the sacred site (or centre) is transformative, and the process is completed by the return of the pilgrim into society, but as a changed person (reaggregation) (Turner 1973: 213). Turner posited pilgrimage as a process pitting structure (everyday, profane life) against anti-structure (the openness of the liminal, spiritual state of the pilgrim). With his wife Edith, Turner wrote *Image and Pilgrimage in Christian Culture* (1978), which drew upon the couple's personal conversion to Catholicism in 1958 and represented the *apogee* of the study of pilgrimage as a highly unified, normative religious practice presented as core to Christianity and yet common to all religions, across historical time and geographical distance (Turner and Turner 1978).

The move away from Turner's single model (arguably a modern metanarrative) to a historically situated, nuanced study of multiple, different pilgrimages was announced in *Contesting the Sacred: The Anthropology of Christian Pilgrimage* (Eade and Sallnow 1991), edited by John Eade and the late Michael Sallnow (1949–90). This ground-breaking volume emphasized the regionalism, theological diversity, variety of practices, social distinctions and the sheer irreducibility of multifarious examples to a unity in one religion, Christianity. The perception of pilgrimage in other religions as a single, common experience crumbled in the wake of a postmodern deconstructive turn. The restricted use of the term to recognize only devotional journeys in the 'world religions' was largely abandoned. Scholars were inspired to shift their focus to unauthorized, heterodox, New Age, Indigenous and many other less well-known and less influential sites and journeys, and the field of pilgrimage studies expanded significantly as a result (see, for example, Bowman 2008; Coats 2009).

Secular pilgrimage and spiritual tourism

The particularization of research into pilgrimage coincided with a plethora of studies that further destabilized the category 'pilgrimage' by identifying resemblances and affinities between this traditionally religious activity and other types of travel. In the 1970s Dean MacCannell and Erik Cohen spearheaded the academic discipline of tourism, previously regarded as an unimportant part of affluent leisurely life, proposing that the tourist was a significant mode of contemporary being, and that the experiences, locations and attractions that tourists encountered were potentially transformative in much the same way as the sacred sites that drew pilgrims. MacCannell focused attention on tourist environments in terms of deliberately constructed 'attractions' and what he termed 'staged authenticity' (MacCannell 1976), whereas Cohen connected tourism to religious journeys and pilgrimage through the development of a five-dimension typology of 'tourist experiences' which distinguished tourists in terms of their relationship with a 'centre' (Cohen 1979). Faith-based, normative accounts of pilgrimage generally failed to recognize, or significantly minimized, the touristic aspects of the activity (commerce, marketing, attractions that were not historically verifiable), which MacCannell foregrounded in *The Tourist*, arguing that tourists simultaneously seek 'authenticity' but participate in an affective and sensory experience that combines staged authenticity and pastiche culture to 'synthesize fiction and reality into a vast symbolism, a modern world' (MacCannell 1999[1976]: 23). Cohen considered tourist motivations from the viewpoint of their individual orientation towards the home culture, or towards the encountered culture(s). He posited that Recreational and Diversionary Tourists were oriented to their own culture and used travel for entertainment and leisure, while Experiential Tourists were alienated from home and 'sought to recapture meaning by a vicarious, essentially aesthetic, experience of the life of others' (Cohen 1979: 187). His final two modes, Experimental and Existential Tourists, have left their home culture behind and in the former case are spiritual seekers participating in activities to self-transform, and in the latter are 'fully committed' to a centre other than the home culture, where 'the only meaningful "real" life is at [that] centre' (Cohen 1979: 190).

This probing of motivations exposed the similarities between traditional religious pilgrims and Cohen's experimental and existential tourists. Robert H. Stoddard defined a pilgrimage as 'an event consisting of longer than local journeys by numerous persons to a sacred place as an act of religious devotion' (Stoddard 1997: 49). This definition presumes the frame of institutional religion, but was easily applied to secular events such as the ceremonies of 'civil religion', for example, the Australian commemoration of the military dead on Anzac Day, 25 April, which involves attendance at war memorials around the country and for many travel to Gallipoli, Turkey to the famous First World War battle site (Seal 2007). Commemoration of the war dead is near-universal, and other events including the Olympic Games, visiting heritage monuments like Stonehenge, or sites of natural wonder like Uluru or Niagara Falls have been proposed as pilgrimage destinations for spiritual seekers and those unaffiliated with religion, who make what Justine Digance termed 'journeys redolent with meaning' (Digance 2006). This paradigm shift was controversial, in that many scholars embraced the extension of the category of pilgrimage as another way to destabilize the theological and normative accounts of the phenomenon, while others (who were often personally religious and methodologically conservative) rejected the validity of 'secular' pilgrimages and the conflation of pilgrimage with certain types of tourism as misleading (Palmer, Begley and Coe 2012). Stoddard's definition, quoted above, was challenged by research into online devotions that were dubbed 'cyber pilgrimages' and involved neither travel, a sacred site, or a community of pilgrims sharing the journey (Hill-Smith 2011).

Pilgrimage and tourism

The next development in pilgrimage studies paralleled the introduction of secular pilgrimage, the identification of what Alex Norman termed 'spiritual tourism' (Norman 2012). Secular pilgrimage transformed the theoretical understanding and explanatory power of a religious phenomenon by applying it to secular activities; spiritual tourism similarly transformed a secular concept, tourism, by interrogating both the destinations and motivations for travel of spiritual seekers, and positing an overarching framework of self-transformation underpinning tourism, and guiding the selection of particular destinations. Norman posited that like being a pilgrim belonging to a religious tradition, 'spiritual tourist' is a self-designation, 'the emic voice is quite clear in its focus on individual self-discovery and wellbeing maintenance' (Norman 2012: 23). Five modes of spiritual tourism are identified: healing, experiment, quest, retreat and collective (Norman 2012). In pursuing these modes, sites of natural beauty, meditation and yoga retreats, prehistoric monuments, historic religious buildings and sites of personal meaning to individuals or distinct subcultures are visited (Cusack 2021). Spiritual tourists draw on the earth energies (say, at Uluru, the Himalayas or Sedona) or the esoteric power of built structures (say, Stonehenge, Manchu Picchu or Glastonbury), and the positive culture of their destination to further their 'self-conscious project of spiritual betterment' (Norman 2012: 20).

Spiritual tourism and pilgrimage are very similar when a non-confessional, secular religious studies lens is applied to both phenomena. Although the goal of pilgrims has generally not been expressed in terms of self-actualization or personal betterment, the transformation wrought by the initiatory journey and encounter with the sacred site (tomb of saint, place of miraculous healing and so on) is in socio-cultural terms a type of spiritual (and in some cases social) improvement of the pilgrim recognized by their home community upon return. Some of the most interesting and challenging research in pilgrimage since 2000 has explicitly addressed the overlap between tourism *simpliciter*, pilgrimage, secular and civil sites and rituals (including fan conventions, pop culture destinations and celebrity worship), spiritual tourism, and religious tourism (within religious traditions, but not explicitly functioning as pilgrimage) (Olsen and Timothy 2006; Norman 2011; Stausberg 2011).

Conclusion

In the study of religion pilgrimage is a contested concept because it emerged as a category in the study of world religions and was initially dominated by a Christian-derived model that privileged scriptural authority and institutionally approved religious journeying such as the Hajj in Islam or the shrines of authorized saints in Roman Catholicism. Compounding this contested state was the emergence of models of pilgrimage such as that of Victor and Edith Turner (Turner 1973; Turner and Turner 1978) that were unitary and arguably unnuanced. However, the rise of less theological approaches to pilgrimage and the documenting of many historically and culturally specific pilgrimages had the effect of opening the concept to include secular and non-institutional (and even non-religious) phenomena, which ensures that pilgrimage remains contested to the present day. It is, however, still a useful term in the study of certain human activities (both within and without religion), provided it is used heuristically and in a careful and empirically supported fashion.

CHAPTER 16
PROPHECY
George D. Chryssides

Why Festinger fails

In the study of millennial movements, scholars typically turn to Leon Festinger and his collaborators' study of prophecy (e.g. Stone 2000; Tumminia and Swatos 2011). Although their *When Prophecy Fails* (1956) remains a seminal work, I wish to suggest that their concept of prophecy as (typically failed) prediction is at best limited, and fails to reflect its wider and multifaceted use among religious communities. By examining the concept's history, I aim to show that its application extends far wider than any predictive aspects.

Festinger's research involved a small UFO group led by a Mrs Keech (a pseudonym), who claimed to receive messages predicting the imminent arrival of extraterrestrials. The researchers aimed to determine what the group would deal with failed prophecy, and they coined the term 'cognitive dissonance' to denote the disparity when contradictory beliefs require reconciliation. Criticism of Festinger has tended to target his methodology, and his conclusion that faith maintenance is the outcome of failed expectations, but little comment has been made on the researchers' assumptions: that Mrs Keech's messages count as prophecy, that prophecy is prediction and that prophecy fails. Prophecy tends to be associated with prediction, both in popular understanding, and among many sociologists of religion. Thus, Joseph F. Zygmunt (1972: 245) defines prophecy as prediction that 'drastic transformation of the existing social order will occur in the proximate future through the intervention of some supernatural agency'. Such a characterization, however, gives a very limited view of prophecy. Even Jehovah's Witnesses, who have achieved notoriety for their alleged failed prophetic dates, regard prediction as one of several aspects of prophecy, offering this definition:

> An inspired message; a revelation of divine will and purpose or the proclamation thereof. Prophecy may be an inspired moral teaching, an expression of a divine command or judgment, or a declaration of something to come. Prediction, or foretelling, is not the basic thought conveyed by the root verbs in the original languages ....
>
> (Watch Tower 2018: 691)

A much more nuanced view of prophecy than Festinger's can be gained by examining historical Christian scholarship on the topic. Isidore of Seville (c. 560–636) distinguished seven kinds of prophecy on the grounds of their mode of reception, and which are mentioned in the Bible: ecstasy, vision, dream, revelation amidst cloud, voice from heaven, oracle and experiencing the 'fullness of the Holy Spirit' (*Etym.* VII, viii, 33). Some centuries later Saint Thomas Aquinas (1225–74) distinguished three types of prophecy: denunciation, foreknowledge and predestination. The first of these involves admonition, and is often accompanied by a prediction conditional on failure to heed the divine warning. Thus Jeremiah writes:

> If at any time I announce that a nation or kingdom is to be uprooted, torn down and destroyed, and if that nation I warned repents of its evil, then I will relent and not inflict on it the disaster I had planned.
>
> (Jeremiah 18:7–8)

God can reconsider his intentions, depending on the nation's response. Foreknowledge involves prediction of a future that is determined by human behaviour, yet can be expected with some certainty, for example the destruction of Jerusalem in 70 CE. By contrast, predestination is accomplished solely by God, uninfluenced by human action; for example, Christ's second coming is expected in God's own time, and cannot be accelerated or retarded by human action.

Turning to more recent pre-Festinger sociological analysis, Max Weber distinguishes the prophet from a number of other religious specialists: the magician, the mystagogue, the guru, the teacher or philosopher and the reformer. The magician has special powers to perform rites, but lacks ethical doctrines; the legislator defines law codes; the philosopher-teacher imparts specific areas of knowledge; a guru transmits traditional sacred teaching and reformers bring about radical changes, but not necessarily new revelation. Weber might profitably have added the clairvoyant, who is far-seeing, the shaman, who offers guidance through contact with spirits, the spirit medium and the channel, who impart communications from the dead or from a brotherhood of adepts, offering messages of comfort, guidance for life and occasionally prediction.

Bearing in mind these categories, Mrs Keech appears to be more of a spirit medium and channel, rather than a prophet. Her spiritual experiences begin with automatic writing, followed by fairly trivial messages purportedly from her deceased father, then from an 'Elder Brother', and finally Sananda, who identifies himself as Jesus. All this sounds more like channelling than prophetic pronouncement. Significantly, in Festinger's text, words like 'prediction' and 'messages' occur much more frequently than the word 'prophecy', and it is thus unclear whether 'prophecy' is Mrs Keech's term or that of the researchers – in other words, whether it is emic or etic vocabulary.

Issues surrounding prophecy

There are other neglected issues surrounding prophecy. What is the career trajectory of the prophet, and how does he or she secure acceptance and sometimes subsequent rejection by the community? Social psychologist Len Oakes (1997) suggests a five-stage pattern: early narcissism, incubation, wakening, mission, decline and fall (Oakes 1997: 42–3). Oakes argues, following Weber, that charisma is not merely an inherent personality trait, but must be recognized by the community. This observation raises the ancillary question of the institutionalization of prophecy, and how the prophets become incorporated into a religion's institutional structures. Prophethood can become a recognized office. Paul writes, 'So Christ himself gave the apostles, the prophets, the evangelists, the pastors and teachers, to equip his people for works of service … ' (Ephesians 4:11–12). Some religious communities, such as the early Pentecostalists understood Paul to be defining an office, and gave formal recognition to the prophet as one who claimed a divine 'calling' and whose charisma was confirmed by the community.

A related issue involves the role of women prophets. The book of Joel, which the apostle Peter quoted on the day of Pentecost, stated that in the last days 'Your sons and daughters will prophesy' (Joel 2:28; Acts 2:17), and the mention of daughters raised the issue of female prophets. The female prophet therefore has created tensions for Pentecostals: Joel mentions daughters prophesying, yet such denominations tend to be male-dominated, and heed Paul's advice that women should remain silent during worship. The Canadian Pentecostal evangelist Aimee Semple McPherson (1890–4) regarded women preachers as a fulfilment of this prophecy, saying, 'When people say a woman should not preach in church, remember thus saith the Scripture', thus employing the concept of prophecy simultaneously in its predictive and homiletic senses (Barfoot and Sheppard 1980: 9).

Controlling prophecy

The prophet, by virtue of his or her calling, often conveys an uncomfortable message to the religious establishment, and religious organizations that accept prophecy therefore need to steer a course between ensuring stability and being open to prophecy. Some evangelical authors have suggested methods of 'discernment', such as the person's lifestyle or his possession of spiritual gifts (Wagner 2020).

A canon of scripture involves closure to subsequent prophecy: no new writings can be admitted, and thus prophecy formally ends. When Muhammad is described as the 'seal of the prophets', this entails that no further prophecies can be added. Subsequent post-canonical prophecy has proved controversial: the Baha'i and the Ahmadiyya, who acknowledge prophets after Muhammad, and leaders such as Joseph Smith, who have added to the Jewish-Christian canon, have grossly offended those who belong to their parent traditions.

Jesus refers on numerous occasions to 'the law and the prophets', indicating that there was an agreed canon of prophetic literature by his time; yet prophecy appears to have continued in the early Church. Writing to the Corinthians, Paul states 'where there are prophecies, they will cease' (1 Corinthians 13:8), and some conservative Christian scholars have taken the view that 'signs and wonders', including prophecy died out after the first generation of apostles. This view is known as cessationism, and has a tradition that goes back to Martin Luther and John Calvin, and has its modern exponents (e.g. Warfield 1918; Gaffin 1979; Ruthven 1993). Some cessationists expect their revival in the last days, in line with Joel's prophecy.

Prophecy as interpretation of the past

Prophecy is frequently thought to be predictive because of the use that Christians subsequently made of it. Popular Christian piety holds that the Bible points to Jesus Christ, and that the Old Testament contains many prophecies foretelling his advent. The vast majority of Christians would therefore claim that, far from prophecy being doomed to failure, the ancient Jewish prophecies have been highly successful. As J. Gordon Melton suggests, failure is not characteristic of prophecy: 'lacking a broad view of millennial groups, [Festinger] fails to understand that *within religious groups, prophecy seldom fails*' (Melton, in Stone 2000: 147; itals original). Scholars of religion, rather than merely discuss failed predictions, might profitably explore how prophecy becomes successful.

Successful prophecy makes use of various strategies. One method was the use of typology. This method of exegesis, which has biblical precedent, involves identifying events or objects mentioned in Hebrew scripture, which are known as 'types', and which are believed to prefigure their 'antitypes'. Jesus says, 'just as Moses lifted up the snake in the wilderness, so the Son of Man must be lifted up' (John 3:14). Thus alluding to an incident – the 'type' – in which the Israelites were bitten by snakes, but miraculously cured by fixing their gaze on a bronze serpent (Numbers 21:6–8). John takes the incident to be a cryptic reference to Jesus being 'lifted up' on the cross – the 'antitype'.

Another strategy was rewriting history to fit prophecy. For example, Micah 5:2 is sometimes taken to be a 'messianic prophecy' on account of its reference to Jesus' presumed birthplace: 'But you, Bethlehem Ephrathah, though you are small among the clans of Judah, out of you will come for me one who will be ruler over Israel … ' When Matthew writes his account of Jesus' nativity, he recounts the Magi visiting King Herod, who asks where the messiah will be born. His advisers mention Bethlehem, quoting Micah's verse (Matthew 2:6). However, Micah does not mention a messiah: messianism only gained momentum in the first and second centuries BCE, while Micah was writing around the end of the eighth century BCE. And was Jesus actually born in Bethlehem? He is typically called Jesus of Nazareth, and John's gospel indicates that there was uncertainty about Jesus' birthplace (John 7:41–43). Present-day scholars are more likely to regard the gospel writers as devising stories that appear to substantiate Old Testament prophecy, or taking genuine incidents in the life of Jesus and the early church, and selecting past Jewish scriptural passages that appear to fit. Prophecy thus becomes retrodiction rather than prediction. In one of Luke's resurrection stories, Jesus appears to two disciples, who have difficulty in believing that the messiah should suffer and die, and explains how such events fulfil ancient prophecy:

> [Jesus] said to them, 'How foolish you are, and how slow to believe all that the prophets have spoken! Did not the Messiah have to suffer these things and then

enter his glory?' And beginning with Moses and all the Prophets, he explained to them what was said in all the Scriptures concerning himself.

(Luke 24:25–27)

Luke is therefore suggesting that prophecy is recognizable by hindsight. It is somewhat like a detective novel, in which the author drops subtle clues throughout the narrative, the significance of which only becomes clear in the final denouement, and which the average reader is annoyed at having missed. Thus, Micah may not have said explicitly that the messiah would be born in Bethlehem, but provides a clue for later generations to recognize.

Some conservative Christians, particularly among the Brethren and in the Adventist tradition, came to talk about a 'lesser' and 'greater' fulfilment of prophecy. In the case of Micah, the 'lesser fulfilment' is the prophet's immediate and intended meaning: he was predicting the destruction of Jerusalem, but offering hope that the city would once again be ruled by a governor, who would be part of a minority community, Bethlehem being only a small village. However, probably unbeknown to Micah, a greater event would later occur – the birth of Jesus Christ, who would not only redeem God's people, but the entire world.

Another Adventist strategy, for which Jehovah's Witnesses are better known, is chronological calculation. The 'failed prophecy' dates of 1925 and 1975 were derived from considering key passages in Hebrew scripture that suggested time periods. The calculations are complex, and different events were highlighted as prophetically predicted in the course of the Watch Tower Society's history. Much of the Adventist and Watch Tower chronological calculations, however, relate to events in the past, and hence are better construed as attempts to make sense of history (Chryssides 2010).

Conclusions

The preceding discussion suggests that it is facile to construe prophecy simply as prediction, and *a fortiori* as failed prediction. Discussion of the nature of prophecy must go wider than simply considering the predictions of minor, insignificant groups like Sananda, whose claim to a religious identity must be questioned. To construe prophecy in this way is to ignore the wider and, I believe, more interesting aspects of prophecy that I have highlighted above. Scholars of religion might profitably return to Weber's taxonomy to determine how prophets relate to these other key religious figures. Recognizing the multifaceted nature of prophecy should enable us to examine issues like recognition and initiation of prophets, their function within religious organizations, the institutionalization of prophecy, the role of women prophets, how prophecy is controlled and how it is generally conceived as successful rather than the reverse. An examination of the concept's history and how it is actually used, particularly within traditional forms of religion, would facilitate better understanding of the concept.

CHAPTER 17
RELIGION
David Morgan

There are perhaps dozens of definitions of religion informing academic enquiry, but I shall consider four prevailing models in order to convey the range of ideas that inform how scholars working in the academic study of religions handle the concept of 'religion'.

Four approaches to the definition of religion:
(1) The naturalistic model of religion

The naturalistic model was formally set out by philosopher David Hume in *The Natural History of Religion* (1757). Hume posited what he called 'the natural progress of human thought' (Hume [1757]1993: 135). For Hume, 'the mind rises gradually, from inferior to superior', beginning with the divine as an anthropomorphic projection that eventually arrives at a conception of 'that perfect Being, who bestowed order on the whole frame of nature' (1993: 136). Religion did not arise 'from a contemplation of the works of nature, but from a concern with regard to the events of life, and from the incessant hopes and fears, which actuate the human mind' (1993: 139). The origin of religion, in other words, resided in the human need to explain what Hume called the 'unknown causes' and the 'invisible agent' that were believed to be at work in the natural events that befell humans (1993: 140).

Hume's influence is evident in a more recent study by the anthropologist Stewart Guthrie, who argued that because human beings tend to recognize patterns of what matters to them most, religions should be regarded as human projections of the divine onto the world (Guthrie 1993: 68–70). Pascal Boyer found Guthrie's work sympathetic to the cognitive science of explaining religion in terms of supernatural agents: 'Religion is about the existence and causal powers of nonobservable entities and agencies' (Boyer 2001: 7). This approach hinges on what has been called 'hyperactive agent detection', that is, the over-interpretation of events or artefacts as agents that may either harm or benefit us. For the conceptualization of religion, it serves as a productive over-interpretation of an event, thing or person. Hyperactive agency detection comes into very handy use every day in discerning the intentions of those one interacts with over large matters and small. It is how human beings presume to know the thoughts or feelings of other humans, a process that they also apply to other animals and even to places and natural events. According to Boyer, this inferential ability is adapted to religious discernments about supernatural beings (Boyer 2001: 146–50).

(2) Religions as systems of beliefs

Whereas the naturalistic approach to religion stresses its singular origin in human perception and neurology, many scholars are more interested in the differences among religions as measured by the plurality of beliefs. The desire to enumerate the range of religious ideas and symbols, and the groups that hallowed them, emerged during the eighteenth century when the European imagination expanded to comprehend the nature and scope of 'culture' and 'cultures' as the colonial enterprise encountered them. Religion and religions were a fundamental ingredient in this. But the emphasis on belief also derives from Christianity in the West, which exhibits a history of debate over right (orthodox) and wrong (heterodox) belief.

The strongly Christian disposition that European thought exhibited during the Enlightenment diminished somewhat as the discipline of ethnography took shape over the course of the nineteenth century. Edward Tylor could insist in his widely influential book, *Primitive Culture* (1871), that 'the thoughts and ideas of modern Christianity are attached to intellectual clues which run back through far pre-Christian ages to the very origin of human civilization, perhaps even of human existence' (Tylor 1920: 421). But Tylor spent far more time in his volume assembling an encyclopedic breadth of non-Christian cultures into a scheme of universal cultural evolution, asserting that 'it has not seemed my proper task to work out in detail the problems thus suggested among the philosophies and creeds of Christendom' (Tylor 1920: 428). He looked instead at a very broad range of non-Christian practices, stories and beliefs for the purpose of comparison, as evidence of the universal structure and progressive evolution of the human mind. Myths were a primary source of information for Tylor's comparative work, which he described as a 'turning of mythology to account as a means of tracing the history of the laws of mind' (Tylor 1920: 275).

It was precisely the deep bias evident in Tylor and many scholars that led Daniel Dubuisson to propose that the very word and concept of 'religion' be retired from use in the academic study of religions. Religion, in Dubuisson's view, is 'a typically Western creation' that has provided the armature about which Western civilization has produced its 'own universe of values and representations', which have in turn shaped how Westerners think about the world. As a result, invoking the category of 'religion' means imposing quite without thinking about it a host of Western presumptions about whatever is placed under a rubric that is by no means neutral (Dubuisson 2003: 39). Religion is what Dubuisson calls the particular 'cosmographic formation' of the West. Other civilizations deploy different formations consisting of their own 'collective conceptions and practices, symbolic constructions, corporeal and mental techniques, discursive and semiotic systems, imaginary worlds or beings' (Dubuisson 2003: 17). Dubuisson urged that scholars focus on describing these different cosmographic formations rather than presuming they all belong to the category of (the Western conception of) religion.

(3) *Sui generis* religion

What is known as the *sui generis* approach to the study of religion presumes that religion is a part of human nature and is therefore universal, though it varies in particular details according to time and place. This has encouraged advocates to speak of 'homo religiosus', that is, humankind as an inherently religious being. In this approach, religion is thought to consist of an irreducible essence in its own right. Such essentialist approaches have often sought to focus on religious experience as a universal datum, which they consider to be the best way to define religion *per se*. In doing so, scholars have often given special attention to intuition, feeling or emotion as the universal medium of religious experience.

A number of influential authors have stressed the importance of feeling as a medium of revelation. In 1799, the Protestant theologian Friedrich Schleiermacher wrote that 'Religion's essence is neither thinking nor acting, but intuition and feeling. It wishes to intuit the universe, wishes devoutly to overhear the universe's own manifestations and actions, longs to be grasped and filled by the universe's immediate influences in childlike passivity' (Schleiermacher [1799]1988: 102). Such intuition generates revelation and its necessity for what Schleiermacher later described as 'the feeling of utter dependence' (1988: 129 n.42). Intuition is the ability to sense the divine. Schleiermacher's characterization of religious experience was particularly important for the twentieth-century German theologian, Rudolf Otto, who maintained that religion originates in a feeling of the 'numinous' constituting a 'mental state' that is 'perfectly *sui generis* and irreducible to any other' (Otto [1917]1950: 7).

The emphasis placed by Schleiermacher and Otto on characterizing religious experience was taken up by Joachim Wach among many others and treated far more systematically as the basis for conducting the history of religions as a comparative study. According to Wach, 'religion is an ubiquitous expression of the *sensus numinis*' (Wach 1958: 38). This sense of the numinous is universal and is part of 'the nature of man' (Wach 1958: 38–9). Genuine religious experience consists of four criteria that must be present for an experience to count as truly religious, according to Wach. The first two criteria appear in the claim that religious experience is 'a total response of the total being to Ultimate Reality' (Wach 1958: 32). To totality and ultimate reality, Wach wrote, must be added 'intensity' and [ethical] 'action'. Intensity refers to the magnitude of the experience, and recalls Otto's emphasis on the sublime character of the numinous: 'Potentially this is the most powerful, comprehensive, shattering, and profound experience of which man is capable' (Wach 1958: 35).

In the *sui generis* approach to defining religion, scholars commonly presume to study what is most profound and inspiring in human beings in addition to what is most universal. Because it stresses the importance of feeling, the *sui generis* approach also frequently has made use of the arts as primary forms of conveying and inspiring religious experience. Otto, for example, maintained that there was a 'hidden kinship between the numinous and the sublime', which encouraged him to collect works of sacred art from many different religious traditions (Otto [1917]1950: 63). Wach turned to the arts in order to register the intensity of religious experience: 'In the modern West a great deal of religious passion is revealed in music, from Palestrina to Bach to Bruckner and Vaughan Williams; in painting, from Rembrandt and El Greco to the Chagall of the Old Testament illustrations and to Rouault; and in literature, from Milton and Bunyan, through Blake and Dostoevsky, to Melville and Rilke – and none of these was a theologian' (Wach 1958: 35–6).

(4) Functionalism

Finally, religion may be framed as a characteristic set of patterns such as rites, institutions, charismatic leaders or various kinds of practices that construct and maintain categories such as sacred, profane, spirit, matter, reality and appearance. The purpose of religion in this functionalist paradigm is to generate and maintain social organization. Émile Durkheim presents the classic case for a functionalist approach in his *The Elementary Forms of Religious Life* ([1912]1995). Here he famously defined religion as 'a unified system of beliefs and practices relative to sacred things, that is to say, things set apart and forbidden – beliefs and practices which unite into one single moral community called a Church, all those who adhere to them' (Durkheim 1995: 44). Religion, in other words, consists of proscriptions that charge something with sacred or special status by protecting it from profanation, or inappropriate contact or use; by ritual practices that join people together by infusing and spreading what Durkheim called 'collective effervescence', or shared feeling, which is invested in symbols of the group, or totems, and by a set of beliefs that members of the group also share. The result is what Durkheim characterized as a moral community. This community maintains its integrity or structure by virtue of these social initiatives. Religions are powerful because they craft a collective sense of reality.

For functionalists, religion helps constitute social order by authorizing shared views of what matters to a community, fixing its symbols in positions of power by various means. But this both recognizes the power of collective representations and acknowledges that their basis in reality is far more dependent on the shared feelings they transmit than on their objective truth. For this reason, the British anthropologist Alfred Radcliffe-Brown, who shared Durkheim's functionalist approach to religion and society, pointed out that although religions are commonly regarded as 'bodies of erroneous beliefs and illusory practices', the better approach is to focus on what religions do, that is, on 'the contribution that they make to their formation and maintenance of a social order' (Radcliffe-Brown 1952: 154).

Contestations

Since the very act of defining a concept such as religion limits the range of its significance, it is not surprising that any definition of religion encounters criticism. To Dubuisson's proposal to eliminate the use of 'religion' altogether, J. Z. Smith might reply that the term itself is 'not a native category', but a 'second-order, generic category', a tool wielded by scholars to do their classificatory and analytical work. According to Smith, religion is 'a term created by scholars for their intellectual purposes and therefore is theirs to define' (Smith 1998: 281). This would urge that scholars need not hesitate in using the concept, but should practise a critical reflexivity in doing so that is the characteristic feature of religious studies as the academic study of religion. Few other fields of enquiry or academic discipline will do so as a matter of principle.

The naturalistic approach to religion has been criticized for failing to account fully for the considerable range of forms of order that comprise religions historically. Neurology cannot explain everything. Reductionism always has its limits. Group dynamics do more to organize and interpret the world than the mind of an individual. The hyperactive inference mechanism may tell me that some agent is threatening or offering me comfort, but to make it into a deity or some other form of superhuman agent, more work is necessary than the organism's overdetermination. Genetic disposition is not enough to generate the kinds of cultural intricacy that characterize a religion (Malley 1995).

Defining a religion as a system of beliefs easily reduces it to a creed or philosophy, missing thereby the importance of practice as well as the embodied life of a religion's material culture (Morgan 2021: 27–53). In this manner, religion becomes something cognitive, within a person's head, thus diminishing the importance of what people do. But as Hamlet told his friend and fellow student at the University of Wittenberg, 'There are more things in heaven and earth, Horatio, than are dreamt of in your philosophy' (Shakespeare 1992: 25). In addition to being embodied, religions are also material in the most robust way, comprised of artefacts, images, architecture, animals, forests, mountains, deserts, oceans, storms and stars. To reduce religions to systems of ideas misses their lived reality.

The *sui generis* approach to studying religion has been criticized for insisting that religion is a universal condition dubbed *homo religiosus*. Such an inherent religious nature is itself a sort of theological commitment (McCutcheon 1997: 15–16). That is very clear in the work of Otto, but also with others such as Eliade and Wach. Russell McCutcheon has also argued that the discourse of the *sui generis* approach needs to be situated within the politics of knowledge-making: what scholars do needs to be 'seen to function in, and contribute to, the maintenance of certain socially and politically charged associations' (McCutcheon 1997: 18) such as the close association of scholarship on religion with elite institutions, many of which are rooted in a religious tradition. And the use of the arts by proponents of *sui generis* religion can easily remove the artefact from its original setting and encode it with aesthetic values that suit the modern scholar, who may be doing little more than projecting the feelings that he or she considers universal and laudable.

Functionalism has been criticized for several reasons. Durkheim's emphasis on beliefs and on their systematic coherence met with rejection early on. Radcliffe-Brown explicitly urged that it was rites that produced social coherence not a system of beliefs, and he called on the formidable work of William Robertson Smith to support this view (Radcliffe-Brown 1952: 155–6). Moreover, societies rarely perform a unified choreography of religious ritual. Durkheim's account misses dissent, difference and plurality. Functionalism is designed to stress stasis and continuity and is less poised to account for change. Religions are often fractious and revolutionary, and individual leaders emerge with charismatic allure that challenges the social organization of dominant groups.

How the concept of religion is utilized may depend on what the academic analyst or interpreter wants to believe about religion. Scholars choose the definition that suits their intellectual purpose. If the point is to defend religion against critique by a cultural elite (such as intellectuals), then one's task is well served by choosing the *sui generis* model. If one is inclined to regard religion as inextricable from other social forces and the discourses that convey ideological commitments, the naturalistic view will be compelling. For those who want to use religion as a tool to understand how societies tend to resist change as a way of maintaining order, functionalism will do nicely. And for those who understand religion as a personal preference obeying a neoliberal logic of self-interest in which religious opinion is insulated from coercion by the state and left to sink or swim in the supermarket of religious ideas, religion as a cognitive system of beliefs works best. What is certain is that none will command an unchallenged privilege. And rightly so since a fundamental truth about studying religion is that we are to some extent always also studying ourselves.

CHAPTER 18
SECULARIZATION
Titus Hjelm

The term 'secularization' has been used in myriad, confusing and contradictory ways. Hence, from early on, some scholars have called for its abandonment altogether. The vagaries of academic fashions have pushed secularization from the position of a master term to a more marginal role. Yet no discussion of religious change can bypass secularization. Therefore, it is important to know the different meanings and coverage of the concept before celebrating or denouncing it wholesale.

In unpacking these meanings and coverage, it is prudent to start by noting that it would be more accurate to talk about a cluster of theoretical concepts than one recognizable 'secularization theory'. Steve Bruce (2011: 26), for example, prefers 'secularization paradigm'. Bryan Wilson's ([1966] 2016: 5) succinct definition of secularization – 'the process whereby religious thinking, practice and institutions lose social significance' – is another useful memento, but needs to be broken down into its component parts for a full understanding of the concept. I will do this by discussing secularization in relation to cognate concepts, the sources and levels of secularization, and some challenges to the secularization paradigm.

Secularization and cognate terms

I want to start with several cognate terms to secularization, as these are frequently mixed up with unfortunate consequences. In sociologically accurate usage, *secularization* refers to the historical social process where religion loses significance as an institution and among individuals. *The Secular* is a broader term, referring to 'something for which religion is not the primary reference point' (Lee 2012: 135). Thus, there is the secular press, for example, in distinction from religious publications. Secular press, politics, education and so on usually emerge as an outcome of secularization. *Secularity* is simply the state of being secular.

The trickiest and most commonly confused cognate term to secularization is *secularism*, which refers to 'an ideology or system of differentiating or allocating religious and secular spheres' (Lee 2012: 136). The French Revolution of 1789, especially in its later forms, was strongly secularist, although France as a society was far from being secularized at the time. The press, politics and education became secular as an outcome of political secularism, but this says little about the decline of religion in terms of individual faith. Secularism can lead to secularization when it is backed by political power (although seventy years of Communist rule in Eastern Europe shows mixed results in this regard), but in liberal democracies secularism as an ideology has been 'no more than, at best, marginal to the momentum of the process of secularisation' (Wilson 1982: 149). Secularization is a structural process involving many unintended consequences rather than a policy outcome (Bruce 2011: 36). Secularization is even less about *atheism* – lack of belief in God or gods – another term often used in conjunction with it. Atheism, like secularism, does not account for the social process of secularization, and only a minority of secular people are atheists. Finally, *non-religion* is a more recent scholarly concept, which interrogates the different meanings of having no religion, especially how the more common categories above may not capture the variety of indifference towards religion (Lee 2012).

Sources of secularization

In sociology, modernization and secularization have been considered intimately linked. The problem, of course, is that both concepts are vague. Often the secularization paradigm is treated as monolithic, when in reality scholars differ significantly in their emphasis on the different sources of secularization (Tschannen 1991). Bruce's (2011: 27) diagram of twenty-two factors of modernity which together lead to secularization shows graphically the complexity of the phenomenon. I will here mention only the main issues.

First, there is *rationalization*, which is often crudely interpreted as the triumph of scientific knowledge over 'superstition'. This ignores the fact that, as Max Weber famously argued, religion itself can be the catalyst for rationalization. Weber tried to understand why capitalism emerged in Europe, but not in other, more advanced civilizations. He ended up arguing that Judaism 'disenchanted' the world by positing a radically transcendent, otherworldly, God. Even as nature ceased to be full of mystery and magic, obedience to God became increasingly a matter of following particular rules. Everyday life became rationalized under such rules. Judaism would not, however, turn out to be the main carrier of rationalization. That fell upon the Protestantism of the Calvinist/ Puritan variety, specifically, which 'divested itself as much as possible from the three most ancient and most powerful concomitants of the sacred – mystery, miracle, and magic' (Berger 1967: 111). Rationalization in turn begat capitalist economy, which in turn fed back to secularization. Weber called this the 'iron cage' of rationalization: 'Religious developments originating in the Biblical tradition may be seen as causal factors in the formation of the modern secularized world. Once formed, however, this world precisely precludes the continuing efficacy of religion as a formative force' (Berger 1967: 128).

Second, as rationalized planning, economic growth and prosperity started to take precedence in states' organization, sticking to religious orthodoxy became a potential hindrance. This led to religious *pluralism*, when churches (in the European case) lost their monopoly status. This aspect of the secularization paradigm was developed especially by Peter L. Berger, who argued that pluralization undermines religious certainty. If salvation ceases to be the sole province of one church, the whole idea of salvation becomes less certain in individual consciousness, Berger says. Somewhat paradoxically, then, faith is strongest when it is invisible. It is invisible because it is unquestioned. Pluralism creates doubt and doubt creates decline of faith.

Third, *individualization* – which is also a residue of the Protestant focus on personal faith – turns previous monopoly church adherents to religious consumers. However, treating religion as a consumer choice is problematic, according to secularization theorists (but not others, as discussed below), because it hinders socialization of the next generation into a religious community. If religion is about choice, then by definition, your children should be able to choose their own religion. Failure to socialize, in turn, is one of the most significant factors in secularization. In other words, secularization is largely a cohort effect.

Levels of secularization

In addition to disagreement over the sources of secularization, there are differing ways of measuring its extent. It is helpful to consider secularization in terms of different levels, as secularization on one level may not be proof of it on another.

Differentiation refers to the process where religion is evacuated from other social institutions and spheres, which become autonomous. So, for example, the state ceases to monitor religious orthodoxy and education is increasingly (although not exclusively) organized by the state rather than churches. There is wide agreement on the differentiating effects of modernization and it is at the heart of different types of secularization theories (Tschannen 1991: 400–1). The level of differentiation in particular societies may be contested, but the usefulness of differentiation as a measure of secularization is less so.

An important claim running parallel to the argument regarding differentiation is that religion may survive in a differentiated society, but only in a *privatized* form. That is, religion ceases to be visible and available in public affairs. This idea has been forcefully challenged by scholars who agree with the differentiation thesis, but who argue that privatization cannot be considered a necessary consequence of former (Casanova 1994). Religion continues to be evoked as justification for political values in many parts of the world, and phenomena like global migration make religion a public 'hot topic' even – or perhaps especially – in highly secularized countries.

Both of these macro developments are related to, but in no straightforward way, to the *decline* of religion on the individual level. The classic secularization paradigm upholds that, providing other key factors (such as freedom of religion) are in place, maintaining a religious worldview becomes increasingly difficult in a highly differentiated society (Bruce 2011). The two do not necessarily correlate, however, so to avoid confusion, it is important to be clear about the level of secularization that is being discussed.

Finally, many secularization theorists talk about *worldliness* (Tschannen 1991), or the 'internal secularization' (Chaves 1994) of religious communities. This refers to the attempts of religious communities to accommodate the prevailing social values and moods. Hence, many Christian churches have accepted the ordination of women and gay marriage, for example, during the last several decades. For many this is primarily a contested theological issue, but it also has social repercussions, as evidence from both the United States and Europe shows that the only growing churches, such as the Pentecostal churches, are the most conservative ones.

Challenges to the secularization paradigm

Such a diverse cluster of concepts has engendered, unsurprisingly, similarly diverse criticisms. Here I will focus on the criticisms that hang on a particular understanding of the concept of secularization. These concern prediction, 'spirituality' as a new form of religion, and understanding secularization as a question of demand or supply.

The first type, which could be called the straw man counterargument, is very common. Such critics claim that the secularization paradigm is first and foremost an exercise in prediction, that the paradigm foretells the demise of religion everywhere. For these critics any sign of religious vitality is a refutation of the secularization paradigm. Migrant churches and the rise of conservative Christianity, for example, have been exhibited as harbingers for secularization. Yet, they do not come close to filling the gap left by decline of religious belief and practice in secularized societies, nor do they reverse the long-term trend in decline. The problem here is not only that arguments like these do not engage with actual theorizations of secularization, but that they present incommensurable data as evidence for refuting secularization. An ethnographic study may well demonstrate the vitality of religion in the case of one church, but it does not say anything about the decline of religion in a population. Similarly, the vitality of religion around the world does not refute what has happened in those societies where the secularizing forces have been in effect for some time. The secularization paradigm is 'an attempt to explain common features of the recent past of modern industrial liberal democracies' (Bruce 2011: 3–4). Thus, what happens in Iran does not refute what has happened in Essex. Sadly, Jeffrey Hadden's (1987: 588) acerbic indictment of the secularization paradigm – 'a taken-for-granted *ideology* rather than a systematic set of interrelated propositions' (emphasis in the original) – now applies equally well to the many straw man arguments against the paradigm.

The second type claims that religion is not declining, but changing form from institutional religion to individualized 'spirituality'. The counterargument to secularization from this angle is, then, methodological and definitional: spirituality (or 'non-churched' religion) is invisible to social scientific counting measures. That is why research that uses standard measures of belief, belonging and practice only measures 'churched religion', but misses swathes of reality that could be categorized under a broader concept of 'religion' (Gauthier 2020). The problem with this kind of definitional sorcery is that it does not offer an alternative to studying religious decline. In fact, it makes secularization seem impossible, which clearly goes against everyday observation. Other approaches, such as that reported in *The Spiritual Revolution* by Paul Heelas and

Linda Woodhead (2005), have the merit of at least attempting to assess the popularity of the spiritual milieu. Heelas and Woodhead found in their study of the British town of Kendall a vibrant alternative spirituality scene with a wide variety of practices. However, as Steve Bruce has noted in several publications (e.g. 2011: 107–11), the claim for any type of 'spiritual revolution' that would balance the decline in traditional churchgoing is not supported by the data. Somewhat tragically, this is exactly what Heelas and Woodhead (2005: 48) themselves say in their book: 'The growth of the (relatively small) holistic milieu is not compensating for the decline of the (considerably larger) congregational domain.' They are a bit more ambiguous regarding future projections, but it looks like when the tide of academic fashion started to turn, many people latched on to the title's claim of a 'spiritual revolution', without checking the argument itself. The positive side of the debate has been an expansion of legitimate topics for the sociological study of religion, but this has little to do with secularization.

The final, and at least seemingly methodologically most robust challenge to the secularization paradigm comes from what is referred to as the rational choice theory (RCT) of religion and now more commonly known as the economics of religion. Referring to Peter Berger's ideas regarding the secularizing effects of religious pluralism (see above), Finke and Stark (1988: 42) say that 'we agree with Berger that pluralism forces religions to compete for adherents. Unlike Berger, however, we view competition as a stimulus for religious growth and not an avenue for its demise.' The RCT approach flips the direction of analysis in the sense that unlike the secularization paradigm, which assesses the demand for religion, RCT assumes demand as constant, but considers the supply of religious 'goods' as the key to a vibrant religious culture (hence the sometime moniker 'supply-side theory of religion'). Thus, competition between multiple providers in the American case is viewed favourably against the stagnant monopoly churches of Europe. RCT was touted as the 'new paradigm' in the sociology of religion from the late 1980s to around 2000, when the field suffered a setback over a mathematical problem in combining religiosity measures with the pluralism indexes most RCT analyses were using. When these technical problems were attended to, evidence suggested that Berger's original claim regarding the secularizing effect of pluralism had stronger support than the RCT approach. What remains unclear, however, is what the mechanism of these effects is (Stoltz 2020).

Conclusion

Secularization is a contested concept because there is disagreement and confusion over the sources of secularization and the appropriate level of measuring the decline of religion. Several traditions for challenging the secularization paradigm have emerged in recent decades. The success or popularity of 'secularization' in the sociology of religion (and the study of religion more broadly) is not, however, simply a matter of theoretical or methodological refinement. It seems to be almost an existential question for many scholars, which makes balanced debate difficult. What is clear, however, is that neither the concept nor the contestations over it are going anywhere anytime soon.

CHAPTER 19
SPIRITUALITY
Steven J. Sutcliffe

Introduction: Mapping the field

The noun 'spirituality' and its adjective 'spiritual' have been widely used by a variety of individuals, groups and institutions in the late modern world, especially since the 'long 1960s' (Marwick 1998). The terminology has a complex history that can be traced back across the twentieth century and even earlier in some traditions of use. Various new, marginalized and 'alternative' groups have found in spirituality a flexibility and expressivity that seem unavailable in the term 'religion'. The latter has historically been associated with mainstream, hegemonic institutions, especially in those countries with an established Christian denomination recognized by the state, particularly in Europe and the Nordic countries. Groups particularly associated with the discourse of spirituality include New Age, Holistic and Human Potential practitioners. This has led some commentators to identify the growth of a new constituency in late modernity of the 'spiritual but not religious' and there are certainly many communities for whom it makes sense – practically, rhetorically or strategically – to draw a clear distinction between the two terms (Mercadante 2014, Parsons 2018). However, many new religions also proselytize using the language of spirituality in order to communicate a 'lived' quality to their practices and doctrines. Furthermore, the global acculturation of the term in late modernity means that Christians and Buddhists (for example) may well now describe themselves as 'spiritual' *as well as* 'religious', perhaps using 'spiritual' to designate the more personal and intimate dimensions of their practice.

Spirituality draws in part on a Christian genealogy: for example, Evangelicals stress the revitalizing power of 'life in the Spirit' and Catholicism has a long-established tradition of 'spiritual direction' (Jones et al. 1986). At the same time, the term 'spirituality' is increasingly in use in secular fields such as medicine and healthcare. For example, the National Health Service in Scotland has replaced 'hospital chaplains' and 'chapels' with 'spiritual care' advisors and 'sanctuaries' (NHS 2021) while in 1999 the Royal College of Psychiatrists in the UK established a 'spirituality and psychiatry' special interest group. And since 'the long 1960s' a range of publications has mapped the many varieties of spirituality: for example, *The New Spirituality* (Lynch 2017) addresses 'progressive belief', *Hermaphrodeities* (Kaldera 2009) works with 'transgender spirituality', and *Queer*

Spiritual Spaces (Browne, Munt and Yip 2010) includes Quaker, Muslim and Buddhist examples of LGBTQ+ spirituality. Secular expressions have been identified in titles like *Spirituality for the Sceptic: the Thoughtful Love of Life* (Solomon 2002) and *The Book of Atheist Spirituality: An Elegant Argument for Spirituality without God* (Comte-Sponville 2008) while a new hybrid of New Age millennialism and conspiracy theories has been dubbed 'conspirituality' (Ward and Voas 2011; Dyrendal 2015). In short, there is a lot of 'it' about.

The terminology of 'spirituality' has also been assimilated into the study of religion(s). The concept is regularly rehearsed in academic media: for example, in the proceedings of the International Network for the Study of Spirituality (INSS) and in numerous journal articles and books: notable examples include *The Spiritual Revolution* by Paul Heelas and Linda Woodhead (2005), who argue from fieldwork data that 'spirituality' is gradually replacing 'religion' amongst certain populations; Boaz Huss (2014), who argues that the term is a 'new cultural category' which complicates the binary between religious and secular; and *Secular Societies, Spiritual Selves?* by Anna Fedele and Kim Knibbe (2020), who triangulate the concept with gender and the secular. The INSS is an instructive academic example since it was founded in 2010 as the British Association for the Study of Spirituality (Hunt 2011) even though there already existed an organization – the British Association for the Study of Religions (BASR), founded in 1954 – that one might expect to include 'spirituality' within the study of 'religion' (Sutcliffe 2004). However, where the BASR is grounded in a broadly 'scientific' perspective based in history, sociology and ethnography, the INSS presents a more 'applied' methodology based in pastoral psychology, healthcare and social work. These divergent methodologies partly explain the co-existence of two associations for similar phenomena, but they also point to a felt semantic difference between 'spirituality' and 'religion' which is attractive and meaningful not only to practitioners but to some scholars. Nevertheless, while 'spirituality' is a widely deployed and recognized emic term, its viability as an analytical or etic term remains a moot point (Sutcliffe 2019).

The range of examples suggests that, first, spirituality functions as a *lingua franca* for a certain kind of cross-cultural sensibility in the sense that it 'pushes back' against the differentiation of 'religions' as discrete entities separate from other cultural activities. The examples also suggest that spirituality in some contexts serves as a form of 'public religion' (Woodhead 2013) rather than describing merely private or domestic interests as traditionally held. This interpretation is supported by the protean capacity of spirituality to communicate late modern sensibilities across 'religious', 'non-religious' and 'secular' fields alike (Heelas and Woodhead 2005). Even if at least one scholar wonders if the term lacks stable meaning, the cumulative ethnographic evidence suggests that it is providing a new register for disciplining the late modern self which is anything but merely 'subjective' (Altglas 2018). That is, various forms of ritual – prayer, meditation, yoga, circle work, tai chi, expressive dance – are increasingly taught in collective groups as 'spiritual practices' to discipline the mind and body.

Spirituality: Entangled genealogies

Consider the term's genealogy. In a classic article written within a Christian hermeneutic, Walter Principe distinguishes two senses of *spiritualitas* or *pneumatikos*: a 'Pauline' sense, based in New Testament interpretation, and a more humanistic 'entitative-psychological' sense. Despite different trajectories, both senses operate at a '*real* or *existential* level' and thus describe a 'lived quality' of experience (Principe 1983: 135; see also Woodhead 2011). According to Principe, the Pauline sense describes an embodied disposition in which '*pneuma* or *spiritus* are set over against *sarx* or *caro*' (the lustful, carnal body) rather than the healthily embodied *soma/corpus*. He also argues that within the 'entitative-psychological' tradition, *spiritualitas* became opposed to the more holistic embodiment of *corporalitas*, resulting in a misleading dualism between spirit and flesh. Principe's admittedly tendentious model captures 'gnostic' forms of spirituality, but not the embodied disposition characteristic of the 'holistic milieu' (Heelas and Woodhead 2005) which surely has more in common with the 'lived quality' of Pauline corporeality. In other words, Principe gives us useful material to think with, but his polarization of interpretations breaks down.

A second genealogy is derived from late nineteenth- and early twentieth-century post-Christian sources as illustrated by the Theosophical Society and its numerous 'children' (Tingay 2000). In 1910, G. R. S. Mead, former secretary to its co-founder H. P. Blavatsky, published 'On the Track of Spirituality' (Mead 1910). It is instructive to consider the substantive qualities of the titular term as described by Mead. Spirituality is 'god-like' and as such is not to be confused with 'intellectuality'. It should not be used to describe 'the path of sanctity or sainthood' (Mead 1910: 148–50) but, rather, describes a property of 'ordinary life and ordinary people, free from ... pietistic and spiritistic presuppositions' (Mead 1910: 162). It expresses a sense of 'freshness; seeking for new ideas and experiences in everything around' (Mead 1910: 149). It is a '"natural" thing' insofar as 'the happy individual feels at his [*sic*] best' and 'in his [*sic*] true and proper place' (Mead 1910: 152). No hierarchy is implied since 'among the spiritual the bond is that of friends' (Mead 1910: 157). Finally, spirituality is both serious and light: its exponents 'should be in earnest and eager' and 'bubbling over with life' (Mead 1910: 151–2).

Spirituality after the 'long 1960s' vividly sounds the mixed note of this joint Principe-Mead Christian-post-Christian genealogy. In their ethnography of an English market town, Heelas and Woodhead (2005) record widespread use of terms like 'energy', 'vibration', 'flow', 'power', 'aura', 'warmth', 'vitality' and 'well-being'. Consider also the responses by Findhorn residents, doyens of the New Age since 1962, who use the word 'spirituality' to express opposition to 'the system', to 'dogma', to 'organized belief' and to 'narrow' outlooks, and positively linked the term with 'living experience' and 'open', 'inner', 'inclusive' and 'natural' ideas (Sutcliffe 2003: 215).

Ethnographically based accounts such as Heelas and Woodhead (2005) give appropriate weight to emic understandings whilst simultaneously providing their own analytical framework. However, for some commentators, 'spirituality' signals everything that is wrong with 'religion' when it becomes de-traditionalized and marketized: for example in *New Age Capitalism: Making Money East of Eden* (Lau 2000) and *Selling Spirituality: the Silent Takeover of Religion* (Carrette and King 2004). Nevertheless the claimed 'fuzziness' of spirituality (Zinnbauer et al. 1997) and the 'problem' of its institutionally diffuse structure (Bruce 2017) are typically of secondary import to practitioners as can be ascertained through the empirical evidence of fieldwork and interview, or philosophical counter-critique (Redden 2016; Clot-Garrell and Griera 2019; Watts 2020). What becomes evident via empirically based enquiry is the ease with which practitioners handle this erstwhile 'fuzzy', 'diffuse' or 'monetized' term, especially via the *lingua franca* described above by Heelas and Woodhead (2005).

Spirituality as a placeholder

Spirituality has a second, meta-level function: as a 'placeholder' to signal via shorthand a moment or quality of experience that cannot easily or satisfactorily be described. Usually this moment or quality is affective and/or corporeal but it may also be noetic: an emotion, something felt in the body, an insight. It is not necessarily transient but may be trained through specific practices, or institutionalized through pedagogies like (Catholic) Ignatian Spirituality (Frederick and Muldoon 2020) or the (Holistic) Diploma in Practical Spirituality and Wellness (Bloom 2018). In these examples the term gets 'filled in' with specific content according to the substantive tradition. However, its placeholder function has arguably strong appeal. To eludicate I turn – perhaps unexpectedly – to Jonathan Z. Smith's discussion of the historiography of the Melanesian term *mana*. According to Smith, *mana* was defined in 1865 in *A Dictionary of the Hawaiian Language* as 'supernatural power … supposed and believed to be an attribute of the gods' and more briefly in 1845, in the *Dictionary of the New Zealand Language*, as 'power, influence' (Smith 2002: 125). In a 1877 letter to F. Max Müller, the missionary Richard Codrington describes *mana* as:

> a force altogether distinct from physical power, which acts in all kinds of ways for good and evil, and which it is of the greatest advantage to possess or control …
> Mana is not fixed in anything, and can be conveyed in almost anything.
>
> (cited in Smith 2004: 126)

These definitions stem from colonial contact so require sensitive treatment. But, as in the case of the recovery of the concept of 'animism' (Harvey 2014), *mana* may assist cross-cultural conceptualization if carefully treated (Meylan 2017, especially Chapters 3 and 7). Here the principal point is that, as Smith concludes, *mana* is 'not a substantive category, it is a linguistic one' in the sense that it represents 'floating or undecided signification' (Meylan 2017: 133). Smith draws on the anthropologist Claude Lévi-Strauss who writes: 'It is the function of notions of the mana-type to oppose themselves to the absence of signification without allowing, by themselves, any particular signification' (cited in Smith 2004: 133). Levi-Strauss's examples include 'the use of nominal "place holders" … for objects not yet encompassed by native taxonomy or nomenclature'. In the philosophy of mathematics a 'placeholder' is a symbol which represents a missing term in an equation, or which marks a purely formal numerical value. By analogy, *mana* denotes 'that whose name and taxon must be deferred' (Smith 2004: 133).

Conclusion: Spirituality as post-Christian religion

'Spirituality' may hold a similar placeholder – or 'x' factor – function as a 'native Western' and 'post-Christian' example of 'that whose name and taxon must be deferred' while simultaneously communicating the power of a substantive 'more' beyond linguistic representation. Similarly Heelas (2014) describes the function of 'spiritualities of life' in 'transgressing the secular' through fine and subtle mechanisms as a response to encroaching secularization. The aim of this second, meta use of 'spirituality' is to defer denotative meaning and to rebuff reductive analysis whether expressed in scientific or theological terms. Although there are substantive trends in the *lingua franca* of spirituality, these may be of secondary interest to practitioners who prefer tactically to deploy the placeholder function to signal the semantic limitation of utterances and thereby to communicate an unmediated and hence 'secularly transgressive' moment. This addresses the title of the article 'Is the term "spirituality" a word that everyone uses, but nobody knows what anyone means by it?' (Rose 2001) but from a different angle from the author's yearning for stable content. More productive is the intuition in Rose's text that 'using the term "spirituality" seems to be *a neat catch-all, intimating… without necessarily revealing*' (Rose 2001: 193; emphasis added). Spirituality is a term which makes excellent sense to its users. It represents a popular concept with a double service: substantive *lingua franca* and functional placeholder. As such, spirituality is the new religion of post-Christian societies.

CHAPTER 20
SUPERSTITION
Amy R. Whitehead

The concept of superstition is unusual. As a term, 'superstition' is pejorative. The concept, however, reflects a rich array of complex practices and customs that both highlights and problematizes the intersections at which religion, 'officialdom', the secular and a whole host of unauthorized, unofficial, lay, 'folk', individual and/or collective traditional beliefs and practices meet. After all, that which may be reduced to the 'stuff of superstitious nonsense' by one, may be viably religious and valuable to another.

The problematic

Prevalent in cultures worldwide, within both popular and scholarly discourse, the concept of superstition persists in conveying sets of beliefs, materialities and practices that are (a) set in opposition to rationalism, (b) put on equal terms pejoratively with 'magic' and (c) deemed 'lesser' than, or a footnote to, so-called 'authentic' or 'true' religion. In other words, so-called superstitions are typically disapproved of (by official governments or religions), associated with lack of education, and understood as 'false'. But what constitutes a superstition? How can we measure the intended outcomes of individual and collective uses of putative superstitions? And how does the concept relate to, or interact with, ritual, religion, magic, belief in miracles and credulity?

In addition to black cats, throwing salt over one's left shoulder, avoiding walking under ladders, warding off the evil eye, or the use or avoidance of certain numbers, commonalities can be found in superstitions cross-culturally (see Oyedeji et al. 2021). Depending on the religious context, so-called superstitions (or 'lesser' practices) provide ritually prescriptive mechanisms through which agents can attempt to influence the outcome of events, causality or some conception of a supernatural force (the divine, spirits, ancestors, ghosts, luck). For example, in Roman Catholic shrines across Spain, touching or making offerings to certain Marian statues is thought to promote fertility. Based on the biblical account of people bringing handkerchiefs that Paul had touched to the sick (Acts 19:11–12), 'holy handkerchiefs' are used by some fundamentalist Christian congregations to aid in healing (Chryssides 2021: 263), and Thai and Japanese Buddhist temples often contain fortune telling machines, the use and practice of which is endorsed by religious authorities. Religious adherents typically engage in other practices such as wearing an amulet, a cross, a hand of Fatima, *vibhuti* (sacred ash applied in three lines across the forehead in honour of Śiva) or a medal of Saint Christopher (which may be blessed by priests). Where, then, do we place belief in ghosts, faith healing, practices of exorcism, ancestor veneration or use of mediums, divination or astrology, the latter of which Nick Campion refers to as an indigenous European religion (Campion 2022)? Are these objects, practices and understandings religious or superstitious, and who has the authority to declare it?

Arguably, and despite the inherent judgement found in the term, so-called superstitious practices can be both 'superstitious' and religious. The question of authority becomes one of positionality, or of who is looking on or practising, and from what angle. The wide range of activities, beliefs, spirituality and practices that superstition covers can result from officially religious, individual and collective interpretations and may, then, be better placed on a sliding scale that works in tandem with current moves in the emerging subfields of vernacular, lived and material religion that are concerned with what people actually do, on the ground, and why.

Historical trajectory

Although that which can readily fall into the category of putative superstitions was being written about by the ancient Hebrews (see Leviticus 19:31 as a warning against consulting mediums), it was the influence of early Greek and Roman understandings that formed the strong current which gained momentum over the centuries alongside the development of different forms of religion (predominantly Christianity) and spread into different parts of Europe, and eventually Asia. The residue of this legacy is with us today. Superstition continues to be defined in relation to that which it is perceived to *not* be, namely 'true religion'.

But, according to Wouter Hanegraaff, this was not always the case. *Superstitio* (relating to practices such as divination and prophecy) is Latin for the Greek *deisidaimonia*, where *deisi* is indicative of 'fear' but also 'awe' or 'respect', and *daimones* could be deities such as gods, goddesses or demigods. As gods and goddesses sat at the heart of ancient Roman religion, emphasis on awe and reverence had positive implications (Hanegraaff 2016: 591). However, in the parallel world of fourth century BCE Greece, *deisidaimonia* was employed by the Greek philosophical elite to pejoratively refer to the nonsensical and 'irrational beliefs about harmful deities, and for cultic practices that reflected a misguided fear of the gods' (Hanegraaff 2016: 591). Practices associated with the Latin *supersitio* later followed suit, and from the first century CE, *superstitio* 'became associated with "depraved, strange, spooky and dishonourable" practices of foreign peoples such as the Egyptians, the Druids or the Chaldaeans' (Martin in Hanegraaff 2016: 592). The association with the common people (*vulgus*), country dwellers (*pagus*) and the lower orders of Roman society became a feature of the concept of superstition (O'Neil 1987). In other words, superstition became a reference for 'other' to that which was agreeable to the hegemonic discourses of the time, including being uneducated, rural (as opposed to sophisticated and urban), poor and worshipping or paying homage in 'the wrong direction'.

In the thirteenth century, Thomas Aquinas, drawing on Augustine, divided ' … superstition into three types – *idolatria, divination, vana observantia* (idolatry, divination, and empty observances)' (Aquinas, ST II. Q92. A2) which further reflects the continuation of early Greek and Roman understandings, but through Christian theology. Idolatry, divination and 'empty observances' are forbidden because they were thought to draw attention away from the 'one true faith'. Leaping ahead to sixteenth-century northern Europe, similar to the thirteenth century, the concept was used to signal beliefs and practices that were not only 'lesser than', but sinful; only in the sixteenth century, both the concept and the term carried associations with witchcraft, signalling that one had become entangled with uncontrollable and potentially diabolic forces.

The concept of superstition also played significant, strategic and polarizing roles within movements such as the Protestant Reformation and Enlightenment philosophy. Protestant Reformers weaponized superstition, using the term pejoratively to label both accredited and non-accredited Catholic material performances and beliefs such as statue and saint devotion, miracle working statues, use of rosaries, holy water, indulgences and relic veneration. Although the Catechism of the Catholic Church states that 'To attribute the efficacy of prayers or sacramental signs to their mere external performance, apart from the interior dispositions that they demand, is to fall into superstition' (*Catechism* 2003), there were understandings about what these things meant, signified or the roles that they played. This resulted in Catholic practices being marked out as remnants from a 'pagan past', the designation of which fuelled the Reformation's 'war on idols', and ensuing anti-Catholic rhetoric. Calvinist Protestantism, with emphasis on 'hearing' the Word of God instead of 'seeing', won pride of place in the hierarchy of religious authenticity. Bias against superstition, it would seem, is intricately related to bias against materiality, religious material cultures, the tangible and ritual.

Superstition and the study of religions

Recent moves in scholarship are revealing a 're-think' of the way that superstition as a concept is being handled, particularly in relation to the modernizing strategies of different nation-states. Hanegraaff (2016) suggests that in the early modern period, 'religion' and 'the secular' defined themselves against one another. From this, a triad was formed, the third part of which he refers to as the 'third domain'. This, he argues, became the category within which a 'whole range of traditional non-secular beliefs and practices that were just as distasteful to Christian orthodox thinkers as they were to their secular critics' (2016: 591) were placed. Rejected by both 'religion' and 'the secular', the third domain is best summed up using the language of '*superstition and magic*', a category that has been mostly overlooked by scholars (Hanegraaff 2016: 591), but one that is needed to adequately understand and conceptualize 'religion'. In fact, arguably, superstition has been overlooked by scholars of religion precisely because it is the difficult to classify, 'wild card' element of Hanegraaff's triad. Superstitious beliefs and practices are so deeply rooted and wide-reaching, that either diminishing them or ignoring them completely in favour of the more controllable and categorizable 'religion' and 'the secular' is understandably a more attractive option. However, in this way, a rich array of phenomena would be invariably left behind.

Jason Ānanda Josephson-Storm (2018) also argues for a 'third term' (superstition) to be introduced into Western Christendom's construction of the 'binary opposition between "religious" and the "secular," ... ' which has succeeded in having global influence and reach (Josephson-Storm 2018: 1). In response to the climate of modernization and contact with 'the West' that began taking place from the 1850s in Japan, some Japanese Buddhist leaders began dividing traditional Buddhist cosmologies and practices into the constructed categories 'superstition' and 'religion'. Buddhist educator and reformer Inoue Enryō (1858–1919), with his reception of Western philosophy, was, according to Josephson-Storm, crucial to this change. While Buddhism began to occupy a space alongside Christianity and Judaism (as an authentic westernized 'religion'), officially sanctioned monastic practices such as exorcisms, healings, banishing monsters, Shinto kami worship and magical rituals, were not approved of by foreigners and government officials and deemed 'not really Buddhism' (Josephson-Storm, 2006: 143).

Josephson-Storm also surveys scholarly works where anti-superstition campaigns have been instigated by governments in China, Vietnam and Haiti. In these places, particularly in the twentieth century, superstitions were regarded as dangerous and widely discouraged (2018: 7–8). Developing costly campaigns to counter superstitions is not only indicative of the disdain felt towards the irrationality associated with them; it is also indicative of a perceived genuine threat that these governments have felt from the powerful roles that so-called superstitions play in the lives of citizens.

Huang Ko-wu traces the historical legacy of superstition in China from the late Qing Dynasty to the early Republic, saying that after May Fourth (the 1919 anti-imperialist political movement), the Chinese intelligentsia, who were influenced by the impact of Western science and knowledge, used science as the ground from which to launch an attack on anything labelled 'superstition', while other figures noted that 'all religion [including Daoism, Confucianism and Buddhism] was superstition' (Ko-wu 2016: 54) or *mixin*. According to Ko-wu, *mixin* is 'translational counterpart of the English term superstition' that focuses on associations with irrational beliefs (2016: 56). In 1928, this movement physically manifested in the Nationalist Party's publication of the 'Standards for the Preservation or Abolishment of Ancestral Temples', intended to launch a nationwide attack on so-called idols and temples (Ko-wu 2016: 56). This echoes the Protestant Reformation's war on Catholic idols, and both 'religion' and 'the secular's' disdain of so-called superstition. The 1949 Communist and subsequent cultural Revolutions under the Communist regime of mainland China (Ko-wu 2016: 56) saw religious superstition as competition with communist idealism and continues to come under severe attack from the Chinese Communist Party. Religion, for the CCP, should not be in a position to interfere with the state's power, nor harm its citizens (Maslakova 2020: 521). In European contexts, acts such as the UK's Fraudulent Mediums Act of 1951 was created to repeal the Witchcraft Act of 1735 and 'to make ... express provision for the punishment of persons who fraudulently purport to act as, spiritualistic mediums or to exercise powers of telepathy, clairvoyance or other similar powers' (Legislation.gov.uk n.d.) guilty of an offence. What is meant by 'other similar powers' is left to speculation.

Alternatively, many contemporary Pagans, the umbrella term under which sits a variety of different earth-traditions, have replaced the pejorative superstition with 'tradition' in their successful disassociation of knocking on wood, crossing fingers, the number 13 and black cats from Christianity's cosmology of devils, bad spirits and evil. These beliefs and practices have been reframed in a positive light due to associations with ancient, pre-Christian, polytheistic traditions and they are arguably part of a reclaiming strategy that is of interest to scholars of religion. As Brent Plate suggests: 'What seems trivial and easily overlooked, in the end, becomes foundational for religious environments and traditions (Plate 2012: 162).

For scholars of religion, then, the concept of superstition reflects etic and emic problems of location, as well as that of authority. First, although many people practise many forms of superstition, most people will not self-identify as superstitious. Some might, however, carry out practices in a variety of shrines and temples that can be deemed superstitions by non-adherents. Further, since the term has pejorative connotations, scholars of religion would not be quick to label the practices of others as 'superstitious' (as in 'superstitious nonsense'), whether those others are Catholics carrying out Marian shrine venerations in Western contexts, Hindus offering milk to statues of Ganesh, use of *vibhuti*, Spiritualists obtaining messages from mediums, or Japanese Buddhists carrying out practices such as distributing healing charms, banishing monsters or performing exorcisms. These are precisely the types of activities that may be understood within modern discourses as superstitious, but that are inherently interesting for scholars in the study of religions. While too pejorative a term for direct scholarly use, it is legitimate for scholars to report on secondary occurrences of the term, when one religious community uses it to describe practices of which it disapproves.

Conclusion

For scholars, the concept of superstition, while highly problematic, is rarely problematized. Although frequently thought of as monolithic, simple and silly 'magical' practices that result from irrationality and ignorance, the nuances of so-called superstitious beliefs and practices are, however, worth considering for the simple fact that the concept raises more questions than it actually answers. The term itself is, however, too pejorative for scholarly use and more than likely beyond rescue. Scholars of religion would rarely describe the practices we see that take place, for example, in Buddhist or Hindu temples, or Catholic shrines, as superstitious. That would go against the underlying creed of our discipline, namely being non-judgemental. On the other hand, it is worth mentioning that religions themselves are judgemental, and their use of the concept of superstition is itself is indeed worthy of note. But as a concept, superstition can be on hand to serve as a guide through which to help navigate the complex assemblages of features found in putative superstitious practices. It can also help in shedding light on the modern biases that continue to be present within our field, as well as serving as a frame for understanding the modernizing attempts of officialdom to suppress traditional lay practices in different cultural contexts. Whether or not the concept re-conceptualized will be able to shed its millennia-old pejorative connotations is yet to be known.

CHAPTER 21
SYNCRETISM
Bettina E. Schmidt

Syncretism is a contested term used to describe the blending of two or more traditions. While originating with Plutarch, it was Erasmus of Rotterdam who applied the term to religion in 1519. Erasmus saw the foreign influences in Christianity, which he described as syncretism, as enrichment. However, the term soon gained negative connotations particularly among Protestant theologians who argued that the Gospel was becoming distorted. This negative implication continued into colonial times. Only later, in the postcolonial period, did the blending of religious traditions begin to be seen as something positive.

While the process of blending is universal and – though less frequently – also applied as a descriptor of cultural adaptations (e.g. Herskovits 1941), syncretism is mainly used to describe the blending of Indigenous religions with Christianity. A prime example is Catholicism in Latin America where scholars note a survival of the worship of Pachamama or other earth mother deities in the guise of the Virgin Mary, for instance as the Virgin of Guadalupe. In postcolonial times this form of syncretism was seen as a sign of resistance against colonial domination by reinterpreting Christian doctrines using local religious practices. Other examples are found in the African-derived religions across the Caribbean islands and the Americas which are generally considered to be syncretic. The Cuban Orisha religion became originally known under the name *Santería* which derived from the Spanish word *santos* (saints) and means literally the devotion of saints. Its more accurate Spanish name, 'la religión de los orichas' (the religion of the orishas), highlights the devotion of orishas, which is the name of deities in the traditional Yoruba religion in Nigeria and Benin. While the orishas merged with Catholic saints, some scholars argue today that this blending was merely superficial, due to the terror and suppression during the time of slavery. Because the hagiography of the Catholic saints reminded the enslaved of the deities of their ancestors, they began to pray to the saints, but addressed in them their songs and prayers to the orishas. However, since this form of religion, like the other African-derived religions, developed from the merging of different traditions, they are usually categorized as syncretic. But there is a problem with this label.

Syncretism and the contested notion of 'purity'

The term 'syncretism' implies the mixture of originally 'pure' traditions such as Christianity and African religions. But what is 'pure'? When Christianity spread through Europe, the missionaries adapted their practices to the agricultural calendar of Europe and incorporated elements from pre-Christian traditions. But it is misleading to regard these pre-Christian traditions or forms of early Christianity as homogenous traditions. Christianity derived from Judaism and incorporated elements from other traditions such as Graeco-Roman festivals. And the pre-Christian cultures in Europe were a mixture of various groups such as the Celts, the Normans and the Saxons. Jumping centuries ahead, to the conquest of the Americas and the brutal capture and transport of Africans to the new European colonies, Christianity was already the result of blending and ongoing influences. The Catholicism that arrived in the Spanish and Portuguese colonies was a form of popular Catholicism of the peninsular with a strong emphasis on the devotion to saints and the Virgin Mary. This was very different from the Christianity that arrived in the British colonies. What, then, is the pure form of Christianity – Catholicism with its emphasis on the devotion to the saints or Protestantism with its focus on the Gospel? The same heterogeneity applies to the African traditions that form the backbone of the African-derived religions in the Americas.

The term 'African Traditional Religions' covers a range of different religions, some with a focus on ancestor worship, a creator god, spirits of nature or a polytheistic system of deities. Some scholars argue that the incredible number of different languages spoken in Africa today is just a fraction of the languages spoken in Africa before the invasion of European slave traders. Each language can be seen as representing a unique cultural and religious tradition. Considering the brutality of the slave trade, which selected people to be sent across the Atlantic and killing the rest, even so, historians identified a vast mixture of cultures in each of the slave transports crossing the Atlantic. Due to the brutal suppression of African cultures and languages during the slave trade in the Americas, which lasted for centuries, no 'pure' African religion could have survived – although historians have confirmed that by the end of the slave trade across the Atlantic, the West African Yoruba made up a high percentage of people transported to the remaining European colonies in the Americas (e.g. Cuba and Brazil). This explains the strong influence of Yoruba culture in the African-derived religions in Latin America today.

We have therefore two heterogeneous religious amalgamations that clashed in the Americas and led over a long period to the formation of African-derived religions, centuries after the first African man put foot on a Caribbean island.

Syncretism and colonialism

Another misleading problem with the concept of syncretism is that it implies a hierarchical order of one dominant religion (i.e. Christianity) and other secondary traditions (i.e. the Indigenous religions). Some scholars even argue that labelling a religion syncretic implies a pejorative view of Indigenous religions and thereby supports the misunderstanding of them. A closer look at an African-derived religion illustrates why the label 'syncretic religions' is a continuation of the colonial oppression and the long-practised custom that the winners dictate how the past is remembered. Charles Long argues that colonialism led to the systemic suppression of people who were left with no place to express their own humanity – apart from religion which allowed the human imagination to blossom as a means of survival. African slaves had to adapt to the conditions of slavery to survive but were able to resist at the same time via the creation of a different reality (1986: 177). Long regards these religions as a creative sphere with a utopian and eschatological dimension, which changed the master—slaves dialectic as the following story of Saint Patrick and Vodou illustrates.

The Christian elements in African-derived religions, such as the use of the iconography of Catholic saints for African deities are often explained by a 'cover theory': during slavery, African beliefs and practices were prohibited, and slaves hid their authentic beliefs by superficially adapting them to the worship of saints. Thus, the term 'syncretic' would be justified albeit with the African religions as dominant and Christianity as the secondary influence. However, scholars today argue against this simplistic understanding of the blending of African deities with Catholic saints. The Irish saint Saint Patrick, who became incorporated into the Vodou pantheon, is linked to Dãmbala, the patron of waters, because of the association with snakes. According to oral tradition, Saint Patrick cleansed Ireland of snakes, while Dãmbala is represented as a snake in Yoruba tradition. However, this analogy goes beyond the visual aspects since it points, within the Caribbean context, to an inner connection between the two. Saint Patrick's hagiography is a story of survival. Born into privilege he was captured by Irish pirates in 406 CE and sold into slavery. After years he escaped back to the continent where later he was chosen to return to Ireland as a missionary. His story resonated with the slaves in the Caribbean; as Joan Dayan writes, 'In St. Patrick's dual sea crossings, back and forth from bondage to escape, from one kind of freedom to another, Haitians remembered how their ancestors died into life, saved by descending into the waters and arriving reborn in Guinea' (2003: 47). The representation of Dãmbala as Saint Patrick is not only a reminder of the atrocities, but also of the transformation of the African Dãmbala into a Haitian deity. Going back to the critique of syncretism, the story of Dãmbala and Saint Patrick illustrates why it is misleading to ignore the creative imagination of the blending of traditions as well as discounting the creativity of the process.

Bricolage vs syncretism

Instead of using the term 'syncretism' the French sociologist Roger Bastide (1970) described the process of creating an African-derived religion with the term bricolage. The term 'bricolage' refers to a method of reflection and discovery that leads to the creation of something new. For Bastide, African-derived religions – and we can apply it to any other religions labelled as syncretic – are new creations that are products of the human imagination. The term 'bricolage' was introduced by the French anthropologist Claude Lévi-Strauss as a metaphor for mythical thinking of Amerindian societies which Lévi-Strauss praised for their methods of observation and reflection. A *bricoleur* is as innovative and creative as an engineer or scientist. With only limited tools at hand, a bricoleur uses whatever is available to solve a problem at hand (Lévi-Strauss 1966: 16–17). Bricolage implies a continuously new arrangement of elements from different systems.

Bastide, who also worked in Brazil like Lévi-Strauss, applied the term 'bricolage' to African-derived religions in order to highlight the fact that those African-derived religions are the result of creativity and innovation. The new religions enabled people to preserve memories and a sense of a distinct identity over a long period of oppression. Adding elements from different traditions helped to fill gaps created by the brutality of the slave trade by preserving the collective memory while, at the same time, reacting to the new environment and local influences. As one of my research partners in Brazil stressed frequently, Candomblé is a Brazilian religion and honours the Amazonian spirits and the African ancestors while having the African deities at its core. This process of conserving memory which Bastide describes as bricolage is not mechanical but depends on its situation, time and environment and constantly renews itself. While it was born out of necessity, it would be misleading to describe bricolage as simply a product of the trans-Atlantic slave trade. The African-derived religions show imaginative and resourceful energy while maintaining the religious core. While syncretism implies a notion of purity and hierarchy, bricolage highlights continuity, creativity and change.

Syncretism and cultural appropriation

This leads to a final point in the critique of syncretism. The term 'syncretism' might explain the creation of new religions (although, as should be evident by now, it does so in a rather superficial and simplistic manner), it does not, however, explain their continuation into the twenty-first century. Haiti became independent and abolished slavery in 1804, more than 200 years ago, and Brazil abolished slavery with the establishment of the Republic in 1888, more than 100 years ago. While the abolition of slavery did not put an end to racism and discrimination against the descendants of the enslaved Africans, we might have expected that, as a result of the abolition of slavery, the links between Catholic saints expressed in African-derived religions for example through prayers to the Virgin Mary or images of Christian saints in a Vodou temple to weaken and wither away. Why then do we still encounter images of Catholic saints in Vodou temples or see devotees of Candomblé or other African-derived religions praying to the Virgin Mary – if we follow the explanation offered by the concept of syncretism? These changes have proved to be more than superficial and have led to the creation of a new, creole religion. African-derived religions – like any other religions labelled as syncretic – are not the result of a simple blending of two systems under oppressive conditions. They constantly adapt and incorporate new elements by keeping the collective memory alive as one can see in the case of the Cuban religion mentioned above. Originally identified as Santería – the worship of saints – it became known as 'la religión de los orichas' or Lucumi religion later on to stress the worship of the African deities instead of Catholic saints. After the Cuban revolution, it migrated to the United States and became popular among African Americas who had not grown up in a primarily Catholic and Spanish-speaking environment, but in English-speaking Black Churches. In this way the religion became identified as the Yoruba religion in the United States.

On the other hand, historically the Yoruba influence in North America was minimal. When African Americans moved from New York to South Carolina and founded the village Oyotunji in 1970 with a Yoruba temple at its core, their lineage could only be traced back to Africa via Cuba. In the first years Oyotunji relied on Cuban priests to conduct some of the ceremonies. Was this therefore a form of cultural appropriation? This question is particularly important in connection with the religious changes, as the following short story illustrates. The role of *Ifá* priests (i.e. *babalawos*) had been restricted to men for centuries. However, with the expansion of the religion from Cuba to the United States, women became interested in *Ifá* and some travelled to Nigeria in order to seek initiation. When I discussed this issue with Cuban and Puerto Rican priests in New York in 1999, I was told that they would walk out of the ceremony if a woman were to enter the room as *babalawo* even though I mentioned that the initiations were carried out in Nigeria, the homeland of the Yoruba. For my Cuban and Puerto Rican partners, the Cuban religion maintained the original religion better than the Yoruba in Nigeria, since in their view, in Nigeria the Yoruba belief had become corrupted by colonialism and Christian missionary activities. However, when I mentioned this comment to a Nigerian scholar one or two years later, he laughed and dismissed the Cuban and Puerto Rican priests as not having the authority to speak for the Yoruba. His reaction echoes the wider debate about authority discussed controversially within the African diaspora and on the African continent. For the African diaspora, the transnational spiritual communities draw on Yoruba cosmology and ritual practices to provide, as Fadeke Castor writes, 'methods to access past generations (the ancestors) and heal historical wounds. This in turn informs a spiritual praxis that extends the healing to current and future generations' (2017: 7). However, this is seen differently in Africa, the motherland of all African-derived religions.

Conclusion

Despite a revitalization of the original positive notion of syncretism in the postcolonial period, syncretism remains highly contested. To some degree, the challenge of syncretism echoes Paul Gilroy's disapproval of normative categories (Gilroy 1993: 188) since the notion of pure roots within syncretic constructs led to misinterpretation of religions created during the colonial times. So-called syncretic religions are not 'just' the result of a blending of two or more religions, but of a slow and creative process with a bricolage of elements from various systems which are equally important. They are highly creative and signs of survival and resistance, reflecting the power of human imagination.

CHAPTER 22
VIOLENCE
Negar Partow

Introduction

Debates on the role of religion in violent incidents and wars around the world have grown steadily in recent decades. Gaining momentum by the United States' 'Global War on Terror' in 2001, major debates on the relationship between religion and violence arose from two major sources of concern. First, the growing number of local and international groups such as the Taliban, al-Qaeda, and Islamic State calls into question the value of religion and its social function. Second, this debate is not specific to religious groups, but engages researchers, politicians and law makers, who have paid attention to the dynamics between religion and violence and have tried to address these issues in their political speeches. For instance, following the September 11 attacks in 2001, President Bush called the US response 'the crusade', which symbolically connected the attack to a history of conflict between Christian and Muslim from 1095 to 1291 CE. By contrast, following attacks in Denmark and France in 2015, President Obama announced that the United States 'was not at war with Islam – we are at war with the people who have perverted Islam', which separated the act of violence from religion. These contrasting political positions have shaped the contemporary global security environment.

Politicians, theologians, non-state religious groups and state militaries use definitions of violence without paying attention to their implications, where they lead, or what impact they have on conflict or reconciliation processes. Discussing parameters and conditions of violence is inevitable in our modern world, as the concept is interconnected with the practice of politics. What makes the concept susceptible to misuse is whether those with authority (religious leaders, politicians, leaders of non-state armed groups and activists) use it well or badly. This means that often those with authority are unaware of the origins of violence or the texts, practices and rituals to which they refer, to justify their positions. Thus, violence is conceptualized contextually without paying attention to the roots of the ideas they promote or considering their theological and religious arguments and counterarguments. It is almost an impossible task to ensure that all actors and agents are aware of the implications and can protect individuals and communities from their effects.

Conceptualizing violence

Conceptualizing violence is problematic. Violence refers to any relational and contextual act that harms an individual or a community. Often definitions posed by sociologists are either limited to physical harm, or are subjective in terms of the advantaging one community or an ideological position over others (Jackman 2001; Hall 2003). Religious definitions of violence often presuppose an understanding of morals and ethical boundaries. For instance, in Abrahamic religious texts, monotheistic belief entails an ethical position, as it prescribes sets of obligations that distinguish good from bad. All Abrahamic religious texts portray the wrath of God as a punishment for those who deviated from the prescribed ethical path, bestowing responsibility on the faithful to 'fight' against evil. Saint Augustine refers to Romans 13:4: '[The rulers] are God's servants, agents of wrath to bring punishment on the wrongdoer', arguing that God has given the sword of government and Christians should fight with their government to fight against wickedness and evil (Augustine [400] 1872: 69–76). Augustine's theological definition and conditions of a permissible war are still read widely by politicians and militaries around the world and set the foundation for the contemporary 'Just War' theory. Definitions of violence have been influenced significantly by twentieth-century political philosophers, who provided secular definitions to define the relationship between violence and religion. Such definitions were motivated by modern science (which takes cause and effect as its fundamental principle) and therefore focus on physical causes and effects as legitimations of violence. Hence, rather than thinking about an act of violence, such as war, as an act to show one's faith to God, philosophers explored what political, economic or social causes instigated a war and why acting or responding with violence is acceptable or even necessary. If God was no longer the ultimate goal for whom a war was to be instigated, who or what was the entity for whom one was to engage in a war?

Religion and violence in modern era

Nearly all modern conceptualizations of violence consider the state – the centralized unit of the modern politics – as the only legitimate authority who could exercise violence (Van der Veer 2013). Prior to the formation of modern nation states in the seventeenth century dying for one's faith would make the person a martyr, but this position in the modern world belongs to those who devote their lives in battles over borders and resources, which are considered to be sacred and worthy of sacrifice.

Among many philosophers, four thinkers impacted the conceptualization and conditions of violence in the twentieth century. One of the greatest sociologists of the twentieth century, Émile Durkheim, considered the main characteristic of modernity to be the loss of religious community (Durkheim 2008). To him, religion had been the term of reference for laws and politics that modern ideas re-traditionalized as the result of industrialization and urbanization (Lash et al. 1996). While religious systems were no longer a vessel for enchanting the world, he noted, they could still function as community centres that develop boundaries and ideals for members. Durkheim's view on the necessity of a community for human social life shaped the centrality of a political state with a unified military force that has hegemony over exercising violence. These are the only forces that can legitimately exercise violence within the geographical borders of a country. This is not only in the context of conflict and war against an external force, but also about the laws that determine 'good' from 'bad' citizens and regulate the punishment for violating norms.

The second figure is Friedrich Nietzsche, the nihilist philosopher of power, who argued that there is nothing left in this world except power (Ansell-Pearson 1994). Nietzsche considered modernity to be identifiable with the death of God and the hegemony of power. If there is no longer a God-given moral code, all we are left with is a contest to determine who is the most powerful. His ideas shaped the discourse of power in modern warfare and became the underpinning philosophy for major international relations theories of Realism, military might, competition and hegemony (Joseph 2017). These concepts are frames of reference for identifying conditions on which exercising violence is permissible.

While Nietzsche's ideas conceptualized and contextualized violence in military power, it was Max Weber (our third example), a sociologist who encouraged the rationalization of these concepts (Anter 2019). He argued that the modern world was disenchanted (that is to say, a world in which awareness of God has diminished), which exclusively relied on rationalization – human reason – as the main tool for defining core concepts such as violence. Weber significantly influenced Hannah Arendt, the fourth thinker, whose book *On Violence* conceptualized violence in connection with institutionalization of power (Arendt 1970). She argues that institutionalized systems like a bureaucratized government have a greater tendency to use violence as a tool for control, and that when a system is fully bureaucratized there is no one person to approach or make accountable. Arendt, a political scientist who escaped the Nazis and witnessed the genocide of the Jewish community in the Second World War, was the first scholar to describe how the practice of violence in a bureaucratic system creates a situation in which individuals are no longer accountable and become deadened to the practice of violence.

The large body of the literature that followed these philosophies can be divided into three groups. They are all theories on the nature, context and conditions of violence and their connection with religion. The first group is interested in describing how religious traditions explain the existence of violence in humans, and contextualize it. René Girard, for instance, views violence in humans as a manifestation of reciprocity and mimetic behaviour (Girard 2007). For this group, the symbolic meaning of an act of violence has prominence over the act. Girard develops his theory of human memetic behaviour in connection with the Christian ritual of the Eucharist, arguing that the symbolic act of drinking the blood and eating the body of Christ adds meaning to his sacrifice. Girard views the roots of all violence to be mimetic behaviour, which is a desire to imitate models of behaviour that makes an object valuable. To him, this desire is the source of rivalry and violence, and forms a collective mimetic.

The second group conceptualizes violence in relation to acts or practices that have religious dimensions and those that are embedded in religious traditions. This group has a strong view on religion and its social and political functions. Atheist authors such as Richard Dawkins identify organized religious traditions as the producers of narratives that instigate violence. They view religious texts and practices as embedded with violent ideas and actions whose function is to legitimize religion and strengthen the boundaries of a community (Dawkins et al. 2019). The second group also includes religious figures like David Fergusson, who oppose atheist scholars by focusing exclusively on the reconciliatory role that religion plays and argue that while religious discourse is used to justify violence, it is often secular reasons that fuel a conflict (Fergusson 2011).

The third group studies the context in which an act of violence happens, either focusing on religious contexts in which such acts are considered permissible or on the wider social and political contexts that justify the exercise of violence. This group relies on religious texts and traditions, predominantly the Judaeo-Christian tradition, to discuss the conditions which make going into a war permissible (*jus ad bellum*) and how violence could be exercised during a war (*jus in bello*). Michael Walzer is the prominent theorist in this group whose 'Just War' theory attempts to translate Saint Augustine's writings on the topic to modern warfare (Walzer et al. 1977). Discussions on the conditions of engaging in a conflict, however, are not limited to the Judaeo-Christian tradition. Ancient Confucianist texts in China (Yao 2011) and the Mahabharata in India (Allen 2020) are examples of Eastern religious texts that delineate the conditions of exercising violence in a conflict. The existing international systems, including the Geneva Convention and the International Court of Justice, which were developed after the Second World War, however, are exclusively based on the Judaeo-Christian tradition in terms of their approach to conflict and its moral principles.

Religious traditions have different terms of reference for conceptualizing violence. In the secular context, violence is interlinked with defining what harm is; therefore, the causes and the effects of an act of violence are both in the material world. On the contrary, religious conceptualization of violence and its rationale rest upon the relationship between the material and non-material. It is in this space that religious traditions conceptualize violence. Thus, an act of violence against oneself is acceptable if it is undertaken to show the submission and loyalty of a person to their religious tenets. In the Shinto tradition in Japan, for instance, living the life of a Samurai requires absolute commitment to the Emperor or the local authority as a sign of discipline and honour. Samurais considered the ritual of hara-kiri (killing oneself for honour), and the practice of kamikaze – ways to restore their honour and dignity.

Globalization and reconceptualizing violence

Many religious traditions recommend practices that could be considered self-harming in secular context. They often consider the body a tool for training one's soul, and their rituals are thus designed to use this tool in a different fashion from everyday life.

Regardless of their views about the nature and conditions of human existence, rituals regarding one's body were formed for self-discipline and for increasing awareness of others and non-material matters. Traditional religious histories are full of accounts of devotees who practised these rituals to extremes. The Roman Catholic nuns of the Middle Ages period, for instance, refrained from eating to the point of no return in the hope their Lord would feed them with heavenly food in their dreams (Bell 2014). Some traditions of Muslim Sufis considered the human body a cage for the soul, and went through long periods of fasting for purification. Some Buddhist monks practise long hours of prostration to demonstrate their devotion to Buddha, Dharma and Sangha (the Buddha, his teachings and the monastic community). In each of these cases, an element of self-harm is evident.

The work of Durkheim and Weber associated violence with sacrifice and loyalty through agency and authority. States resemble religious communities with their territorial boundaries, their monopoly over violence and the identity-making process that relies on individuals' sense of belonging. Religious traditions have disciplining methods and community engagement norms that are different from states. The human body in religious traditions is the tool that these practices and traditions use, based on specific philosophical positions. For instance, in Buddhism, detachment from the material world is the tool for achieving nirvana and there are sets of practices that facilitate this process after endless rebirths. These include meditation, practising detachment, prostration and fasting to end suffering (Dalai Lama 2018). Hinduism considers one's body a wild ram that requires a yoke (yoga) and thus encourages the practice of yoga (in the sense of following a spiritual path), fasting, abstinence from speaking and seclusion as rituals that assist a Hindu to achieve 'the state of liberation' – *moksha* (Varenne 1989). The ideas of sacrifice, devotion and self-discipline were changed by the ideals of nationalism in the twentieth century and once again by globalization and the rise of communication technology in the twenty-first century. The most significant impact of globalization and information technology on the definition of violence is the spread of a new form of connectivity that, to an extent, changes the definition and boundaries of nationalism based on which individuals were connected. For instance, online harassment and 'radicalizing' recruits to fight against an ideology are transnational phenomena, moving beyond the geographical and jurisdictional borders of a state. The new ideals of belonging and community are now discussed more in the context of morality and ethical principles rather than national identity or the power of a state through its military might.

As societies become more culturally and religiously plural, conceptualizing violence, considering why it is exercised and the conditions under which it is permissible to use violence, involve dealing with fundamental problems about ethics and human behaviour. Who has the right and the authority to define the conditions and limitations of violence? Politicians, civilians, media and states are all engaged in these discussions daily. One of the major problems in such discussions is ambiguity in terms of the impact a definition could have on a religious community and the conceptual problems that it creates for its associated notions such as identity, religiosity and the authority for exercising violence. Conceptualizing violence as an act that is practised in human interaction, with each other and with their environment, separates the concept from its religious context and thus makes agreeing on a common definition more challenging. It also allows diverse groups and individuals to use or misuse the concept.

Examining the concept of violence in the study of religion is important, particularly in terms of the boundaries that religious communities have developed around the notion and exercise of violence (in both individual and communal terms) and in relation to topics such as sacrifice, dedication, loyalty and identity.

Conclusion

Violence – causing harm – is an action that is open to different interpretations in religious and secular contexts. Scholars hold conflicting positions while explaining the nature and characteristics of violence. In religious contexts, the reason for an act of violence is submission to God or religious convictions, and not revenge. It is performed for a particular reason and with associated rituals, such as offering sacrifice, or showing one's devotion or disciplining oneself. These rituals could be extremely unreasonable in a secular context, particularly as the authority of sanctifying an act of violence moved from religious leaders to politicians. The state's perspective on disciplining oneself or establishing community norms derives from the narrative of nationalism and influences the interpretation of ideas of sacrifice, devotion and self-discipline.

Conceptualizing violence with reference to religion remains extremely complicated with the rise of smart technologies and globalization. Innovation in communication technology has changed the norms of community engagement as well as the concept of belonging and identity. Politicians, theologians, non-state religious groups and state militaries define acts of violence without paying attention to the meanings attached to those acts in theological context. However, it is difficult for all agents to be aware of the contextual and theological meanings of violence. It is therefore vital to continue studying the notion of violence in religious contexts to minimize the risks of misinterpretations that affect individuals and communities.

CHAPTER 23
WORLD RELIGION
Teemu Taira

If one regards 'religion' as a problematic category, as many scholars do, then the term 'world religion' cannot be any less complicated. As Tomoko Masuzawa (2005: 313) wrote, 'the discourse of world religions takes for granted the idea of "religion itself" as a "unique sphere of life," and … it presumes that this sphere is prevalent throughout the world and its history'. If one thinks that 'religion' has at least some heuristic use, then it remains an open issue of whether 'world religion' has that, too.

'World religion' has been one of the key organizing concepts throughout the academic study of religion. It has been applied outside academia from governmental procedures to education and non-governmental organizations. The concept has been successful, but it has also become one of the most criticized concepts in the study of religion – to the point that it is difficult to find scholars who would defend the concept without serious qualifications. This, however, does not mean that the concept and the idea have been abandoned, or that those who criticize the concept are unanimous about what is wrong with it.

Arbitrary classificatory tool?

As evidenced in the blank spots in world religion maps, the 'world' in 'world religion' does not mean any religion in the world. The 'world' in 'world religion' is similar to 'world class', referring to the significance or status among the members of the category. If so, then the term 'world religion' is far from an innocent descriptive term; it has a history that is entangled with several challenges. The term itself has previous mentions in medieval and early modern times (Smith, W. C. 1991; Smith, J. Z. 1998; Chidester 2018), but it becomes a widely established part of English language in the twentieth century (Geaves 2014). For the formation of the discourse itself, the late nineteenth century is crucial.

One way to challenge the concept of world religion is to examine whether it is used and applied consistently. It has turned out that even in the early applications in the academic study of religion, world religion was understood in an idiosyncratic manner and the number of the members of the category changed fast and quite randomly. On the basis of his *Outlines of the History of Religion to the Spread of Universal Religions* (1877), Dutch scholar Cornelius P. Tiele suggested in *Encyclopedia Britannica* in 1885 that there are three 'universal religions' or 'world religions' – Christianity, Islam and Buddhism, based on the criteria that their mission is not tied to a particular nation or ethnic group. Friedrich Max Müller did not use the term 'world religion', at least not widely, but he made a list of eight religions that comprise the 'library of the sacred books of the east' (Masuzawa 2005: 107–20; Sun 2013: 61–2; Taira 2016: 80; Chidester 2018). The list from 1889 consisted of:

(1) the *Vedic*, both ancient and modern; (2) *Buddhism*, Northern and Southern Gainism; (3) the *Zoroastrian* religion of the Avesta; (4) *Confucianism*; (5) *Taoism*; (6) the *Jewish*; (7) the *Christian*; and (8) *Mohammedan* religions.

(Müller 1907: 549)

While Tiele's list looks like an ancient curiosity based on the criteria we now regard irrelevant, Müller's list is starting to look like the typical list of the twentieth-century world religions textbook, with three main exceptions: first, later Sikhism and in some cases Shinto have taken the place of Zoroastrianism; second, the terms have been modernized; third, the status of Confucianism and Daoism has fluctuated. The contrast with the first appearances of plural 'religions' in the English language in the 1590s is striking: then there were only two, Protestant and Catholic (Harrison 1990: 39). In brief, the histories of 'religion', 'religions' and 'world religion' have been about expanding the list of candidates that are included in the categories.

Multiple criteria have been suggested for world religions, such as the number of adherents, universal mission not limited to a particular nation or ethnicity and influence. Practically all selections have combined more than one criterion in order to include preferred candidates. Influence has been highlighted in the case of Judaism, because popularity and mission would not apply favourably; the number of adherents were considered significant in order to include Hinduism, because arguably it does not offer a universal message or do missionary work. Given the difficulty to apply clearly defined criteria for establishing boundaries between world religions and whatever is outside them, it is not surprising that the actual lists of world religions have varied in time and space.

Exclusion and inclusion

'World religion' is not only an arbitrary classificatory term. It has systematically excluded some groups and traditions, particularly those we nowadays call 'indigenous'. Many textbooks cover them briefly – usually by lumping wildly different traditions under one category as if suggesting that they have enough in common. They have been called 'primitive', 'primal', 'basic' and, increasingly, 'indigenous' and their role has been to exemplify what was earlier or simpler form of religiosity and what has been superseded by proper world religions (Chidester 2018: 46). The list of excluded candidates extends to new religious movements, Satanism, Paganism and so on. Simply put, they have not been significant 'geopolitical entities' (Smith 1998: 280) with which colonial and imperial powers would have had to deal with, either as partners or enemies. The inclusion has been based on 'Western influence' and a world religion is 'a religion that the west accepted to recognize as such by imposing its forms and values' (Dubuisson 2019: 138).

The exclusion is only part of the problem. The discourse on world religions has tended to represent the included traditions in a peculiar manner. It has textualized, essentialized and reified complex and heterogeneous traditions. Our representations are always based on deliberate choices and exclusions that construct order from chaotic details, but the way in which religious traditions have been represented as world religions has followed a standard procedure in giving preference to textual authority over everyday practices, to presumed stability over historical change, to ideas that are close to 'our' values. Therefore, the Hinduism of world religions is closer to Brahmanism than village practices (King 1999; Owen 2011). Similarly, the British representations of Buddhism in the Victorian era ignored and even despised Buddhism as practised, while constructing an idealized image of pristine Buddhism based on ancient texts – the kind that sat comfortably within Victorian values (Almond 1988). In addition, world religions are typically represented as separate from each other, whereas ethnographic evidence consistently demonstrates that people do not conform to these boundaries. Representations are typically based on the assumption of single belonging, whereas there is evidence that multiple belonging is normal for some, and even accepted in some contexts. Such representations also convey the idea of what particular religion truly is, thus making it possible for some to challenge the beliefs and practices of self-identifying adherents (e.g. 'true Muslims do not drink wine', whereas some self-identifying Muslims do). For these reasons, it can be said that the world religions discourse is largely Protestant and has constructed the world according to its own image. What is more, this has led some colonized communities to 'self-essentialize' themselves according to the expected image (Geaves 2014: 203), thus, while strategically useful for some communities in limited contexts, enhancing the tendency towards problematic generalizations within the overall field of representations concerning world religions.

It could also be argued that the world religions discourse changed the attitude Europeans had towards people elsewhere by admitting that others have great religions worth studying. This would be a way of reading the expansion of world religions to fit the current values of diversity and multiculturalism. However, critical scholars have argued that while this has been the stated intention of some proponents of world religions, this view hides the fact that world religions discourse extended modern European conceptual systems to elsewhere. In the binaries that were operative in such a discourse, Christianity was always on top, marking the more valuable or more developed example (Dubuisson 2003). Even when world religions included several members, Christianity maintained its special status. Religions were supposed to develop in history from more primitive to the most civilized one. Most world religions were considered somewhere between *Natur* (nature) and *Geist* (spirit), whereas Christianity – Protestant Christianity, in particular – was closest to the perfection (Murphy 2007: 78–96). Even Müller, who in many ways was fascinated about the Indian religiosity, suggested that the comparative work in the science of religion will 'assign to Christianity its right place among the religions of the world', given that it shows the 'unconscious progress towards Christianity' (Müller 1867: xx).

In addition to the conceptual domination for which world religions discourse contributed to a great detail, the domination was also quite concrete. The classification of others and the introduction of discourse on religion facilitated the establishment of colonial command, often jointly with the local officials (e.g. in Japan; see Josephson 2012). There are even statements that explicitly connect world religions discourse to imperial relations. British theologian F. D. Maurice suggested in 1848 that studying religions of the world was useful for a nation that was 'engaged in trading with other countries, or in conquering them, or in keeping possession of them' (cited in Chidester 2018: 47) and Huston Smith, the US scholar of religion, justified the study of world religions in 1958 by suggesting that it provides knowledge for military personnel who might find the peoples they were studying as 'allies, antagonists, or subjects of military occupation' and assist our need to be able 'to predict their behavior, conquer them if worse came to worst, and control them' (cited in McCutcheon 1997: 179–80).

The future of 'world religion'

The term 'world religion' has been under critical scrutiny at least since the 1990s and increasingly so in the twenty-first century. The term is not used that much any more by scholars of religion, but the idea persists in the academic study programmes, in religious education and elsewhere in society. Students do not always have a strong investment in the term – they are not sure why some are called world religions – but they are convinced that there are 'religious traditions' in the world. Many students want to learn about major religious traditions and feel that that is what is expected from them if they are going to be successful in the job market.

Multiple scholars have provided alternative solutions to what should be done with the category and courses carrying 'world religions' in their titles. While the solutions are many, ranging from dropping the term altogether from our vocabulary to imaginative and innovative ways in which world religion and the discourse that has supported the category can be an object of critical analysis (Cotter and Robertson 2016). When it comes to the question of whether the concept should be kept or discarded, my view is clear: there is nothing good the concept of world religion is doing in our efforts to study the world we live in. It does not add to our intellectual efforts in comparison and it has been a tool in the maintenance of power relations. The term 'world religion' has all the problems the term 'religion' has and more. Even when academic commitment to the term 'religion' may be seen by some as strategically wise move in a contemporary crisis and diminishing resources of universities and humanities in particular, the term 'world religion' does not help much in playing that game either. The endless extension of the list of items studied under 'world religions' does not solve the problem (Taira 2016: 82–3).

If one considers typical examples of world religions more worthy of a study than other religions, there may well be ways to justify one's preferences, but it should not take place through the concept of world religion. If the term 'world religion' was properly established by religious studies scholars in the first part of the twentieth century, it is the task of contemporary scholars to disestablish it and the types of representations it has maintained. The problem is that genie is already out of the bottle – the discourse is alive and well despite the criticism.

To get rid of the term 'world religion' should not be taken as a recommendation to forget everything that has been written in the name of it. What should be done is to study critically what work such a category has done and still does. In practice, this could open several interesting prospects, such as the study of the emergence and function of the category 'world religion', the processes by which some candidates came to be understood and classified as religions and world religions (or how such naming was denied or contested) by scholars, colonial administrators, government officials, missionaries, media professionals and adherents themselves. This is also one possibility to subvert the content of traditional world religions courses (Taira 2016), and an opportunity to scrutinize the very designator 'religion' itself (of which 'world religion' would be a sub-type), but this would require the scholars of religion to be able to convey to students clearly what intellectual and social capital is gained by thinking differently from some of our predecessors.

CHAPTER 24
WORSHIP
Christina Welch

In everyday society the meaning of the term 'worship' appears relatively unproblematic, but for scholars of religion, trying to pin the concept of worship down is not as simple as it might seem. A quick run through of online dictionaries suggests that even in the public domain, what worship might be is not easily explained. According to Wikipedia, worship is 'an act of religious devotion usually directed towards a deity. For many, worship is not about emotions, it is more about a recognition of God'. However, according to the Cambridge English Dictionary emotion is key; here worship is defined as a 'strong feeling of respect and admiration for God or a god', and is done with others in a special place. Yet, no mention of a building appears in the Merriam-Webster Dictionary where worship is 'reverence offered a divine being or supernatural power' and 'a form of religious practice with its creed and ritual'. Here the inclusion of 'creed' suggests something doctrinal, even dogmatic, and that worship relates to belief.

Thus, in the public domain we find that worship is a ritual activity usually done with others, typically in a special building, that may or may not involve emotion but has a routine element, and comprises displaying one's high esteem of or to a beyond-human single entity (often termed God) in whom one believes. There are a good few problems with this, not least because the terms associated with worship (many of which are covered in this volume), are more or less problematic in and of themselves. Additionally, we need to consider that there is a history to the term 'worship' that lends it particular baggage and gives this God a particular Abrahamic religious bias.

Problematizing worship in the Abrahamic traditions

The Hebrew Bible uses worship in specific ways to determine appropriate worship behaviour (e.g. worship of the One God, not other gods – Exodus 20:3), and incites the slaughter of those who do otherwise (such as King Jehu instructing eighty men to kill the worshippers of Baal – 2 Kings 10: 18–27). Robert A. Warrior argues that Christian colonialism weaponized this concept, supported by the conquest narrative of Deuteronomy (7:1–2), to aid the cultural genocide (and in some cases physical genocide) of indigenous peoples living in colonized lands (Warrior 1996: 97). In the Americas and Australia for instance, indigenous peoples were taught to worship according to colonial norms as part of the assimilation-by-education process, and enslaved Africans were forced to worship (at least outwardly) the God of their enslavers. Some of these peoples accepted Christianity, and theologies developed where this God was worshipped differently; for instance, with an Indigenous mindset and locally grounded sacraments, with emotion front and centre, where issues of race and gender are key, and where the impact of colonialism has to be reckoned with; worship is not a neutral term, and worshipping is not a neutral act (Budden 2011; Clark 2012; Boyd 2016; Martin 2016; Liew and Segovia 2018). As Tovey (2004) notes in a Christian context, in order to be authentic to the worshipper, worship with all it entails in terms of ritual and liturgy has to be part of culture; even within one religious tradition, there will be multiple ways to worship.

It would, however, be inaccurate to place the common usage of the term 'worship' solely within a Christian, or an Abrahamic framework, but of course even within this, there are differences. Judaism, for instance, was once a religion where worship included the sacrifice of animals and the high priest was the chief religious functionary. Following the destruction of the Second Temple (70 CE) however, animal sacrifice ended, and public worship focused around synagogues with a rabbi officiating as necessary. In Islam, though, worship practice is largely unchanged from the days of Muhammad, although the physical act of *salat* (performance of prayers) differs slightly between Sunni and Shi'a Muslims, with Sufi Muslims, depending on geographical location, including music and dance.

Problematizing worship beyond the Abrahamic traditions

In terms of what worshipping as an activity might entail, the collection of short essays *Worship* by Jean Holm with John Bowker (1994) covers a wide range of religious traditions and, although perhaps overly uncritical of the term 'worship' itself, provides a good overview of what different people do when they perform ritual worship acts. The chapter by Xinzhong Yao on Chinese religion highlights many of the problems with using worship to describe the wide range of rituals that have adapted socially and politically over the centuries in both China and with Chinese people living in diaspora. He notes that in Chinese Religions, defined as 'a syncretism of Confucianism, Taoism, Buddhism, primitive practices and animistic beliefs' (1994: 159), worship can be officially sanctioned or popular folk-based, done alone or in a group, done at fixed times or whenever suits and can include acts of worship to family ancestors or natural phenomena. None of this fits neatly into the online dictionary definitions noted above. Indeed, given the missionary origin of the term 'ancestor worship', there are of course issues around the acceptability of the term today, but, beyond that, the conceptual mapping of the act is relevant: is this act worship, or is it honouring or veneration, and how are these different from worship? Academic language matters, given it is the medium we use to reflect what we see, and this in turn is reflected back as expectations of that act.

In exploring more academic definitions, as in the *Encyclopedia of Religion* (Eliade 1987), worship is defined as 'the practical expression of religious life and related to ritual (religious activity) … religious communities (social organisation) [and] interior forms of worship such as prayerful contemplation' (Hoffman 1987: 445). This definition is open-ended, although of course quite what counts as religious activity is questionable: for instance, would ritual activity conducted around a museum artefact count as worship? This is no mere technical question because museums, as holders of material and visual expressions of religious significance, are increasingly having to grapple with this issue. In 2016, flowers and coins were left as offerings to the Ganesha images on display in the Birmingham Museum and Art Gallery when it hosted the 'Celebrating Ganesha' touring exhibition. The images of this elephant-headed deity were blessed by a local mandir priest in a ritual that blurred the traditional boundary between a secular (museum/art gallery) and spiritual (Hindu Temple) context (Jaffer 2016). However, the problematics of worship and museums goes further, with Gretchen Buggeln, Crispin Paine and S. Brent Plate suggesting that in increasingly secular Western societies, museums can be seen to have 'replaced the house of worship as the place where citizens seek the transcendent' (2017: 11). This statement implies that worship is tied to notions of transcendency, but many people perform acts of worship towards the spiritual within the everyday here-and-now world, with many traditional African/African-Caribbean, and Indigenous religions exemplifying this. Further, celebrities are routinely worshipped, from living and dead pop idols to media figures such as the natural history broadcaster David Attenborough, whom Peter Ward explores as a worshipped individual who makes no claims to specialness (2020: 2–4).

Worship of the worldly has historically been associated with primitive animism and even savagery through a view propagated by early anthropologists like E. B. Tylor (1871) and James Frazer (1890). Yet contemporary animists reject the dualism that these evolutionary rationalists posited and seek to normalize the worship (loosely defined) of the natural immanent wider-than-human-world, full of other-than-human persons such as animals, plants, and rocks (Harvey 2000). Worship then, as Douglas Davies explains in his introduction to the edited book of that name, 'is not always the best word to use when describing the actions of … ' – and here we head into problematic terminology again – ' … devotees in some religions' (1994: 1). Many people who perform ritual actions that loosely could be defined as worship are not best described as devotees. Devotion suggests belief in, as well as an almost exclusive commitment to, someone – being devoted to a god is generally socially acceptable, while being devoted to a rock or animal may not be. Here Ninian Smart's argument that intent in the ritual act is key (1972: 3–4), although ritual is another problematic term.

Problematizing worship as ritual

Davies notes that the closest definition of worship is 'patterns of human behaviours expressing what people believe to be the most important aspects of life' (1994: 3). Here perhaps we are closer to a useable definition of worship, as 'believe' suggests having confidence in a something, supposing it to be true within whatever is culturally normal. An example would be the Kumari of Nepal. Here a young unblemished girl is 'permanently housed and regularly worshipped' as a living goddess and the embodiment of Shakti, the feminine form of energy and vitality, until she hits puberty when she loses her divinity (Majupuria and Roberts 2007: 17). A glimpse of a Kumari is believed to bring good fortune, and devotees who have regular access to her officially worship her through *puja* (ceremonial worship rituals), but for those who only see her during a rare appearance in street parades, or briefly at the window of her residence, worship is difficult to describe. Worship here is more about just being in the presence of a Kumari and accepting that she, at that time, embodies the divine. As with Hinduism there is a two-way relationship between the deity (or image of the deity) and the person that engages with this earthly representation of the divine (*darshan*). Hinduism, however, is highly varied and such worship can include making ritual offerings to rivers or trees as representations of the divine, as well as to super-human deities. But making ritual offerings is not necessarily worship even if it might look that way to an outsider, as offering rituals is common within the different Buddhist traditions, but worship as a term is highly problematic in Buddhism. For monks and nuns, Buddhism is typically about engaging with the Buddha as an enlightened being and the way of living he represents, whilst for many lay people, engagement can be for everyday pragmatic benefits such as healing or a successful outcome to an activity.

If, then, worship as a concept is imperfectly explained as performing a specific ritual act towards something that embodies what is held very vitally important, such as a god or God (gendered or otherwise, multiple or singular, human-like or not), then next we should return to where this ritual act takes place. The dictionary definitions largely suggest a specific set-aside place, typically a building. But determining a building as a place for worship can be as much a legal designation as anything else (Bradney 2014), and a worship space can be a home altar, a street shrine or an engagement with nature. Japanese religion being a case in point here (Ellwood 2008) but even in Christianity we find the Bible noting worship taking place in various locations; Abraham's servant prayed beside a public well (Genesis 24:26), and the Magi travel to worship at Jesus' home (Matthew 2:1–12). Further, the assumption that worship or worship-style activity has a set-asideness from everyday spaces and activities was blown aside by the introduction of televized worship. Although in 1999, when Wolff conducted his study comparing in-church worship to worshipping-by-television, participants felt the latter 'less satisfying' than the former (1999: 232), technology has moved on, meaning that worshipping-by-television is now more interactive. Further, with the Internet and social media proving Internet/cyber-churches, live-streamed real-world services and spaces for prayer-tweets, remaining at home whilst connecting with a worship community is the new normal, particularly in the wake of global Covid-19 pandemic lockdowns. But the notion that one must be physically present to worship has long been problematic. In medieval Christian Europe it was possible to take a pilgrimage in-thought rather than in-deed or send someone to pray for you (Rudy 2011), and chantry chapels allowed you to get the benefits of worship even if you were dead. A contemporary version of this exists today in the form of prayer-bots that post Muslim's prayers online, even after death, automatically allowing one to gain extra merit post-mortem (Öhman, Gorwa and Flordi 2019).

Conclusion

Overall then, the concept of worship is problematic if the starting point is a dictionary or encyclopaedia definition, even if that source of the definition is an academic one rather than popular. A large part of this problem is the colonial baggage that the term carries, along with the other concepts that help shape the definition of worship. Worship does not have to be, or has necessarily ever been, towards super-natural phenomena or a deity (or deities) in a specially designated building, nor does that the object of worship (however it is defined) have to be supernatural forever, and indeed the activity does not even have to be carried out by the living. A homogenous description of the concept of worship is not useful. However, contextualizing the many and varied rituals (mental as well as physical), and what or to whom these rituals are addressed, may bring us closer to grasping the significance of the act taking place. Worship may be better conceptualized as an umbrella term than a definition, although perhaps one that does not keep out all the rain.

CHAPTER 25
CONCEPTS IN PRACTICE
George D. Chryssides and Amy R. Whitehead

Some years ago one of the authors attended Wesak celebrations in Wolverhampton Town Hall. For those who are less familiar with Buddhism, it may be helpful to explain that the festival, which is celebrated at full moon in May by Buddhists worldwide, marks the birth, enlightenment and demise of Siddhartha Gautama, the historic founder of the religion, who lived and taught in India in the fifth century BCE. Traditionally, these three events are reckoned to have occurred in the same calendrical date, which is therefore an occasion for great celebration. Although an anniversary marking the Buddha's death may sound like a sober occasion, the Buddha instructed his disciples not to weep, but to preserve his teachings (the Dharma) and maintain his monastic community (the Sangha). While Buddhists will typically perform devotional acts at Wesak, and listen to the monks' teachings, it is also a day for rejoicing and partying. At the town hall, therefore, the women had prepared tea and cakes, and the children provided singing and dancing. A number of distinguished guests got up on the platform to make short speeches, and one or two monks gave brief spiritual instruction. All were upbeat and cheerful, apart from one Western monk – we shall call him the Venerable Devadatta (not his real name) – who mounted the stage and told the audience that it was all very well to have a tea party with entertainments, but this would not help them to make any progress towards enlightenment, and that they ought to improve their spirituality instead by practising the teachings of the Buddha.

We should like to use this incident to highlight a number of concepts which have been discussed by the contributors to this volume. Their various analyses are not merely pieces of theory, but can help us to understand the different levels at which religion and religious commitment operate, and how we ought to interpret Buddhism accordingly. The ensuing discussion aims to demonstrate practically how this anthology can be utilized to problematize concepts as they emerge within lived religions.

First, we highlight the concepts of conversion and diaspora (Chapters 3 and 5). The incident highlights an important distinction between the way in which a diaspora community practises its religion, and its uptake by a Western convert. There are problems in describing the audience as diaspora Buddhists: as Knott points out (Chapter 5), the concept of a religious diaspora is problematic, since Buddhism lacks an identifiable home country. Although Buddhism began in India, Buddhists now merely consist of around 0.8 per cent of the country's population, while Theravada Buddhism is now the dominant religion of Sri Lanka, Thailand, Laos and Cambodia. As she suggests, their diasporic nature denotes their identity as a migrant minority, and their desire to maintain traditional community bonds. It might probably be more accurate to speak of the Burmese and Thai audience as communities, rather than Buddhists, in diaspora, and to regard them as practising their culture, which includes their religion. We do not know Devadatta's life history, but if he is like the majority of Western Buddhists, he would have read literature about the religion, gone along to a Buddhist group consisting largely of Western adherents and teachers, and been introduced to meditational practices, which he then assumed to be normative. He is a Buddhist convert through choice and conviction, rather than for the other reasons that Bromley identifies, such as marital convenience or political coercion (see Chapter 3). Devadatta therefore does not belong to this diasporic community: he is very much the outsider, although welcomed by the diasporic community. Nonetheless, despite being the outsider, Devadatta appeared to regard his own version of Buddhism as normative, and his audience's version as inferior and debased. Yet, if one compares the practice of the majority of Theravada Buddhists in Asian countries, one would find less similarity to Devadatta's version and more to that of the audience, who consisted mainly of first- and second-generation migrants who were lay Buddhists from Thailand and Burma, in contrast with Devadatta, who is a Westerner and a first-generation convert.

Devadatta's outsider status is also evidenced in different attitudes to myth. Both he and the Thai community are of course familiar with the story of the Buddha's demise. The Thai diaspora, however, draw on the Buddha's mandate to rejoice rather than weep, whereas Devadatta, having received monastic ordination, prefers to emphasize his instruction that the Dharma and Sangha should act as his successors. Devadatta appears to subscribe to the view, as one Western author has put it, that 'the only complete and logical Buddhist is the monk, for he renounces his worldly goods … to attain liberation from suffering' (Masson 1977: 17). Note the masculine gender in this quotation: if this were correct, it would exclude women from being true Buddhists (at least in the Theravada tradition), as well as the preponderance of Buddhist men and children. In Bowman's terms, this view privileges the religious specialist over the vernacular religion that is pursued by the vast majority of lay practitioners.

We have not personally visited Devadatta's community, but the Bodh Gaya Monastery (name changed), to which he belongs can be viewed online, and differs markedly from the Thai monasteries that one finds in the Far East. In Thailand the entrance of almost every home, business and temple has a spirit house (the Christian churches are notable exceptions), at which offerings are regularly made to hungry ghosts. At a Thai temple, one typically finds in the forecourt an image of a hermit physician offering healing, facilities for fortune-telling, the sale of good luck charms and the availability of ceremonies for health and longevity. Invariably, in Thailand one finds the central Buddha rupa flanked by portraits of the country's King and Queen. One of the authors was told, when visiting Thailand, that monks only practised meditation in a quarter of its monasteries.

These observations also point to the concept of syncretism. It is easy to assume that these popular features are accretions that have been added on to a purer expression of Buddhism that has become eroded over the centuries. One recent popular article states:

But upon strolling through the temple-adorned cities and villages, it becomes hard to distinguish if everything you see is connected to traditional Buddhism. In fact, Thai people classify themselves as adherents to Buddhism, but many things they believe and practice, are inherently part of Brahmanism, an early form of Hinduism, as well as folk animist religions. Such folk animist religions are better known as Animism.

(Carter 2021)

This analysis seems to suggest that there were once 'pure' religious systems, namely Hinduism, animism and 'traditional Buddhism', which somehow merged syncretistically, and that 'orthodox' or original Buddhism became contaminated, and therefore needs to be restored to its untainted original form. In Chapter 21 however, Schmidt challenges the concept of 'syncretism' by complexifying the idea that any 'pure form' of religion has ever existed. The notion of bricolage, she suggests, more accurately reflects how different elements and conditions of religious systems combine to create something 'new' (a revelation to which Devadatta was clearly not privy).

The influential Japanese Buddhist reformer Inoue Enryō (1858–1919), in response to contact with the nineteenth-century modernizing attempts of the West, sought to discourage lay Buddhist practices by reducing them to superstition, akin to the attitude expressed by Devadatta. According to Jason Ānanda Josephson-Storm (2006: 143), during this time, Japanese Buddhism was beginning to be recognized as an 'authentic' religion on par with Christianity, Judaism and other religions who sit within the contested 'world religions paradigm', but on one condition: it must leave behind the beliefs and practices that were deemed disagreeable by government officials and foreigners. These beliefs and practices included the officially sanctioned monastic practices of exorcisms, healings, burning 'ghost money', selling good luck charms, practising ancestor worship and magical rituals. Arguably, attempts at modernizing religions can be understood as attempts at cleansing or even sanitizing them of their lay, vernacular or folk practices, which can readily be judged to be inferior. This not only raises the question what religion is, but the extent to which Japanese Buddhism is authentic; even with Inoue Enryō's purges, it is still very different from its Theravada counterpart, which is generally regarded as closer to the historical Buddha's teaching and practice.

Another Western Buddhist reformer in roughly the same period was Colonel Henry Steel Olcott (1837–1907), co-founder of the Theosophical Society in the United States. Unlike Inoue Enryō, Olcott was a convert to Buddhism, but believed that the Christian missionaries had seriously damaged its authentic practices, which he sought to revive. One of his contributions was to design a Buddhist flag, which is now displayed in many Buddhist temples worldwide. He also compiled a *Buddhist Catechism*, setting out what he regarded as the basic tenets of the religion. Olcott was also concerned about superstitious elements that he believed had crept into Buddhism, and he was particularly disparaging of the Sacred Tooth relic, which is housed at the Temple of the Tooth in Kandy, contending that it was no more than a piece of deer horn. This suggestion greatly offended Anagarika Dharmapala, a prominent Sinhalese Buddhist leader, who described Olcott, not as a welcome reformer, but as 'an enemy of our religion' (Prothero 1996: 165–8).

These controversies not only raise the question of whether a dividing line can be drawn between superstition and popular practice and, as Whitehead argues (Chapter 20), the former term is not really helpful in the study of religion. There is the further, related issue of authenticity – another contested concept which might well have featured in this anthology. Devadatta obviously thought he was practising 'true Buddhism', which he equated with the mandates of Buddhist scriptures and the quest for nirvana rather than the way it is practised in the East, where monks meditate relatively seldom, and are not averse to practices such as handling money, using horoscopes to define auspicious wedding dates, helping to promote good fortune and good luck or ordaining trees (a Thai Buddhist practice).

It is sometimes stated, misleadingly, in some of the more simplistic books on religion, that Buddhism is an offshoot of Hinduism, and certainly it is customary for standard textbooks to have separate chapters on each, presupposing the World Religions Paradigm, thus indicating that they are separate religions. However, the terms 'Hinduism' and 'Buddhism' are both Western-imposed categorizations. Many Theravada Buddhist temples in the East display images of Ganesha, sometimes carved into their exterior walls, and in Sri Lanka 'Buddhist' temples often have 'Hindu' annexes – adjoining rooms portraying Hindu deities. Conversely, Hindu temples sometimes contain Buddhist annexes and Buddhist imagery. It could be argued that, since one cannot identify any point in history at which there was a 'pure' version of Buddhism, distinct from what has been called Hinduism, brahmanism, animism and folk magic, the totality of religious practice which we find in a country like Thailand is all part of the country's 'lived religion'.

Indeed, it could reasonably be contended that Devadatta is the syncretist, rather than the Thai diaspora. Arguably, it is Western Buddhism that has appropriated Western practices; although many Western Buddhists are critical of Christianity, much of 'White Buddhism', as it is sometimes called, adopts Christian ways of thinking, for example regarding texts as authoritative, aiming at salvation/liberation, attempting to involve the entire laity in overtly devotional practices (as in Christianity), giving teachings based on scriptures and taking on board aspects of Western ideologies, such as non-violence and vegetarianism. Apart from Western converts, Buddhists are not typically vegetarian. Despite professed opposition to killing, Buddhists do not regard eating an animal as killing, and the association between the two reflects Western rather than Eastern thinking on ethics (Chryssides 1988).

Much of our discussion raises questions of how Buddhism and Western Buddhism should be categorized. If, as we have argued, Western Buddhist practices are innovative, should forms of Western Buddhism be regarded as new religious movements rather than traditional forms of religion? Certainly, the anticult movement has listed several Buddhist and Buddhist-related movements as 'cults', for example Vipassana (although, strictly, this is a practice rather than a movement or organization), the Soka Gakkai, the New Kadampa Tradition and Tritratna (formerly Friends of the Western Buddhist Order), with some of their leaders being described as gurus.

Others might be led to a different conclusion. If one attempts to strip off all the accretions, folk practices and presumed superstitions, with what is one left? Arguably, it could be suggested that one is no longer left with a religion but with a philosophy, or a 'way of life' (a phrase that is popularly used, but which has no real clear meaning). All depends on how one defines religion. David Morgan's discussion (Chapter 17) identified four models, and their contestations, that convey how 'religion' is usually handled by scholars of religion: the naturalist model (as set out by David Hume), religions as systems of beliefs, religion as a *sui generis* category, and functionalism. If one accepts the old-fashioned definition that it is worship of a creator God, then of course Buddhism would not qualify. However, if one accepts, following Durkheim, that it is 'a unified system of beliefs and practices relative to sacred things, that is to say, things set apart and forbidden—beliefs and practices which unite into one single moral community', then there can be little doubt that Buddhism broadly counts as a religion.

Is Buddhism a world religion? As Teemu Taira's discussion (Chapter 23) has shown, this much-employed term encounters serious problems, and there are different ways of deciding what would count as a world religion. In terms of numerical allegiance, Buddhism has attracted approximately 7 per cent of the world's population, and ranks either fourth or sixth in terms of popularity, depending on whether one counts Chinese religions as a single category, and non-religion. It has reached most countries, although most forms of Buddhism do not seek actively to convert the world, in the way evangelical Christian mission has done.

Turning to the notion of spirituality, Devadatta seemed to thinelak that true Buddhism could be separated off from what he might regard as lesser, inauthentic, folk practice. But were not the women and children practising Buddhism too, maybe even in a more authentic way than Devadatta? They were not just having fun – they were celebrating because it was Wesak, an important Buddhist festival. Devadatta seemed to imply that his version of Buddhism offered spiritual practice, while dancing and preparing refreshments, did not. The Christian writer George Herbert composed the hymn 'Teach me, my God and King/In all things thee to see', which included these lines: 'A servant with this clause/Makes drudgery divine,/Who sweeps a room, as for thy laws/Makes that and th' action fine.' This echoes the famous Zen quote: 'Before enlightenment, chop wood, carry water. After enlightenment, chop wood, carry water', which is meant to reappraise one's understanding of success and achievement, the mundane and the ordinary. Life's work and activities do not end simply because one has become enlightened, the point being to be in the moment and to live one's everyday life as an expression of spirituality.

Religion can be practised at different levels, as Milford Spiro (1970) distinguished in his study of Burmese Buddhism, and which he labels nibbanic, kammic and apotropaic, corresponding respectively to the spiritual virtuoso who aims at enlightenment, those who more modestly aim for better rebirth, and those who engage in practices aimed to fend off evil and promote good fortune. This last category comes closest to what we described at the Wolverhampton Wesak festival, which some might describe as folk religion, but is better described, as Bowman argues, as lived or vernacular religion (Chapter 6). The concept highlights Devadatta's implicit distinction between 'true Buddhism' and the lay activities of enjoying food and singing. From a lived, or vernacular, religion perspective, these practices are authentically Buddhist and as justifiable as the practices of the Western monk. While we might not agree with Devadatta's implicit distinction between 'authentic' and 'inauthentic' Buddhism, his attitude informs us as to the nature of the Western Buddhism, and also reflects the fact that much of the scholarly study of Buddhism remains text-based and concerned with metaphysics.

In fact, most of the concepts problematized in this anthology can be applied to our brief account of Devadatta and Wesak. In addition to 'cult', 'syncretism', 'new religious movement', 'folk religion', 'world religion' and 'superstition', we could have further engaged with Jonathan Z. Smith's argument about 'religion' being a term for scholarly use that signals colonial positionality (Smith 1998: 269). Deeper engagement with 'diaspora' would reveal the tensions (sometimes creative, sometimes not) between host communities and the religious practices that are brought from elsewhere, and naturally, how they adapt in relation to location. Since a form of modernization, perhaps by way of colonial influence if not colonization, is at play, these discussions might have also invited the concept of 'Indigenous religion' into closer proximity so that we might address wider notions of community, belonging, 'authenticity', tradition and appropriation. But even this would be an oversimplification. Buddhism has migrated in different forms across Eastern and Western cultures and has successfully put down roots and changed in accordance with the existing local traditions and locations in which it finds itself. Are putative 'new' local renditions of Buddhism with their nuances, complexities and practices (as exemplified through the case of Japanese Buddhism) any less religious, authentic or valid than that which emerged with the Buddha's enlightenment at Bodh Gaya in ancient India?

Inevitably not all of the contested concepts that feature in this anthology have contributed to our case study. Not all are relevant, although others could usefully be discussed in connection with other aspects of Western Buddhism. For example, should some organizations be included as part of the New Age? Is 'worship' an apt characterization of Buddhist devotion? Regarding violence, how do Buddhists reconcile commitment to the First Precept (to refrain from killing) with the fact that Buddhist countries all have armies like other nations? In the end, concepts in the study of religions such as those highlighted in this volume (and more), raise more critical questions than they answer. We hope that this brief case study chapter has demonstrated how we might explore, contest and problematize these concepts which are often taken for granted. We invite scholars, students and the wider public alike to take these discussions further into the rich variety of religious contexts which are present in the world today.

REFERENCES

Introduction: What is a contested concept?

Bowker, John (1983), *Worlds of Faith: Religious Belief and Practice in Britain Today*, London: British Broadcasting Corporation.

Buggeln, Gretchen, Crispin Pain and S. Brent Plate (2017), *Religion in Museums: Global and Multidisciplinary Perspectives*, London: Bloomsbury.

Hinnells, John R. (1978), *Zoroastrians and the West*, The Open University, Man's Religious Quest, Course Unit 27', in John R. Hinnells (ed.), *Spanning East and West*, 1–41, Milton Keynes: Open University Press.

Hughes, Aaron W. (2012), *Abrahamic Religions: On the Uses and Abuses of History*, Oxford: Oxford University Press.

Leuba, James H. (1912), *A Psychological Study of Religion*, New York: Macmillan.

Ling, Trevor (1968), *A History of Religion East and West*, London: Macmillan.

Saleh, Walid A. (2019), 'Prophecy and Revelation in Islam', *Discovering Sacred Texts* (British Library), 23 September. Available online: www.bl.uk/sacred-texts/articles/prophecy-and-revelation-in-islam (accessed 27 September 2021).

Smith, Jonathan Z. (1982), *Imagining Religion: From Babylon to Jonestown*, Chicago, IL and London: University of Chicago Press.

Smith, Jonathan Z. (1998), 'Religion, Religions, Religious', in Mark Taylor (ed.), *Critical Terms for Religious Studies*, 269–84, Chicago, IL and London: The University of Chicago Press.

Uddin, Asma (2019), 'The Baffling Argument That Has Become Mainstream under Trump: "Islam Is Not a Religion"', *The Washington Post*, 19 March. Available online: www.washingtonpost.com/religion/2019/03/19/baffling-argument-that-has-become-mainstream-under-trump-islam-is-not-religion (accessed 27 September 2021).

Chapter 1: Belief

Batson, C. Daniel and W. Larry Ventis (1982), *The Religious Experience: A Social-Psychological Experience*, Oxford: Oxford University Press.

Belter, Ronald and Erwin H. Brinkmann (1981), 'Construct Validity of the Nowicki-Strickland Locus of Control Scale for Children', *Psychological Reports*, 48: 427–32.

Bennett, Gillian (1987), *Traditions of Belief: Women, Folklore and the Supernatural Today*, London: Penguin.

Bok, Bart J. and Margaret W. Mayall (1941), 'Scientists Look at Astrology', *The Scientific Monthly*, 52: 233–44.

Campion, Nicholas (2015), *Astrology and Popular Religion in the Modern West: Prophecy, Cosmology and the New Age Movement*, London: Routledge.

Connor, Steve (2001), 'Human Evolution Is Heading in a New Direction Claims Study into Childbirth', *The Independent*, 23 April: 9.

Evans-Pritchard, E. E. ([1951] 1967), *Social Anthropology*, London: Cohen and West.

References

Glick, Peter and Mark Snyder (1986), 'Self-Fulfilling Prophecy: The Psychology of Belief in Astrology', *The Humanist*, 46 (3), May–June: 20–25, 50.

Gollob, Harry F. and James E. Dittes (1965), 'Effects of Manipulated Self-Esteem on Persuasability Depending on Threat and Complexity of Communication', *Journal of Personality and Social Psychology*, 2 (2): 195–201.

Harvey, Graham (2005), *Ritual and Religious Belief: A Reader*, London: Routledge.

Hornsby-Smith, Michael (1991), *Roman Catholic Beliefs in England: Customary Catholicism and Transformations in Religious Authority*, Cambridge: Cambridge University Press.

Jevons, Frank (1896), *Introduction to the History of Religions*, London: Methuen.

Joosse, Paul (2017). 'Max Weber's Disciples: Theorizing the Charismatic Aristocracy', *Sociological Theory* 35 (4): 334–58.

Myers, David G. (1990), *Social Psychology*, 3rd edn, New York: McGraw Hill.

Park, Robert (2000), *Voodoo Science: The Road from Foolishness to Fraud*, Oxford: Oxford University Press.

Rice, Tom W. (2003), 'Believe It or Not: Religious and Other Paranormal Beliefs in the United States', *Journal for the Scientific Study of Religion*, 42 (1), March: 95–106.

Roof, Wade Clark (1993), *A Generation of Seekers: The Spiritual Journeys of the Baby Boom Generation*, San Francisco CA: Harper Collins.

Ryle, Gilbert ([1949] 1990), *The Concept of Mind*, Harmondsworth, Middlesex: Penguin.

Schwitzgebel, Eric (2019), 'Belief', in Edward N. Zalta (ed.), *The Stanford Encyclopedia of Philosophy*. Available online: https://plato.stanford.edu/archives/fall2019/entries/belief/ (accessed 22 April 2021).

Stark, Rodney and William Simms Bainbridge (1985), *The Future of Religion: Secularization, Revival and Cult Formation*, Berkeley, CA: University of California Press.

Stark, Rodney and William Simms Bainbridge (1987), *A Theory of Religion*, New Brunswick, NJ: Rutgers University Press.

Stark, Rodney (1999), 'Atheism, Faith, and the Social Scientific Study of Religion', *Journal of Contemporary Religion*, 14 (1): 41–62.

Tylor, Edward Burnett (1873), *Primitive Culture*, vol. 1, London: John Murray.

Wilson, Colin (2001), 'Why I Now Believe Astrology IS a Science', *Daily Mail*, 22 March: 13.

Wuthnow, Robert (1976), *The Consciousness Revolution*, Berkeley, CA: University of California Press.

Chapter 2: Charisma

Barker, Eileen (1993), 'Charismatization: The Social Production of 'an Ethos Propitious to the Mobilisation of Sentiments'', in Eileen Barker, James Beckford, and Karel Dobbelaere (eds), *Secularization, Rationalism and Sectarianism: Essays in Honour of Bryan R. Wilson,* 181–201, Oxford: Clarendon Press.

Barnes, Douglas F. (1978), 'Charisma and Religious Leadership: An Historical Analysis', *Journal for the Scientific Study of Religion*, 17 (1): 1–18.

Bromley, David G. (2014), 'Charisma and Leadership: Charisma and Charismatic Authority in New Religions Movements', in George D. Chryssides and Benjamin E. Zeller (eds), *The Bloomsbury Companion to New Religious Movements*, 103–16, New York: Bloomsbury.

Chryssides, George D. (2021), 'Charisma—Elusive or Explanatory?: A Critical Examination of Leadership in New Religious Movements', *Fieldwork in Religion*, 16 (1): 35–54.

Friedland, W. H. (1964). 'For a Sociological Concept of Charisma', *Social Forces* 43: 18–26.

Joosse, Paul (2017). "Max Weber's Disciples: Theorizing the Charismatic Aristocracy." *Sociological Theory* 35 (4), 334–358.

Oakes, Len (1997), *Prophetic Charisma: The Psychology of Revolutionary Religious Personalities*, Syracuse, NY: Syracuse University Press.

Potts, John (2009), *A History of Charisma*, New York: Palgrave Macmillan.

Prophet, Erin (2016), 'Charisma and Authority in New Religious Movements', in. James R. Lewis and Inga Tallefsen (eds), *The Oxford Handbook of New Religious Movements: Vol. II*, 36–49, Oxford and New York: Oxford University Press.

Radkau, Joachim (2009), *Max Weber: A Biography*, trans. Patrick Camiller, Cambridge, UK: Polity Press.

Schlesinger, Jr., Arthur M. (1960), 'On Heroic Leadership', *Encounter*, 3–11.

Schlesinger, Jr., Arthur M. (1964), 'On Heroic Leadership', in *The Politics of Hope*, London: Eyre and Spottiswoode.

Wolpe, Harold (1968), 'A Critical Analysis of Some Aspects of Charisma', *The Sociological Review* 16: 305–18.

Weber, Max ([1921] 1968), *Economy and Society: An Outline of Interpretive Sociology*, New York: Bedminster Press.

Weber, Max ([1930] 2001), *The Protestant Ethic and the Spirit of Capitalism*, trans. Talcott Parsons, London and New York: Routledge.

Worsley, Peter ([1957] 1970), *The Trumpet Shall Sound: A Study of 'Cargo' Cults in Melanesia*, London: Paladin.

Chapter 3: Conversion

Barker, Eileen (1988), 'Defection from the Unification Church: Some Statistics and Distinctions', in David G. Bromley (ed.), *Falling from the Faith*, 166–84, Beverly Hills, CA: Sage.

Braden, Charles (1949), *These Also Believe: A Study of Modern American Cults & Minority Religious Movements*, New York: Macmillan.

Bromley, David G. (2016), 'As It Was in the Beginning: Developmental Moments in the Emergence of New Religions', in James R. Lewis and Inga B. Tøllefsen (eds), *The Oxford Handbook of New Religious Movements, Volume II*, 98–113, New York: Oxford University Press.

Ellwood, Robert (1981), *Alternative Alters: Unconventional and Eastern Spirituality in America*, Chicago, IL: University of Chicago Press.

Korzybski, Alfred (1995), *Science and Sanity. An Introduction to Non-Aristotelian Systems and General Semantics*, Forest Hills, NY: Institute for General Semantics.

Scott, James (1985), *Weapons of the Weak: Everyday Forms of Peasant Resistance*, New Haven, CT: Yale University Press.

Swidler, Ann (1986), 'Culture in Action: Symbols and Strategies', *American Sociological Review*, 51 (2): 273–86.

Chapter 4: Cult

Ashcraft, W. Michael (2018), *A Historical Introduction to the Study of New Religious Movements*, London: Routledge.

Bainbridge, William Sims and Rodney Stark (1980), 'Client and Audience Cults in America', *Sociological Analysis*, 41 (3): 199–214.

Barker, Eileen (2017), 'From Cult Wars to Constructive Cooperation – Well, Sometimes', in Eugene V. Gallagher (ed.), *'Cult Wars' in Historical Perspective: New and Minority Religions*, 9–22, London: Routledge.

References

Campbell, Colin (1972), 'The Cult, the Cultic Milieu and Secularization', in Michael Hill (ed.), *A Sociological Yearbook of Religion in Britain* 5, 119–36, London: SCM.

Chryssides, George D. and Benjamin E. Zeller (2014), *The Bloomsbury Companion to New Religious Movements*, London: Bloomsbury.

Cowan, Douglas E. and David G. Bromley (2015), *Cults and New Religions: A Brief History*, 2nd edn, Malden, MA: Wiley Blackwell.

Galanter, Marc (1989), *Cults: Faith, Healing, and Coercion*, Oxford: Oxford University Press.

Kaplan, Jeff and Heléne Lööw (2002), *The Cultic Milieu: Oppositional Subcultures in an Age of Globalization*, Walnut Creek, CA: AltaMira Press.

McCloud, Sean (2004), *Making the American Religious Fringe: Exotics, Subversives, and Journalists, 1955-1993*, Chapel Hill, NC: University of North Carolina Press.

Oliver, Paul (2012), *New Religious Movements: A Guide for the Perplexed*, London: Continuum.

Pietsch, Andreas and Sita Steckel (2018), 'New Religious Movements before Modernity?: Considerations from a Historical Perspective', *Nova Religio*, 21 (4): 13–37.

Richardson, James T. (1985), 'The Active vs. Passive Convert: Paradigm Conflict in Conversion/Recruitment Research', *Journal for the Scientific Study of Religion*, 24 (2): 163–79.

Sarno, Charles and Helen Shoemaker (2016), 'Church, Sect, or Cult? The Curious Case of Harold Camping's Family Radio and the May 21 Movement', *Nova Religio*, 19 (3): 6–30.

Smith, Jonathan Z. (1988), 'Religion, Religions, Religious', in Mark C. Taylor (ed.), *Critical Terms for Religious* Studies, 269–84, Chicago, IL: University of Chicago Press.

Stark, Rodney and Roger Finke (2000), *Acts of Faith: Explaining the Human Side of Religion*, Berkeley, CA: University of Chicago Press.

Chapter 5: Diaspora

Baumann, M. (2000), 'Diaspora: Genealogy of Semantics and Transcultural Comparison', *Numen: International Review for the History of Religions*, 47 (3): 313–37.

Baumann, M. (2010), 'Exile', in K. Knott and S. McLoughlin (eds), *Diasporas: Concepts, Intersections, Identities*, 19–23, London and New York: Zed Books.

Boyarin, D. and J. Boyarin (1993), 'Diaspora: Generation and the Ground of Jewish Identity', *Critical Inquiry*, 19: 693–725.

Brah, A. (1996), *Cartographies of Diaspora: Contesting Identities*, London: Routledge.

Clifford, J. (1994), 'Diasporas', *Cultural Anthropology*, 9 (3): 302–38.

Cohen, R. (1997), *Global Diasporas: An Introduction*, London: Routledge.

Gilroy, P. (1993), *The Black Atlantic: Modernity and Double Consciousness*, Cambridge, MA: Harvard University Press.

Hall, S. (1990), 'Cultural Identity and Diaspora', in J. Rutherford (ed.), *Identity: Community, Culture, Difference*, 222–37, London: Lawrence and Wishart.

Johnson, P. C. (2013), 'Religions of the African Diaspora', in A. Quayson and G. Daswani (eds), *A Companion to Diaspora and Transnationalism*, 509–23, Oxford: Wiley Blackwell.

Levitt, P. (2007), *God Needs No Passport: Immigrants and the Changing American Religious Landscape*, New York and London: The New Press.

McLoughlin, S. (2013), 'Religion, Religions, and Diaspora', in A. Quayson and G. Daswani (eds), *A Companion to Diaspora and Transnationalism*, 125–38, Oxford: Wiley Blackwell.

Smart, N. (1987), 'The Importance of Diasporas', in S. Shaked, R. Y. Werblovsky, D. D. Shulman and G. A. G. Strounka (eds), *Gilgul: Essays on Transformation, Revolution and Permanence in the History of Religions*, 288–95, Leiden: Brill.

Tölölyan, K. (1996), 'Rethinking Diaspora(s): Stateless Power in the Transnational Moment', *Diaspora*, 5 (1): 3–36.

Tweed, T. A. (2006), *Crossing and Dwelling: A Theory of Religion*, Cambridge, MA: Harvard University Press.

Vásquez, M. A. (2010), 'Diasporas and Religion', in K. Knott and S. McLoughlin (eds), *Diasporas: Concepts, Intersections, Identities*, 128–33, London and New York: Zed Books.

Vertovec, S. (2004), 'Religion and Diaspora', in P. Antes, A. W. Geertz and R. Warne (eds), *New Approaches to the Study of Religion: Textual, Comparative, Sociological, and Cognitive Approaches*, 275–303, Berlin and New York: Verlag de Gruyter.

Chapter 6: Folk religion

Bowman, Marion (2000), 'Contemporary Celtic Spirituality', in Amy Hale and Philip Payton (eds), *New Directions in Celtic Studies*, 69–91, Exeter: Exeter University Press.

Bowman, Marion (2004), 'Phenomenology, Fieldwork and Folk Religion', in Steven Sutcliffe (ed.), *Religion: Empirical Studies*, 3–18, Aldershot, UK: Ashgate.

Bowman, Marion and Ülo Valk (2012),'Vernacular Religion, Generic Expressions and the Dynamics of Belief: Introduction', in Marion Bowman and Ülo Valk (eds), *Vernacular Religion in Everyday Life: Expressions of Belief*, 1–19, Sheffield and Bristol, CT: Equinox.

Boyes, Georgina (1993), *The Imagined Village*, Manchester: Manchester University Press.

Gomme, G. L. (1891), 'The Folk-Lore Society', *Folk-Lore*, 2 (3): 2.

Gomme, G. L. and Alice Gomme (1916), *British Folk-Lore, Folk Songs, and Singing Games*, London: National Home-Reading Union.

Hakamies, Pekka, and Anneli Honko (eds) (2013), *Theoretical Milestones: Selected Writings of Lauri Honko*, Helsinki: Academia Scientiarum Fennica.

Howard, Robert Glenn (2013), 'Vernacular Authority: Critically Engaging "Tradition"', in Trevor J. Blank and Robert Glenn Howard (eds), *Tradition in the Twenty-First Century: Locating the Role of the Past in the Present*, 72–99, Logan, UT: Utah State University Press.

Illman, Ruth and Mercedesz Czimbalmos (2020), 'Knowing, Being, and Doing Religion: Introducing an Analytical Model for Researching Vernacular Religion', *Temenos: Nordic Journal of Comparative Religion*, 56 (2): 171–99.

Kapaló, James A. (2013), 'Folk Religion in Discourse and Practice', *Journal of Ethnology and Folkloristics*, 7 (1): 3–18.

Lubbock, John (1870), *The Origin of Civilisation and the Primitive Condition of Man*, London: Longmans, Green & Co.

Piggott, S. (1989), *Ancient Britons and the Antiquarian Imagination: Ideas from the Renaissance to the Regency*, London: Thames and Hudson.

Primiano, Leonard Norman (1995), 'Vernacular Religion and the Search for Method in Religious Folklife', *Western Folklore* (Special Issue: *Reflexivity and the Study of Belief*), 54 (1): 37–56.

Primiano, Leonard Norman (2012), 'Afterword – Manifestations of the Religious Vernacular: Ambiguity, Power and Creativity', in Marion Bowman and Ülo Valk (eds), *Vernacular Religion in Everyday Life: Expressions of Belief*, 382–94, Sheffield and Bristol, CT: Equinox.

Tylor, Edward (1871), *Primitive Culture: Researches into the Development of Mythology, Philosophy, Religion, Language, Art and Custom*, London: John Murray.

Walker, Geoffrey (2001), 'Clergy Attitudes to Folk Religion in the Diocese of Bath and Wells', unpublished PhD thesis, University of Bristol.

Yoder, Don (1974), 'Toward a Definition of Folk Religion', *Western Folklore*, 33 (1): 2–15. Reprinted 1990 in Don Yoder *Discovering American Folklife: Studies in Ethnic, Religious and Regional Culture*, 67–84, Ann Arbor: UMI Research Press.

References

Chapter 7: Fundamentalism

Arora, Vishal (2014), 'Connecting the Dots on Buddhist Fundamentalism', *Diplomat*, 30 May. Available online: https://thediplomat.com/2014/05/connecting-the-dots-on-buddhist-fundamentalism (accessed 20 May 2021).

Bauder, K. (2008), 'Calvinism, Arminianism, Biblicism', *In the Nick of Time*, 29 April. Available online: https://sharperiron.org/article/calvinism-arminianism-biblicism (accessed 20 April 2021).

Bebbington, D. W. (2004), *Evangelicalism in Modern Britain: A History from the 1730s to the 1980s*, Philadelphia, PA: Taylor and Francis.

Beecher, H. W. (1882), 'Mr. Beecher', *Brooklyn Daily Eagle*, 15 October: 1.

Bereza, S. (2017), *The Right Kind of Music: Fundamentalist Christianity as Musical and Cultural Practice*. PhD thesis, Duke University, Durham, North Carolina. Available online: https://dukespace.lib.duke.edu/dspace/handle/10161/14433 (accessed 20 April 2021).

Combined Wire Services (1990), 'Soviet Troops Sent to Azerbaijan', *Hartford Courant*, 4 January: 1 & 19.

Finucane, J. (2014), 'Proselytizing, Peacework, and Public Relations: Soka Gakkai's Commitment to Interreligious Harmony in Singapore', in R. M. Feener (ed.), *Proselytizing and the Limits of Religious Pluralism in Contemporary Asia*, 4: 103–23, Singapore: Springer Singapore.

Oxford English Dictionary (2021), 'Fundamentalism', *OED Online*. Available online: https://www.oed.com/view/Entry/75498 (accessed 12 September 2021).

Graham, B. (1997), *Just as I Am: The Autobiography of Billy Graham*, San Francisco, CA: Harper.

Hofstadter, R. (1963), *Anti-Intellectualism in American Life*, New York: Knopf Doubleday.

Jones, R. R. Jr. (1976), *Word of Their Testimony: Sermons Delivered at the Congress of Fundamentalists*, Greenville, SC: Bob Jones University Press.

Lewis, C. (2021), '"The Bounds of their Habitation": Bob Jones' Rhetorical Duel with Billy Graham', *Fides et Historia*, 53 (1), Winter/Spring: 37–59.

Marsden, G. (1991), *Understanding Fundamentalism and Evangelicalism*, Grand Rapids, MI: Eerdmans.

Marty, M. E. (1970), *Righteous Empire: The Protestant Experience in America*, New York City: Dial Press.

Marty, M. E. (1997), *Modern American Religion, Volume 2: The Noise of Conflict, 1919–1941*, Chicago, IL: University of Chicago Press.

Marty, M. E. and R. S. Appleby (1991), *Fundamentalisms Observed*, Chicago, IL: University of Chicago Press.

Mitchell, D. R. (1982), 'Book Report', *Fundamentalist Journal*, December: 47.

New York Times News Service (1992), 'Hindu Opposition Plans to Agitate India Vote', *Chicago Tribune*, 31 December: 36.

Ramakrishna, K. (2021), 'The Global Threat Landscape in 2020', *Counter Terrorist Trends and Analyses*, 13 (1): 1–13. Available online: www.jstor.org/stable/26979984 (accessed 20 May 2021).

Russell, C. T. (1886–1904), *Millennial Dawn* (later renamed *Studies in the Scriptures*), 6 vols., Brooklyn, NY: Watch Tower Bible and Tract Society.

Shelter, S. G. (1967), 'Bishop Voices Concern over Modern-day Church', *Intelligencer Journal*, 4 February: 10.

Smith, J. I. and Y. Y. Haddad (2014), *The Oxford Handbook of American Islam*, New York City: Oxford University Press.

Sparks, J. (1987), 'More Trouble on the Mount', *Spokesman-Review*, 11 January: 18.

Torrey, R. A. et al. (eds) (1910–1915), *The Fundamentals: A Testimony to the Truth*, Chicago, IL: Testimony Publishing Company.

Watson, A. (1944), 'Utah Purge of Plural Marriage Uncovers Domestic Difficulties', *Daily News*, 19 March: 41.

Wood, S. and D. H. Watt (2014), *Fundamentalism: Perspectives on a Contested History*, Columbia, SC: University of South Carolina Press.

Chapter 8: Guru

Copeman, Jacob and Aya Ikegame (2014), 'The Multifarious Guru: An Introduction', in J. Copeman and Aya Ikegame (eds), *The Guru in South Asia: New Interdisciplinary Perspectives*, 1–45, London: Routledge.

Feltmate, David (2012), 'The Humorous Reproduction of Religious Prejudice: Cults and Religious Humour in *The Simpsons, South Park and King of the Hill*', *Journal of Religion and Popular Culture*, 24 (2): 201–16.

Flood, Gavin (2005), 'Introduction: Establishing the Boundaries', in G. Flood (ed.), *The Blackwell Companion to Hinduism*, 1–19, Oxford: Blackwell.

Iwamura, Jane Naomi (2011), *Virtual Orientalism: Asian Religion and American Popular Culture*, Oxford: Oxford University Press.

Iwamura, Jane Naomi (2017), 'The Oriental Monk in American Popular Culture', in B. D. Forbes and J. H. Mahan (eds), *Religion and Popular Culture in America*, Oakland, CA: University of California Press, 51–70.

Jacobs, Stephen (2015), *The Art of Living Foundation: Spirituality and Wellbeing in the Global Context*, Farnham, UK: Ashgate.

Mallinson, James and Mark Singleton (eds) (2017), *Roots of Yoga*, London: Penguin.

Mlecko, Joel D. (1982), 'The Guru in Hindu Tradition', *Numen*, 29 (1): 33–61.

Rollings, Grant. (2019), 'Like a Madhouse', *The Sun*. Available online: https://www.thesun.co.uk/news/10022134/abuse-violence-terror-bhagwan-sex-cult (accessed 27 November 2021).

Storr, Anthony (1996), *Feet of Clay. Saints, Sinners and Madmen: A Study of Gurus*, New York: The Free Press.

Swami Nityānanda (2020), *Śrī Guru Gītā*, Walden, NY: Shanti Mandir.

Tian, Charlie (2017), *Invest Like a Guru*, Hoboken, NJ: John Wiley.

The Family Survival Trust (2019), 'What Is a Cult', Available online: www.thefamilysurvivaltrust.org/what-is-a-cult (accessed 10 April 2021).

The Social Media Guru (2016), *The Social Media Guru: A Practical Guide for Small Businesses*, n.p.: eBook Partnership.

Vaudeville, Charlotte (1987), '*Sant Mat*: Santism as the Universal Path to Sanctity', in K. Schomer and W. H. McLeod (eds), *The Sants: Studies in a Devotional Tradition of India*, 21–40, Delhi: Motilal Banarsidas.

Warrier, Maya (2005), *Hindu Selves in a Modern World*, London: Routledge.

Weber, Max (1978), *Economy and Society*, Berkley, CA: University of California Press.

Chapter 9: Indigenous religions

Clifford, James (2013), *Returns: Becoming Indigenous in the Twenty-First Century*, Cambridge, MA: Harvard University Press.

Cox, James L. (2007), *From Primitive to Indigenous: The Academic Study of Indigenous Religions*, Aldershot, UK: Ashgate.

References

Hartney, Christopher and Daniel J. Tower (eds) (2017), *Religious Categories and the Construction of the Indigenous*, Leiden: Brill.

Kraft, Siv Ellen et al. (2020), *Indigenous Religion(s): Local Grounds, Global Networks*, London: Routledge.

Newcomb, Steven (2008), *Pagans in the Promised Land: Decoding the Doctrine of Christian Discovery*, Golden, CO: Fulcrum Publishing.

Olupona, Jacob (2004), *Beyond Primitivism: Indigenous Religious Traditions and Modernity*, London: Routledge.

Chapter 10: Magic

Belier, W. W. (1995), 'Religion and Magic: Durkheim and the Année sociologique group', *Method and Theory in the Study of Religion*, 7 (2): 163–84.

Bohak, Gideon (2008), *Ancient Jewish Magic: A History*, Cambridge: Cambridge University Press.

Bremmer, J. N. (1999), 'The Birth of the Term "Magic"', *Zeitschrift für Papyrologie und Epigraphik*, 126: 1–12.

Collins, D. (2008), *Magic in the Ancient Greek World*, New York: John Wiley and Sons.

De Martino, E. (2007), *Il mondo magico: prolegomeni a una storia del magismo*, Torino: Bollati Boringhieri.

Frazer, J. G. ([1890] 2001), *The Golden Bough*, Basingstoke: Palgrave Macmillan.

Greenwood, S. (2013), 'Feminist Witchcraft: A Transformatory Politics', in N. Charles and F. Hughes-Freeland (eds), *Practising Feminism*, 109–34, London and New York: Routledge.

Lurker, M. (2004), *The Routledge Dictionary of Gods and Goddesses, Devils and Demons*, London: Routledge.

Preston Blier, S. (1993), 'Truth and Seeing: Magic, Custom, and Fetish in Art History', in R. H. Bates, V. Y. Mudimbe, and J. O'Barr (eds), *Africa and the Disciplines*, 139–66, Chicago, IL: University of Chicago Press.

Puca, A. (2018), '"Witch" and "Shaman": Discourse Analysis of the Use of Indigenizing Terms in Italy', *International Journal for the Study of New Religions*, 9 (2): 271–84.

Rountree, K. (2004), *Embracing the Witch and the Goddess: Feminist Ritual-Makers in New Zealand*, London: Routledge.

Sempruch, J. (2004), 'Feminist Constructions of the "Witch" as a Fantasmatic Other', *Body and Society*, 10 (4): 113–33.

Toy, C. H. (1899), 'Relation between Magic and Religion', *Journal of the American Oriental Society*, 20: 327–31.

Wax, M. and Wax, R. (1963), 'The Notion of Magic', *Current Anthropology*, 4 (5): 495–518.

White, E. Doyle (2016), *Wicca: History, Belief, and Community in Modern Pagan Witchcraft*, Brighton, UK and Chicago, IL: Sussex Academic Press.

Young, M. W. (ed.) (2017), *The Ethnography of Malinowski (1979): The Trobriand Islands 1915–18*, London: Routledge.

Chapter 11: Millennialism

Cohn, N. (1962), 'Medieval Millenarianism: Its Bearing on the Comparative Study of Millenarian Movements', in S. L. Thrupp (ed.), *Millennial Dreams in Action: Essays in Comparative Study*, 31–43, The Hague: Mouton.

Chryssides, G. D. (2022), *Jehovah's Witnesses: A New Introduction*, London: Bloomsbury.

Doyle, C., with C. Wessinger and M. D. Wittmer (2012), *A Journey to Waco: Autobiography of a Branch Davidian*, Lanham, MD: Rowman and Littlefield.

Ellwood, R. (2000), 'Nazism as a Millennialist Movement', in C. Wessinger (ed.), *Millennialism, Persecution, and Violence: Historical Cases*, 241–60, Syracuse, NY: Syracuse University Press.

Kaplan, U. (2021), 'Preparing for the Confucian Millennium: The Korean New Religious Movement Kaengjŏngyudo', *Nova Religio*, 25 (1): 64–86.

Landes, R. (2011), *Heaven on Earth: The Varieties of the Millennial Experience*, New York: Oxford University Press.

Lowe, S. (2000), 'Western Millennial Ideology Goes East: The Taiping Revolution and Mao's Great Leap Forward', in C. Wessinger (ed.), *Millennialism, Persecution, and Violence: Historical Cases*, 220–40, Syracuse, NY: Syracuse University Press.

Redles, D. (2011), 'National Socialist Millennialism', in C. Wessinger (ed.), *The Oxford Handbook of Millennialism*, 529–48, New York: Oxford University Press.

Rosenfeld, J. E. (2011), 'Nativist Millennialism', in C. Wessinger (ed.), *The Oxford Handbook of Millennialism*, 89–109, New York: Oxford University Press.

Salter, R. C. (2000), 'Time, Authority, and Ethics in the Khmer Rouge: Elements of the Millennial Vision', in Year Zero, in C. Wessinger (ed.), *Millennialism, Persecution, and Violence: Historical Cases*, 281–98, Syracuse, NY: Syracuse University Press.

Sarno, C. and H. Shoemaker (2016), 'Church, Sect, or Cult? The Curious Case of Harold Camping's Family Radio and the May 21 Movement', *Nova Religio*, 19 (3): 6–30.

Wessinger, C. (2000), *How the Millennium Comes Violently: From Jonestown to Heaven's Gate*, New York: Seven Bridges Press.

Wessinger, C. (2011a), 'Millennial Glossary', in C. Wessinger (ed.), *The Oxford Handbook of Millennialism*, 717–23, New York: Oxford University Press.

Wessinger, C. (2011b), 'Millennialism in Cross-Cultural Perspective', in C. Wessinger (ed.), *The Oxford Handbook of Millennialism*, 3–23, New York: Oxford University Press.

Wessinger, C., (ed.) (2011c), *The Oxford Handbook of Millennialism*, New York: Oxford University Press.

Wojcik, D. (2011), 'Avertive Apocalypticism', in C. Wessinger (ed.), *The Oxford Handbook of Millennialism*, 66–88, New York: Oxford University Press.

Zeller, B. E. (2014), *Heaven's Gate: America's UFO Religion*, New York: New York University Press.

Chapter 12: Myth

Adas, Michael (1989), *Machines as the Measure of Men: Science, Technology, and Ideologies of Western Dominance*, Ithaca, NY: Cornell University Press.

Arnason, Johann P. (2013), 'Review of Robert Bellah: Religion in Human Evolution: From the Paleolithic to the Axial Age', *The Review of Politics*, 75 (1): 143–9.

Bellah, Robert N. (2011), *Religion in Human Evolution: From the Paleolithic to the Axial Age*, Cambridge, MA: The Belknap Press of Harvard University Press.

Boyd, Richard (1993), 'Metaphor and Theory Change: What Is "Metaphor" a Metaphor For?', in Andrew Ortony (ed.), *Metaphor and Thought*, 2nd edn, 481–532, Cambridge: Cambridge University Press.

Brisson, Luc (2004), *How Philosophers Saved Myths: Allegorical Interpretation and Classical Mythology* (1996), trans. Catherine Tihanyi, Chicago, IL: University of Chicago Press.

Cohen, P. S. (1969), 'Theories of Myth', *Man N.S.*, 4 (3): 337–53.

Donald, Merlin (1991), *Origins of the Modern Mind: Three Stages in the Evolution of Culture and Cognition*, Cambridge, MA: Harvard University Press.

References

Fowler, Robert L. (2011), 'Mythos and Logos', *The Journal of Hellenic Studies*, 131 (45): 45–66.

Johansen, T. K. (1999), 'Myth and Logos in Aristotle', in R. G. A. Buxton (ed.), *From Myth to Reason? Studies in the Development of Greek Thought*, 279–91, Oxford: Oxford University Press.

Klostermaier Klaus K. (2007), *A Survey of Hinduism*, 3rd edn, Albany, NY: State University of New York Press.

Lévi-Strauss, Claude (1966), *The Savage Mind* (1962), trans. Doreen and John Weightman, Chicago, IL: University of Chicago Press.

Lévy-Bruhl, Lucien ([1910] 1926), *How Natives Think*, trans. Lilian A. Clare, New York: Alfred A. Knopf.

Lévy-Bruhl, Lucien ([1949] 1975), *The Notebooks on Primitive Mentality*, trans. Peter Rivière, New York: Harper and Row.

Lloyd, G. E. R. (1990), *Demystifying Mentalities*, Cambridge: Cambridge University Press.

Midgley, Mary (1985), *Evolution as a Religion: Strange Hopes and Stranger Fears*, London: Methuen.

Sprat, Thomas (1734), *The History of the Royal Society of London for the Improving of Natural Knowledge*, London: Printed for J. Knapton et al.

Tofighian, Omid (2016), *Myth and Philosophy in Platonic Dialogues*, London: Palgrave Macmillan.

Tylor, Edward B. (1913), *Primitive Culture: Researches into the Development of Mythology, Philosophy, Religion, Art, and Custom*, vols. 1 & 2, 5th edn, London: John Murray.

Witzel, E. J. Michael (2012), *The Origins of the World's Mythologies*, Oxford: Oxford University Press.

Chapter 13: New Age

Aupers, Stef and Dick Houtman (2010), 'Beyond the Spiritual Supermarket: The Social and Public Significance of New Age Spirituality', in Stef Aupers and Dick Houtman (eds), *Religions of Modernity: Relocating the Sacred to the Self and the Digital*, 135–60, Leiden: Brill.

Bailey, Alice (1948), *The Reappearance of the Christ*, New York: Lucis.

Bruce, Steve (2002), *God Is Dead: Secularization in the West*, Oxford: Blackwell.

Bruce, Steve (2017), *Secular Beats Spiritual: The Westernization of the Easternization of the West*, Oxford: Oxford University Press.

Campbell, Colin (1972), 'The Cult, the Cultic Milieu and Secularization', in Michael Hill (ed.), *A Sociological Yearbook of Religion in Britain*, 5th edn, 119–36, London: SCM.

Campion, Nicholas (2012), *Astrology and Popular Religion in the Modern West*, Farnham, UK: Ashgate.

Durkheim, E. (1915/1971), *The Elementary Forms of Religious Life*, London: George Allen and Unwin.

Frisk, Liselotte, Ingvild Sælid Gilhus and Siv Ellen Kraft (2016), 'The New Age', in James R. Lewis and Inga B. Tøllefsen (eds), *The Oxford Handbook of New Religious Movements, Volume II*, 469–81, Oxford: Oxford University Press.

Hanegraaff, Wouter (1996), *New Age Religion and Western Culture: Esotericism in the Mirror of Secular Thought*, Leiden: Brill.

Heelas, Paul (1996), *The New Age Movement: The Celebration of the Self and the Sacralization of Modernity*, Oxford: Blackwell.

Heelas, Paul and Linda Woodhead (2005), *The Spiritual Revolution: Why Religion Is Giving Way to Spirituality*, Oxford: Blackwell.

Lewis, James R. and J. Gordon Melton (eds) (1992), *Perspectives on the New Age*, Albany, NY: SUNY Press.

Newcombe, Suzanne (2019), *Yoga in Britain: Stretching Spirituality and Educating Yogis*, Sheffield: Equinox.

Partridge, Christopher (2004), *The Re-Enchantment of the West: Alternative Spiritualities, Sacralization, Popular Culture, and Occulture, Volume I*, London: Clark International.

Partridge, Christopher (2005), *The Re-Enchantment of the West: Alternative Spiritualities, Sacralization, Popular Culture, and Occulture, Volume II*, London: Clark International.

Possamai, Adam (2005), *In Search of New Age Spiritualities*, Aldershot, UK: Ashgate.

Prohl, Inken (2007), 'The Spiritual World: Aspects of New Age in Japan', in Daren Kemp and James R. Lewis (eds), *Handbook of New Age*, 359–74, Leiden: Brill.

Robertson, Roland (1992), *Globalization: Social Theory and Global Culture*, London: Sage.

Ruah-Midbar, Marianna and Adam Klin-Oron (2010), 'Jew Age: Jewish Praxis in Israeli New Age Discourses', *Journal of Alternative Spiritualities and New Age Studies*, 5: 33–63.

Sutcliffe, Steven (2003), *Children of the New Age: A History of Spiritual Practices*, London: Routledge.

Sutcliffe, Steven (2007), 'The Origins of "New Age" Religion between the Two World Wars', in Daren Kemp and James R. Lewis (eds), *Handbook of New Age*, 51–75, Leiden: Brill.

Sutcliffe, Steven (2013), 'New Age, World Religions and Elementary Forms', in Steven J. Sutcliffe and Ingvild Sælid Gilhus (eds), *New Age Spirituality: Rethinking Religion*, 17–34, London: Routledge.

Sutcliffe, Steven (2014), 'New Age', in George D. Chryssides and Benjamin E. Zeller (eds), *The Bloomsbury Companion to New Religious Movements*, 41–5, London: Bloomsbury.

Sutcliffe, Steven J. and Ingvild Sælid Gilhus (2013), 'Introduction: "All Mixed Up" – Thinking about Religion in Relation to New Age Spiritualities', in Steven J. Sutcliffe and Ingvild Sælid Gilhus (eds), *New Age Spirituality: Rethinking Religion*, 1–16, London: Routledge.

Vincett, Giselle and Linda Woodhead (2016), 'Spirituality', in Linda Woodhead, Christopher Partridge, and Hiroko Kawanami (eds), *Religion in the Modern World: Traditions and Transformations*, 3rd edn, 323–44, London: Routledge.

Woodhead, Linda (2010), 'Fuzzy Spirituality? Taking Sides in the Sociology of Religion', in Stef Aupers and Dick Houtman (eds), *Religions of Modernity: Relocating the Sacred to the Self and the Digital*, 31–48, Leiden: Brill.

York, Michael (1995), *The Emerging Network: A Sociology of the New Age and Neo-Pagan Movements*, Lanham, MD: Rowman and Littlefield.

Chapter 14: New religious movements

Barker, Eileen (1989), *New Religious Movements: A Practical Introduction*, London: HMSO.

Beckford, J. (ed.) (1986), *New Religious Movements and Rapid Social Change*. London: Sage.

Berner, Ulrich (2000), 'Reflections upon the Concept of "New Religious Movement"', *Method and Theory in the Study of Religion*, 12 (1/2): 267–76.

Clarke, Peter (ed.) (1987), *The New Evangelists*, London: Ethnographica.

Ellwood, Robert S. and Harry B. Partin ([1973] 1988), *Religious and Spiritual Groups in Modern America*, 2nd edn, Englewood Cliffs, NJ: Prentice Hall.

Melton, J. Gordon and Robert L. Moore (1982), *The Cult Experience: Responding to the New Religious Pluralism*, New York: Pilgrim Press.

Miller, Timothy (1995), *America's Alternative Religions*, Albany, NY: State University of New York Press.

References

Minority Rights Group International (2020), World Directory of Minorities and Indigenous Peoples, Available online: https://minorityrights.org/country/united-kingdom (accessed 1 May 2021).

Needleman, Jacob (1970), *The New Religions*, Garden City, NY: Doubleday.

Nelson, Geoffrey K. (1987), *Cults, New Religions, and Religious Creativity*, London: Routledge and Kegan Paul.

Sutcliffe, Steven (2003), *Children of the New Age*, London: Routledge.

Chapter 15: Pilgrimage

Bowman, Marion (2008), 'Going with the Flow: Contemporary Pilgrimage in Glastonbury', in Peter Jan Margry (ed.), *Shrines and Pilgrimage in the Modern World: New Itineraries into the Sacred*, 241–80, Amsterdam: Amsterdam University Press.

Coats, Curtis (2009), 'Sedona, Arizona: New Age Pilgrim-Tourist Destination', *CrossCurrents*, 59 (3): 383–9.

Cohen, Erik (1979), 'A Phenomenology of Tourist Experiences', *Sociology*, 13 (2): 179–201.

Collins-Kreiner, Noga (2018), 'Pilgrimage-Tourism: Common Themes in Different Religions', *International Journal of Religious Tourism and Pilgrimage*, 6 (1): 8–17.

Cusack, Carole M. (2021), 'A New Spiritual Marketplace: Comparing New Age and New Religious Movements in an Age of Spiritual and Religious Tourism', in Daniel H. Olsen and Dallen J. Timothy (eds), *Routledge Handbook of Religious and Spiritual Tourism*, 79–89, London and New York: Routledge.

Digance, Justine (2006), 'Religious and Secular Pilgrimage: Journeys Redolent with Meaning', in Daniel H. Olsen and Dallen J. Timothy (eds), *Tourism, Religion and Spiritual Journeys*, 36–48, London, New York: Routledge.

Duffy, Eamon (2017), *Reformation Divided: Catholics, Protestants and the Conversion of England*, London and New York: Bloomsbury.

Eade, John and Michael Sallnow (eds) (1991), *Contesting the Sacred: The Anthropology of Christian Pilgrimage*, London and New York: Routledge.

Geary, David and Kiran Shinde (2021), 'Buddhist Pilgrimage and the Ritual Ecology in the Indo-Gangetic Region', *Religions*, 12 (6): 385.

Hill-Smith, C. (2011), 'Cyberpilgrimage: The (virtual) Reality of Online Pilgrimage Experience', *Religion Compass* 5(6): 236–46.

MacCannell, Dean ([1976] 1999), *The Tourist: A New Theory of the Leisure Class*, Berkeley, Los Angeles, CA: University of California Press.

Norman, Alex (2011), *Spiritual Tourism: Travel and Religious Practice in Western Society*, London and New York: Continuum.

Norman, Alex (2012), 'The Varieties of the Spiritual Tourist Experience', *Literature and Aesthetics*, 22 (1): 20–37.

Olsen, Daniel H. and Dallen J. Timothy (2006), 'Tourism and Religious Journeys', in Daniel H. Olsen and Dallen J. Timothy (eds), *Tourism, Religion and Spiritual Journeys*, 1–21, London and New York: Routledge.

Palmer, Craig T., Ryan O. Begley and Kathryn Coe (2012), 'In Defence of Differentiating Pilgrimage from Tourism', *International Journal of Tourism Anthropology*, 2 (1): 71–85.

Peters, F. E. (1994), *The Hajj: The Muslim Pilgrimage to Mecca and the Holy Places*, Princeton, NJ: Princeton University Press.

Seal, Graham (2007), 'ANZAC: The Sacred in the Secular', *Journal of Australian Studies*, 31 (91): 135–44.

Stausberg, Michael (2011), *Religion and Tourism: Crossroads, Destinations and Encounters*, London and New York: Routledge.

Stoddard, Robert H. (1997), 'Defining and Classifying Pilgrimages', in Robert H. Stoddard and Alan Morinis (eds), *Sacred Places, Sacred Spaces: The Geography of Pilgrimages*, 41–60, Baton Rouge, LA: Louisiana State University.

Turner, Victor (1973), 'The Center Out There: Pilgrim's Goal', *History of Religions*, 12 (3): 191–230.

Turner, Victor and Edith Turner (1978), *Image and Pilgrimage in Christian Culture*, New York: Columbia University Press.

Vacaru, Cristian (2015), 'The Biblical Foundations of the Pilgrimage', *International Letters of Social and Humanistic Sciences*, 65: 58–67.

Chapter 16: Prophecy

Barfoot, Charles H. and Gerald T. Sheppard (1980), 'Prophetic vs. Priestly Religion: The Changing Role of Women Clergy in Classical Pentecostal Churches', *Review of Religious Research*, 22 (1): 2–17.

Chryssides, G. D. (2010), 'How Prophecy Succeeds: Jehovah's Witnesses and Prophetic Expectations', *International Journal for the Study of New Religions*, 1 (1): 27–48.

Festinger, Leon, Henry W. Riecken and Stanley Schachter (1956), *When Prophecy Fails*, San Francisco: Harper and Row.

Gaffin, Richard B., Jr. (1979), *Perspectives on Pentecost: Studies in New Testament Teaching on the Gifts of the Holy Spirit*, Grand Rapids, MI: Baker.

Oakes, Len (1997), *Prophetic Charisma: The Psychology of Revolutionary Religious Personalities*, Syracuse, NY: Syracuse University Press.

Ruthven, Jon (1993), *On the Cessation of the Charismata: The Protestant Polemic on Post-Biblical Miracles*, New York City: Continuum.

Stone, Jon R., (ed.) (2000), *Expecting Armageddon: Essential Readings in Failed Prophecy*, London: Routledge.

Tumminia, Diana G. and William H. Swatos Jr., eds (2011), *How Prophecy Lives*, Boston: Brill.

Wagner, Janice E. (2020), *Office of the Prophet: A Comprehensive Study*, Bloomington, IN: WestBow Press.

Warfield, B. B. (1918), *Counterfeit Miracles*, New York: Charles Scribners.

Watch Tower (2018), 'Prophecy', in *Insight on the Scriptures*, Brooklyn, NY: Watch Tower Bible and Tract Society of Pennsylvania.

Weber, Max ([1922] 1963), *The Sociology of Religion*, Boston: Beacon Press.

Zygmunt, Joseph F. (1972), 'When Prophecies Fail: A Theoretical Perspective on the Comparative Evidence', *American Behavioral Scientist*, 16 (2): 245–68.

Chapter 17: Religion

Boyer, Pascal (2001), *Religion Explained: The Evolutionary Origins of Religious Thought*, New York: Basic Books.

Dubuisson, Daniel (2003), *The Western Construction of Religion: Myths, Knowledge, and Ideology*, trans. William Sayers, Baltimore, MD: Johns Hopkins University Press.

Durkheim, Émile ([1912] 1995), *The Elementary Forms of Religious Life*, trans. Karen E. Fields, New York: The Free Press.

Guthrie, Stewart Elliott (1993), *Faces in the Clouds: A New Theory of Religion*, New York: Oxford University Press.

References

Hume, David ([1757] 1993), *Dialogues and Natural History of Religion*, ed. J. C. A. Gaskin, Oxford: Oxford University Press.

Malley, B. E. (1995), 'Explaining Order in Religious Systems', *Method and Theory in the Study of Religion*, 7 (1): 5–22.

McCutcheon, Russell T. (1997), *Manufacturing Religion: The Discourse on Sui Generis Religion and the Politics of Nostalgia*, New York: Oxford University Press.

Morgan, David (2021), *The Thing about Religion: An Introduction to the Material Study of Religions*, Chapel Hill, NC: University of North Carolina Press.

Otto, Rudolf ([1917] 1950), *The Idea of the Holy: An Inquiry into the Non-Rational Factor in the Idea of the Divine and Its Relation to the World*, 2nd edn, trans. John W. Harvey, London: Oxford University Press.

Radcliffe-Brown, A. R. (1952), *Structure and Function in Primitive Society: Essays and Addresses*, New York: The Free Press.

Schleiermacher, Friedrich ([1799] 1988), *On Religion: Speeches to Its Cultured Despisers*, trans. Richard Crouter, Cambridge: Cambridge University Press.

Shakespeare, William ([1604] 1992), *Hamlet*, Norton Critical Edition, 2nd edn, New York: W. W. Norton.

Smith, Jonathan Z. (1998), 'Religion, Religions, Religious', in Mark C. Taylor (ed.), *Critical Terms for Religious Studies*, 269–84, Chicago, IL: University of Chicago Press.

Tylor, Edward B. ([1871] 1920), *Primitive Culture: Researches into the Development of Mythology, Philosophy, Religion, Language, Art, and Custom*, London: John Murray and New York: G. P. Putnam's Sons.

Wach, Joachim (1958), *The Comparative Study of Religions*, ed. Joseph M. Kitagawa, New York: Columbia University Press.

Chapter 18: Secularization

Berger, P. L. (1967), *The Sacred Canopy*, Garden City, NY: Anchor Books.

Bruce, S. (2011), *Secularization: In Defence of an Unfashionable Theory*, Oxford: Oxford University Press.

Casanova, J. (1994), *Public Religions in the Modern World*, Chicago, IL: University of Chicago Press.

Chaves, M. (1994), 'Secularization as Declining Religious Authority', *Social Forces*, 72 (3): 749–74.

Finke, R. and Stark, R. (1988), 'Religious Economies and Sacred Canopies: Religious Mobilization in American Cities, 1906', *American Sociological Review*, 53 (1): 41–9.

Gauthier, F. (2020), '(What Is Left of) Secularization? Debate on Jörg Stolz's Article on Secularization Theories in the 21st Century: Ideas, Evidence, and Problems', *Social Compass*, 67 (2): 309–14.

Hadden, J. (1987), 'Toward Desacralizing Secularization Theory', *Social Forces*, 65 (3): 587–611.

Lee, L. (2012), 'Research Note: Talking about a Revolution: Terminology for the New Field of Non-religion Studies', *Journal of Contemporary Religion*, 27 (1): 129–39.

Stolz, J. (2020), 'Secularization Theories in the Twenty-first Century: Ideas, Evidence, and Problems. Presidential Address', *Social Compass*, 67 (2): 282–308.

Tschannen, Olivier (1991), 'The Secularization Paradigm: A Systematization', *Journal for the Scientific Study of Religion*, 30 (4): 395–415.

Wilson, Bryan (1982), *Religion in Sociological Perspective*, Oxford: Oxford University Press.

Wilson, Bryan ([1966] 2016), *Religion in Secular Society: Fifty Years On*, Oxford: Oxford University Press.

Chapter 19: Spirituality

Altglas, Véronique (2018), 'Spirituality and Discipline: Not a Contradiction in Terms', in V. Altglas and M. Wood (eds), *Bringing Back the Social into the Sociology of Religion*, 79–107, Leiden: Brill.

Bloom, William (2018), 'A New Vocational Qualification in Spirituality and Health', *Journal for the Study of Spirituality*, 8 (1): 91–6.

Browne, Kath, Sally R. Munt, Andrew K.T. Yip (eds) (2010). *Queer Spiritual Spaces: Sexuality and Sacred Places,* Abingdon: Ashgate.

Browne, Kath et al. (eds) (2010), *Queer Spiritual Spaces: Sexuality and Sacred Places*, London: Routledge.

Bruce, Steve (2017), *Secular Beats Spiritual: The Westernization of the Easternization of the West*, Oxford: Oxford University Press.

Carrette, Jeremy and Richard King (2004), *Selling Spirituality: The Silent Takeover of Religion*, London: Routledge.

Clot-Garrell, Anna and M. Griera (2019), 'Beyond Narcissism: Towards an Analysis of the Public, Political and Collective Forms of Contemporary Spirituality', *Religions*, 10 (579): 1–15.

Comte-Sponville, André (2008), *The Book of Atheist Spirituality: An Elegant Argument for Spirituality without God*, London: Bantam Press.

Dyrendal, Asbjørn (2015), 'Norwegian "Conspirituality": A Brief Sketch', in James R. Lewis (ed.), *Handbook of Nordic New Religions*, 268–90, Leiden: Brill.

Fedele, Anna and Kim Knibbe (eds) (2020), *Secular Societies, Spiritual Selves? The Gendered Triangle of Religion, Secularity and Spirituality*, London: Routledge.

Frederick, Thomas and Timothy Muldoon (2020), 'Ignatian Spirituality and Psychotherapy', *Journal of Psychology and Christianity*, 39 (1): 12–23.

Harvey, Graham (ed.) (2014), *Handbook of Contemporary Animism*, London: Routledge.

Heelas, Paul (2014), 'On Transgressing the Secular: Spiritualities of Life, Idealism, Vitalism', in Steven J. Sutcliffe and Ingvild S. Gilhus (eds), *New Age Spirituality: Rethinking Religion*, 66–83, London: Routledge.

Heelas, Paul and L. Woodhead (2005), *The Spiritual Revolution: Why Religion Is Giving Way to Spirituality*, Oxford: Blackwell.

Hunt, Cheryl (2011), 'Editorial'. *Journal for the Study of Spirituality*, 1 (1): 5–9.

Huss, Boaz (2014), 'Spirituality: The Emergence of a New Cultural Category and Its Challenge to the Religious and the Secular', *Journal of Contemporary Religion*, 29 (1): 47–60.

Jones, Cheslyn, G. Wainwright and E. Yarnold (eds) (1986), *The Study of Spirituality*, New York: Oxford University Press.

Kaldera, Raven (2009), *Hermaphrodeities: The Transgender Spirituality Workbook*, Hubbardston, MA: Asphodel Press.

Lau, Kimberly (2000), *New Age Capitalism: Making Money East of Eden*, Philadelphia, PA: University of Pennsylvania Press.

Lynch, Gordon (2017), *The New Spirituality: An Introduction to Progressive Belief in the Twenty-first Century*. London: I.B. Tauris.

Marwick, Arthur (1998), *The Sixties: Cultural Revolution in Britain, France, Italy and the United States, 1958–1974*, Oxford: Oxford University Press.

Mead, G. R. S. (1910), 'On the Track of Spirituality', in G. R. S. Mead (ed.), *Some Mystical Adventures*, 148–62, London: John M. Watkins.

Mercadante, Linda (2014), *Belief without Borders: Inside the Minds of the Spiritual but Not Religious*, New York: Oxford University Press.

Meylan, Nicholas (2017), *Mana: A History of a Western Category*, Leiden: Brill.

References

NHS (2021), *Spiritual Care Matters: An Introductory Resource for all NHS Scotland Staff*, Edinburgh: NHS Education for Scotland.

Parsons, William B. (ed.) (2018), *Being Spiritual but Not Religious: Past, Present, Future(s)*, Abingdon, UK and New York: Routledge.

Principe, Walter (1983), 'Toward Defining Spirituality', *Studies in Religion/Sciences Religieuses*, 12 (2): 127–41.

Redden, G. (2016), 'Revisiting the Spiritual Supermarket: Does the Commodification of Spirituality Necessarily Devalue It?', *Culture and Religion*, 17 (2): 231–49.

Rose, S. (2001), 'Is the Term "Spirituality" a Word that Everyone Uses, But Nobody Knows What Anyone Means by It?', *Journal of Contemporary Religion*, 16 (2): 193–207.

Smith, J. Z. (2002), 'Manna, Mana Everywhere and/~/~/~', in Nancy K. Frankenberry (ed.), *Radical Interpretation in Religion*, 188–212, Cambridge: Cambridge University Press.

Solomon, R. (2002), *Spirituality for the Sceptic: The Thoughtful Love of Life*, New York: Oxford University Press.

Sutcliffe, Steven J. (2004), 'Introduction: Qualitative Empirical Methodologies – An Inductive Argument', in S. Sutcliffe (ed.), *Religion: Empirical Studies – A Collection to Mark the 50th Anniversary of the British Association for the Study of Religions*, xvii–xliii, Aldershot: Ashgate.

Sutcliffe, Steven J. (2019), 'The Emics and Etics of Religion: What We Know, How We Know It and Why This Matters', in George D. Chryssides and Stephen E. Gregg (eds), *The Insider/Outsider Debate: New Perspectives in the Study of Religion*, 30–52, Sheffield: Equinox.

Tingay, Kevin (2000), 'Madame Blavatsky's Children: Theosophy and Its Heirs', in S. Sutcliffe and M. Bowman (eds), *Beyond New Age: Exploring Alternative Spirituality*, 37–50, Edinburgh: Edinburgh University Press.

Ward, Charlotte and David Voas (2011), 'The Emergence of Conspirituality', *Journal of Contemporary Religion*, 26 (1): 103–21.

Watts, Galen (2020), 'Making Sense of the Study of Spirituality: Late Modernity on Trial', *Religion*, 50 (4): 590–614.

Woodhead, Linda (2011), 'Spirituality and Christianity: The Unfolding of a Tangled Relationship', in Guiseppe Giordan and William H. Swatos (eds), *Religion, Spirituality and Everyday Practice*, 3–21, Dordrecht: Springer Netherlands.

Woodhead, Linda (2013), 'New Forms of Public Religion: Spirituality in Global Civil Society', in W. Hofstee and A. van der Kooij (eds), *Religion beyond Its Private Role in Modern Society*, 29–52, Leiden: Brill.

Zinnbauer, Brian J. et al. (1997), 'Religiousness and Spirituality: Unfuzzying the Fuzzy', *Journal for the Scientific Study of Religion*, 36 (4): 549–64.

Chapter 20: Superstition

Aquinas. T. (1920), *Summa Theologica*. I, 2nd rev. ed., trans. Fathers of the English Dominican Province, New Advent [Online] Available online: www.newadvent.org/summa/3092.htm (accessed 12 August 2021).

Campion, Nicholas (2022, forthcoming), 'The Universe and Human Destiny', in James Evans (ed.), *The Cultural History of the Universe*, vol. 6, London: Bloomsbury.

Catechism of the Catholic Church, 2003. Available online: www.vatican.va/archive/ENG0015/_INDEX.HTM (accessed 10 August 2021).

Chryssides, George D. (2021), 'Handling Things Unseen: Tactile Aspects of the Christian Faith', in C. Welch and A. Whitehead (eds), *Religion and Touch*, 253–75, Sheffield and Bristol: Equinox.

Hannegraaff, Wouter, J. (2016), 'Reconstructing "Religion" from the Bottom Up', *Numen*, 63: 576–605.

Josephson-Storm, Jason Ānanda (2006), 'When Buddhism Became a "Religion": Religion and Superstition in the Writings of Inoue Enryō', *Japanese Journal of Religious Studies*, 33 (1): 143–68.

Josephson-Storm, Jason Ānanda (2018), 'The Superstition, Secularism, and Religion Trinary: Or Re-Theorizing Secularism', *Method and Theory in the Study of Religion*, 30 (1): 1–20.

Ko-wu, Huang (2016), 'The Origin and Evolution of the Concept of Mixin (Superstition): A Review of May Fourth Scientific Views', *Chinese Studies in History*, 49 (2): 54–79.

Legislation.gov.uk. (n.d.), 'Fraudulent Mediums Act 1951'. Available online: www.legislation.gov.uk/ukpga/Geo6/14-15/33/enacted (accessed 10 August 2021).

Maslakova, Magdelena (2020), 'The New Regulation on Religious Affairs and Its Possible Impact on the Catholic Church in China', *Journal of Church and State*, 62 (3): 421–42.

Plate, S. B. (2012), 'The Skin of Religion: Aesthetic Mediations of the Sacred', *CrossCurrents*, 62 (2): 162–80.

O'Neil, Mary R. (1987), 'Superstition', in Lindsay Jones (ed.), *The Encyclopedia of Religion*, vol. 13, 8864–7, Farmington Hills, MI: Thomson Gale.

Oyediji A. Ayonrinde, Anthi Stefatos, Shadé Miller, Amanda Richer, Pallavi, Nadkarni, Jennifer She, Ahmad Alghofaily and Nomusa Mngoma (2021), 'The Salience and Symbolism of Numbers across Cultural Beliefs and Practice', *International Review of Psychiatry*, 33 (1–2): 179–88.

Chapter 21: Syncretism

Bastide, Roger (1970), 'Mémoire collective et sociologie du bricolage', *L' Année Sociologique*, 21: 65–108.

Castor, N. Fadeke (2017), *Spiritual Citizenship: Transnational Pathways from Black Power to Ifá in Trinidad*, Durham, NC and London: Duke University Press.

Dayan, Joan (2003), Querying the Spirit: The Rules of the Haitian lwa', in Allan Greer and Jodi Bilinkopf (eds), *Colonial Saints: Discovering the Holy in the Americas, 1500–1800*, 31–50, New York and London: Routledge.

Gilroy, Paul (1993), *The Black Atlantic: Modernity and Double Consciousness*, Cambridge: Harvard University Press.

Herskovits, Melville J. (1941), *The Myth of the Negro Past*, New York and London: Harper and Brothers.

Lévi-Strauss, Claude (1966), *The Savage Mind (La pensée sauvage)*, London: Weidenfeld and Nicolson.

Long, Charles H. (1986), *Signs, Symbols, and Images in the Interpretation of Religion*, Philadelphia: Fortress Press.

Chapter 22: Violence

Allen, N. (2020), 'Just War in the Mahābhārata', in N. Allen, *The Ethics of War*, 138–49, London: Routledge.

Ansell-Pearson, K. (1994), *An Introduction to Nietzsche as Political Thinker: The Perfect Nihilist*, Cambridge: Cambridge University Press.

References

Anter, A. (2019), 'The Modern State and Its Monopoly on Violence', in Edith Hanke, Lawrence
   Scaff, and Sam Whimster (eds), *The Oxford Handbook of Max Weber*, 227–36, Oxford: Oxford
   University Press.
Arendt, H. (1970), *On Violence*, Orlando FL: Houghton Mifflin Harcourt.
Augustine ([400] 1872), *Reply to Faustus the Manichaean*, trans. Richard Stothert, Christian
   Classics Ethereal Library. Available online: https://ccel.org/ccel/schaff/npnf104/npnf104.iv.ix.
   xxiv.html (accessed 21 December 2021).
Bell, R. M. (2014), *Holy Anorexia*, Chicago, IL: University of Chicago Press.
Dalai Lama and Thubten Chodron (2018), *Samsara, Nirvana, and Buddha Nature*, Somerville,
   MA: Wisdom Publications.
Dawkins, R., D. C. Dennett, S. Harris and C. Hitchens (2019), *The Four Horsemen: The
   Discussion that Sparked an Atheist Revolution*, London: Bantam.
Durkheim, E. ([1915] 2008), *The Elementary Forms of the Religious Life*, trans. J. W. Swain,
   London: George Allen and Unwin.
Fergusson, D. (2011), *Faith and Its Critics*, Oxford: Oxford University Press.
Girard, R. (2007), *Violence and the Sacred*, Durham: Duke University Press.
Hall, J. R. (2003), 'Religion and Violence: Social Processes in Comparative Perspective', in
   Michele Dillon (ed.), *Handbook of the Sociology of Religion*, 359–84. Cambridge: Cambridge
   University Press.
Jackman, M. R. (2001), 'License to Kill: Violence and Legitimacy in Expropriative Social
   Relations', in John T. Jost and Brenda Major (eds), *The Psychology of Legitimacy: Emerging
   Perspectives on Ideology, Justice, and Intergroup Relations*, 437–67, Cambridge: Cambridge
   University Press.
Joseph, J. (2017), 'Hegemony', in B. S. Turner (ed.), *The Wiley-Blackwell Encyclopedia of Social
   Theory*, 1–3, Chichester, UK: Wiley-Blackwell.
Lash, Scott, Paul Heelas and Paul Morris (1996), *Detraditionalization: Critical Reflections on
   Authority and Identity*, Oxford: Blackwell.
van der Veer, P. (2013), 'Nationalism and Religion', in John Breuilly (ed.), *The Oxford Handbook
   of the History of Nationalism*, 655–71, Oxford: Oxford University Press.
Varenne, J. (1989), *Yoga and the Hindu Tradition*, Delhi: Motilal Banarsidass.
Walzer, M. (1977), *Just and Unjust Wars: A Moral Argument with Historical Illustrations*, New
   York: Basic Books.
Yao, F. (2011), 'War and Confucianism', *Asian Philosophy*, 21 (2): 213–26.

Chapter 23: World religion

Almond, Philip C. (1988), *The British Discovery of Buddhism*, Cambridge: Cambridge University
   Press.
Chidester, David (2018), 'World Religions in the World', *Journal for the Study of Religion*, 31 (1):
   41–53.
Cotter, Christopher R. and Robertson, David G. (eds) (2016), *After World Religions:
   Reconstructing Religious Studies*, London: Routledge.
Dubuisson, Daniel (2003), *The Western Construction of Religion: Myths, Knowledge, and Ideology*,
   Baltimore, MD: The Johns Hopkins University Press.
Dubuisson, Daniel (2019), *The Invention of Religions*, Sheffield: Equinox.
Geaves, Ron (2014), 'Colonialism and Postcolonialism in the Study of Religion', in George D.
   Chryssides and Ron Geaves (eds), *The Study of Religion: An Introduction to Key Ideas and
   Methods*, 183–209, 2nd edn, London: Bloomsbury.

Harrison, Peter (1990), *'Religion' and the Religions in the English Enlightenment*, Cambridge: Cambridge University Press.

Josephson, Jason Ānanda (2012), *The Invention of Religion in Japan*, Chicago, IL: University of Chicago Press.

King, Richard (1999), *Orientalism and Religion*, London: Routledge.

Masuzawa, Tomoko (2005), *The Invention of World Religions*, Chicago, IL: The University of Chicago Press.

McCutcheon, Russell T. (1997), *Manufacturing Religion: The Discourse on Sui Generis Religion and the Politics of Nostalgia*, Oxford: Oxford University Press.

Müller, Friedrich Max (1867), *Chips from a German Workshop. Volume 1: Essays on the Science of Religion*, London: Longmans, Green & Co.

Müller, Friedrich Max (1907), *Natural Religion*, London: Longmans, Green & Co.

Murphy, Tim (2007), *Representing Religion: Essays in History, Theory and Crisis*, London: Equinox.

Owen, Suzanne (2011), 'The World Religions Paradigm: Time for a Change', *Arts & Humanities in Higher Education*, 10 (3): 253–68.

Smith, Jonathan Z. (1998), 'Religion, Religions, Religious', in Mark C. Taylor (ed.), *Critical Terms for Religious Studies*, 269–84, Chicago, IL: The University of Chicago Press.

Smith, Wilfred Cantwell (1991), *The Meaning and End of Religion*, Minneapolis, MN: Fortress Press.

Sun, Anna (2013), *Confucianism as a World Religion: Contested Histories and Contemporary Realities*, Princeton, NJ: Princeton University Press.

Taira, Teemu (2016), 'Doing Things with "Religion": Discursive Approach in Rethinking the World Religions Paradigm', in Christopher R. Cotter and David G. Robertson (eds), *After World Religions: Reconstructing Religious Studies*, 75–91, London: Routledge.

Tiele, Cornelius Petrus (1877), *Outlines of the History of Religion to the Spread of the Universal Religions*, London: Trübner and Co.

Chapter 24: Worship

Boyd, Stacy C. (2016), *Black Men Worshipping: Intersecting Anxieties of Race, Gender, and Christian Embodiment*, New York: Palgrave Macmillan.

Bradney, Anthony (2014), 'Legal Issues', in George D. Chryssides, and Benjamin E. Zeller (eds), *The Bloomsbury Companion to New Religious Movements*, 179–93, London: Bloomsbury.

Budden, Chris (2011), *Following Jesus in Invaded Space: Doing Theology on Aboriginal Land*, Cambridge: James Clarke & Co.

Buggeln, Gretchen, Crispin Paine and S. Brent Plate (2017), 'Introduction: Religions in Gretchen Buggeln', in Crispin Paine, and S. Brent Plate (eds), *Museums, Museums as Religion, Global and Multidisciplinary Perspectives*, 1–8, London: Bloomsbury.

Clark, Jawanza E. (2012), *Indigenous Black Theology: Towards an African-centered Theology of the African-American Religious Experience*, New York: Palgrave Macmillan.

Davies, Douglas (1994), 'Introduction: Raising the Issues', in Jean Holm with John Bowker (eds), *Worship*, 1–8, London: Pinter.

Eliade, Mircea (ed.) (1987), *The Encyclopedia of Religion*, New York: Collier Macmillan.

Ellwood, Robert (2008), *Introducing Japanese Religion*, New York: Routledge.

Frazer, James G. ([1890] 1922), *The Golden Bough: A Study in Magic and Religion*, New York: Macmillan.

Harvey, Graham (ed.) (2000), *Indigenous Religions: A Companion*, London: Cassell.

Hoffman, Lawrence A. (1987), 'Worship and Cultic Life', in Mircea Eliade (ed.), *The Encyclopedia of Religion*, vol. 15, 445–7, New York: Macmillan.

References

Holm, Jean, with John Bowker (eds) (1994), *Worship*, London: Pinter.

Jaffer, Adam (2016), 'Ganesha in Birmingham', *Birmingham Museums*, 10 October. Available online: www.birminghammuseums.org.uk/blog/posts/ganesha-in-birmingham (accessed 13 September 2021).

Liew, Tat-Siong B. and Fernando F. Segovia (eds) (2018), *Colonialism and the Bible: Contemporary Reflections from the Global South*, Lanham, MD: Lexington Books.

Majupuria, Indra and Patricia Roberts (2007), *Kumari: Living Virgin Goddess*, Bangkok: Craftsman Press.

Martin, Lee R. (ed.) (2016), *Towards a Pentecostal Theology of Worship*, Cleveland, TN: CPT Press.

Öhman, Carl, Robert Gorwa and Luciano Flordi. (2019), 'Prayer-bots and Religious Worship on Twitter: A Call for a Wider Research Agenda', *Minds and Machines*, 29: 331–8.

Rudy, Kate (2011), *Virtual Pilgrimages in the Convent: Imagining Jerusalem in the Late Middle Ages*, Turnhout, Belgium: Brepols.

Smart, Ninian (1972), *The Concept of Worship*, London: Macmillan.

Tinker, George T. (2008), *American Indian Liberation: A Theology of Sovereignty*, Maryknoll, NY: Orbis.

Tovey, Phillip (2004), *Inculturation of Christian Worship: Liturgy, Worship and Society*, Aldershot, UK: Ashgate.

Tylor, Edward B. (1871), *Primitive Culture: Researches into the Development of Mythology, Philosophy, Religion, Art and Custom*, 2 vols., London: John Murray.

Ward, Pete (2020), *Celebrity Worship*, London: Routledge.

Warrior, Robert A. (1996), 'Canaanites, Cowboys, and Indians, Deliverance, Conquest, and Liberation Theology Today', in James Treat (ed.), *Natives and Christians*, 93–104, New York: Routledge.

Wolff, Richard F. (1999), 'A Phenomenological Study of In-Church and Televised Worship', *Journal for the Scientific Study of Religion*, 38 (2): 219–35.

Yao, Xinzhong (1994), 'Chinese Religions', in Jean Holm with John Bowker (eds), *Worship*, 159–71, London: Pinter.

Chapter 25: Concepts in practice

Carter, Anne (2021), 'Thailand's Fusion of Religious Beliefs: Buddhism, Animism and Brahmanism', *The Thaiger*, 23 March. Available online: https://thethaiger.com/news/national/thailands-fusion-of-religious-beliefs-buddhism-animism-and-brahmanism (accessed 17 September 2021).

Chryssides, George D. (1988), 'Buddhism Goes West', *World Faiths Insight*, New Series 20, October: 37–45.

Josephson-Storm, Jason Ānanda (2006), 'When Buddhism Became a "Religion": Religion and Superstition in the Writings of Inoue Enryō', *Japanese Journal of Religious Studies*, 33 (1): 143–68.

Masson, Joseph (1977), *The Noble Path of Buddhism*, Milton Keynes, UK: The Open University Press.

Prothero, Stephen (1996), *The White Buddhist: The Asian Odyssey of Henry Steel Olcott*, Bloomington and Indianapolis, IN: Indiana University Press.

Smith, Jonathan Z. (1998), 'Religion, Religions, Religious', in Mark Taylor (ed.), *Critical Terms for Religious Studies*, 269–84, Chicago, IL and London: The University of Chicago Press.

Spiro, Melford E. (1970), *Buddhism and Society: A Great Tradition and Its Burmese Vicissitudes*, New York: Harper and Row.

INDEX

Adventism 28, 103
Africa 35–6, 59, 129–33, 149
American Academy of Religion 59
Amritanandamayi, Mata 54
Anabaptists 16
animism 61, 84, 120, 148–9, 155, 156
anthropology 11, 22, 49, 59, 70, 77, 94, 149
anthroposophy 82
anticult movement 55, 156
apostasy 22
Appleby, R. Scott 45, 47
Aquinas, Thomas 100, 125
Arendt, Hannah 137
Aristotle 76–7
Ashcraft, W. Michael 27–8, 31
astrology 10, 81, 87, 89, 124
atheism 10, 70, 112, 138
Augustine 15, 125, 136, 138
authenticity 5, 7, 19, 58, 60, 95, 125–6, 131, 148, 155–8

Bach, Marcus 28
Bailey, Alice 81–2
Bainbridge, W.S. 11–12, 29
Barker, Eileen 18m 23, 29, 88
Bastide, Roger 131–2
Batson, C. Daniel 11
Bauder, Kevin 49
Bebbington, D.W. 45–6
Beckford, James 88
Beecher, Henry Ward 45, 48
belief 6, 9–13, 30, 41, 43, 65, 75, 106, 114, 149
Bellah, Robert 77–8
Belter, Ronald 12, 119
Bennett, Gillian 12
Bereza, Sarah 48–9
Berger, Peter L. 112–13, 115
bhakti 52–3
Bible 5, 45, 47, 49, 100, 102, 150
    Hebrew 65, 93, 102, 147
    New Testament 9, 33, 69, 119
Blavatsky, H.P. 18, 119
Bok, Bart J. 11
Bourdieu, Pierre 17
Bowman, Marion 154, 157
Boyer, Pascal 105
Brah, Avtar 33

brainwashing 7, 25, 31, 51, 55
Branch Davidians 70
Brazil 130, 132
Bremmer, J.N. 63–4
bricolage 131–3, 155
Brinkmann, Erwin U. 12
Bromley, David 18, 24, 30, 154
Bruce, Steve 83, 84, 111–12, 115, 120
Buddha 48, 55, 93, 139, 150, 153
Buddhism 7, 45, 62, 90, 117, 126, 139, 142–3, 150, 153–8
    fundamentalist 48
    Japanese 123, 126, 127, 155, 158
    Theravada 153–6
    Tibetan 89
    Western 90, 155–8
    Zen 1, 89, 157

calendar customs 40, 42
Campbell, Colin 29
Candomblé 132
Castor, Fadeke 133
Celts 41, 130
channelling 100
charisma 1, 15–20, 23, 31, 52, 54, 61, 84, 101
China 1, 70, 77, 126, 138, 148
Christian Identity 71
Christianity 9, 12, 15–18, 70, 83, 90, 94, 106, 129–30, 143–4
    fundamentalist 45–9, 123
    Orthodoxy 35, 94
    Protestantism 16, 28–9, 41, 45–9, 112–13, 125–6, 143
    Roman Catholicism 12, 28, 65, 94, 96, 117, 123, 125, 131–3
Chryssides, George 1, 18, 28, 70, 103, 123
Clarke, Peter 88
Clifford, James 33, 61
climate change 60
Codrington, Richard 120
cognitive dissonance 99
Cohen, Erik 94–5
Cohen, Robin 33
Cohn, Norman 69–70
colonialism 5, 58–60, 130, 133, 147–8
colonization 57, 143, 147, 158
Communism 70, 73, 112, 126

Index

Confucianism 74, 91, 126, 138, 142, 148
conversion 21–5, 45, 48, 91, 94, 153
Copeman, Jacob 51
Covid 48, 150
Cowan, Douglas E 30
Cox, James 59
Crawford, Dan 47
creeds 9, 90 106, 109, 147
cult 1, 7, 27–31, 51, 55, 87, 91, 158
cultic milieu 29, 84

Daoism 1, 91, 126, 142
Davies, Douglas 149
Dawkins, Richard 138
Dayan, Joan 131
De Martino, Ernesto 66
decolonization 59, 61
deprogramming 23, 25
deviancy 24, 28–31
Dharmapala, Anagarika 155
diaspora 7, 33–7, 59, 133, 148, 153–4, 156, 158
Digance, Justine 95
Dittes, James 11
Dixon, A.W. 46
Donald, Merlin 77
Drews, Paul 42
Druids 41, 42, 124
Dubuisson, Daniel 106, 143
Durkheim, Émile 64, 84, 108, 136, 139, 157

Eade, John 94
Ellwood, Robert 22, 73, 88, 150
Enlightenment 9, 63, 65, 106, 125
Enryō, Inoue 126, 155
Erasmus 129
esotericism 52, 63, 82,85, 91, 96
ethnicity 2, 4, 33, 35, 66, 142
ethnography 106, 118, 119
Evangelicalism 31, 35, 45–9, 90, 101, 117, 157
exorcism 23, 124, 126, 127, 155
extraterrestrials 70, 99

Falwell, Jerry 49
Family Action Information and Rescue 87, 91
Family Radio movement 71
fasting 139
Fedele, Anna 118
feminism 2, 65–6
Fergusson, David 138
Festinger, Leon 99–100, 102
fieldwork 4, 11, 41, 43, 66, 118, 120
Findhorn 119
Finke, Roger 29, 31, 115
Finucane, Juliana 48
Flood, Gavin 52
folklore 40–3

Francis of Assisi 16
Frazer, James 64, 149
Freud, Sigmund 55
fundamentalism 45–9, 123

Galanter, Marc 30
Ganesha 127, 149, 156
Garvey, Marcus 35
gender 2, 4, 42, 60, 61, 66, 85, 118, 148, 154
ghosts 39, 123–4, 154
Gilhus, Ingvild 82–3, 85
Gilroy, Paul 33, 35, 133
Girard, Rene 137
Glick, Peter 10
globalization 35, 56, 82, 139–40
glossolalia 15, 18
Gollob, Harry F. 11
Gomme, George Lawrence 40
Graham, Billy 47
Greenwood, Susan 66
gurus 1, 6, 51–6, 84, 100, 156
Guthrie, Stewart 105
Gyatso, Kelsang 18

Hadden, Jeffrey 114
Haiti 126, 131–2
Hall, Stuart 33
Hanegraaff, Wouter 81, 124–5
Hartney, Christopher 60, 61
Harvey, Graham 9, 120, 149
healing 15, 29, 41–2, 89, 96, 123–4, 127, 133, 150, 154–5
Heaven's Gate 2, 70
Heelas, Paul 82, 83, 114–15, 118–20, 121
higher criticism 46
Hinduism 5, 35, 48, 51–4, 90, 139, 142, 143, 150, 155–6
Hofstadter, Richard 46–7
Hornsby-Smith, Michael 12
Human Potential 82, 117
Hume, David 105, 157
Huss, Boaz 118

Ikegame, Aya 51
indigenous religion 39, 40–1, 57–62, 85, 94, 124, 129–30, 142, 149, 158
Internet 84, 150
Isidore of Seville 99
ISKCON (International Society for Krishna Consciousness) 88, 89
Islam 3–4, 35, 39, 45, 49, 59, 96, 135, 142–3, 148
Iwamura, Jane 51, 54

Japan 83, 89, 126, 138, 144
Jehovah's Witnesses 28, 70, 87, 89, 90, 99, 103
Jesus Christ 15, 45, 55, 71, 72, 81, 101–3, 137, 150

Jevons, Frank 10
Johnson, Paul Christopher 36
Jones, Bob 47
Joose, Paul 118
Josephson-Storm, Jason Ānanda 126, 155
Judaism 34, 45, 70, 76, 112, 126, 130, 142, 148, 155
Jung, Carl 55

Kabir 53
Kaplan, Uri 29, 74
Khmer Rouge 70, 73
King, Martin Luther 47
Klin-Oron, Adam 82
Knibbe, Kim 118
Knott, Kim 153
Ko-wu, Huang 126
Kumari 149–50
Kumbha Mela 93

Landes, Richard 72–3
Lanternari, Vittorio 28
Latin America 129–30
Laws, Curtis Lee 46–7
Lévi-Strauss, Claude 78, 120–1, 131–2
Levitt, Peggy 36–7
Lévy-Bruhl, Lucien 77–9
Lewis, James R. 82
LGBTQ+ community 65–6, 118
Lloyd, G.E.R. 79
Long, Charles 130–1
Lubbock, John 49
Lucia, Amanda J. 85

MacCannell, Dean 94–5
magic 10, 63–7, 112, 123, 125, 156
Mahesh Yogi, Maharishi 54
Malinowski, Bronislaw 64
mana 120–1
Marsden, G. 47
Marty, Martin E. 45, 47
Masuzawa, Tomoko 141
material culture 39, 41–2, 109
Maurice, F.D. 144
McCutcheon, Russell 109, 144
McIntire, Carl 47
McLoughlin, Sean 34–5
McPherson, Aimee Semple 101
McVeigh, Timothy 71
Mead, G.R.S. 119
meditation 23, 89, 90, 96, 118, 139, 154
mediums 100, 124, 126–7
Melton, J. Gordon 82, 88, 102
messiah 70–2, 102–3
migration 33–7, 113
millennialism 69–74, 81, 118
Miller, Timothy 89

Millerism 28, 71
mission 34, 35 129, 142, 145, 155, 157
Mlecko, Joel D. 51
modernity 45, 47, 61, 65, 77, 82,84, 112,
    117, 136–7
Moon, Sun Myung 18
Mormonism 28, 30, 46, 48, 98, 90
Müller, Friedrich Max 120, 142, 143–4
museums 5–6, 149
Myers, David 10
myth 2, 34, 61, 75–9, 154

nationalism 71, 139–40
nativist 71–2, 74
Needleman, Jacob 88, 89
Nelson, Geoffrey 88
New Age 6, 11, 23, 42, 60, 81–5, 91, 117, 158
new religious movements 7, 18, 31, 58, 70, 81,
    87–91, 142, 156
New Thought 82, 88
Newcombe, Suzanne 84
Nietzsche, Friedrich 137
Norman, Alex 96

Oakes, Len 18, 100–1
Olcott, Henry Steel 155–6
Oliver, Paul 30
Olupona, Jacob 59, 60
Otto, Rudolf 107

Paganism 4, 28, 41, 58, 65–6, 82, 83, 125,
    127, 142
paranormal 11
Park, Robert 10
Partin, Harry B 88
Partridge, Christopher 83
Paul the Apostle 15–19, 101, 119, 123
Pentecostalism 17, 18, 90, 101, 114
Peoples Temple 28, 30
pilgrimage 12, 42, 61, 93–7, 150
Plate, S. Brent 6, 127, 149
Plato 76
pluralism 112–13, 115
popular culture 51, 55, 73, 83, 84
Possamai, Adam 83
Potts, John 17–19
prayer 64, 74, 118, 125, 129, 132, 149, 150
Primiano, Leonard 39, 43
Principe, Walter 119
Prohl, Inken 83
prophecy 3, 15, 71, 99–103, 124
Prophet, Elizabeth Clare 19
Prophet, Erin 19
Protestantism 16, 28–9, 41, 45–9, 112–13,
    125–6, 143
psychology 10, 17, 27, 29, 30, 118

Index

QAnon 71
Quakers 15, 118

race 2, 148
Radcliffe-Brown, Alfred 108–9
radicalization 25, 139
Rajneesh 18, 51
Rastafari 35
rationalism 16, 39, 65, 123
rationalization 112, 137
Redles, David 73
Reformation 35, 88, 125
religion
    African 35, 59, 129–33, 149
    Chinese 1, 148, 157
    as concept 4–6, 9–10, 21, 24, 85, 89, 105–10, 141
    folk 1, 6, 39–43, 157, 158
    Greek and Roman 124
    indigenous 39, 40–1, 57–62, 85, 94, 124,
        129–30, 142, 149, 158
    lived 7, 12, 39, 41–3, 59, 61–2, 109, 124, 156–8
    vernacular 12, 43, 62, 84, 124, 154, 157–8
    world 2, 3, 141–5, 157–8
revelation 99–100, 107, 155
Revelation, Book of 69, 72–3
Rice, Tom 11
rites of passage 89, 94
rituals 13, 23, 34, 56, 67, 126, 138–40, 150–1, 155
    reversal rituals 23, 25
Roof, Wade Clark 11
Roman Catholicism 12, 28, 65, 94, 96, 117, 123,
    125, 131–3
Rountree, Kathryn 66
Ruah-Midbar, Marianna 82
Russell, Charles Taze 18, 46
Ryle, Gilbert 13

Sallnow, Michael 94
salvation 34, 69–74, 93, 112–13, 156
santeria 129, 132
sants 53
satguru 53
scepticism 10
Schiffer, Irvine 17
Schleiermacher, Friedrich 107
Schlesinger, Arthur 17
Schmidt, Bettina 155
Schwitzgebel, Eric 9
science 10, 13, 63–4, 77–8, 105, 112, 126, 136
Scientology 28, 88, 89, 90
Scopes Trial 47
Second Coming 71, 72, 81, 100
secularism 111–12
secularization 49, 84, 111–15, 121
Shakerism 28
shamanism 67, 100

Shankar, Sri Sri Ravi 54
Shinto 4, 126, 138, 142
Sikhism 4, 6, 34, 35, 53, 90, 142
slavery 33, 35, 129–32
Smart, Ninian 34–5
Smith, Huston 144
Smith, J.Z. 5, 108–9, 120–1, 158
Smith, Joseph 18, 101
Smith, William Robertson 109
Snyder, Mark 10
sociology 17–18, 29, 83–4, 100, 112, 115, 118
Spiritualism 28, 29, 87, 88
spirituality 1, 41, 61, 88, 114–15, 117–21, 124,
    153, 157
    New Age 81–5
Spiro, Milford 157
Stark, Rodney 10–12, 29, 31, 115
Stewart, Lyman and Milton 46
Stoddard, Robert H. 93, 95
Storr, Anthony 55
Sufis 35, 60, 89, 139, 148
Sunday, Billy 46
superstition 7, 10, 64, 112, 123–8, 155–6, 158
Sutcliffe, Steven 81–5, 87, 118, 119
syncretism 1, 3, 41, 128–33, 148, 154–5, 158

Taira, Teemu 142, 144, 145
television 150
Thailand 48, 153–4, 156
theology 5, 6, 15, 17, 42, 35, 59, 94, 125, 136
Theosophy 28, 81–2, 87, 88, 119, 155
Tiele, Cornelius P. 141–2
Torrey, R.A. 46
tourism 93–6
    spiritual 93, 96
Tovey, Philip 148
Tower, Daniel 60
Toy, C.H. 64
Transcendental Meditation 28, 54, 98
Troeltsch, Ernst 29
Trump, Donald 27, 71–2
Tucker, Robert 17
Turner, Harold W. 87
Turner, Victor and Edith 94, 96
Tweed, Thomas 37
Tylor, Edward 10, 40, 64, 77, 106, 149
typology 23, 29, 33, 95, 102

Unification Church 18, 28, 88, 89, 90
Unitarians 88–9
United Nations 57
United States 27, 28, 36–7, 49, 65, 88–9, 90, 114,
    132–3, 135

Vedas 52–4
vegetarianism 156

Ventris, W. Larry 11
vernacular religion 12, 43, 62, 84, 124, 154, 157–8
Vertovec, Steve 35–6
violence 2, 4, 48, 135–40, 158
Vipassana 88, 156
Virgin Mary 27, 129, 139, 132
Vodou (Voodoo) 28, 35, 131–2

Wach, Joachim 107–8, 109
Walzer, Michael 138
War 33, 95, 135–8
    American Civil 45, 47
    Second World 88, 137, 138
    on Terror 135
Warrior, Robert A. 147
Weber, Max 15–19, 29, 54, 100–1, 112, 137, 139
Wesak 153, 157–8
Wessinger, Catherine 70–4
white supremacists 71, 74, 91
Whitehead, Amy 156
Wicca 42, 66, 91
Wilson, Bryan 17
Wilson, Colin 10

witchcraft 64–7, 125, 126
Wolff, Richard 150
Wood, Simon 49
Woodhead, Linda 83, 84,115, 118–20
Wolpe, Harold 17
World Council of Churches 90
world religion 2, 3, 141–5, 157–8
World Religions Paradigm 3, 6, 60, 83, 155, 156
World Trade Center 48
worldview 65, 72, 113
worship 4, 5, 17–18, 51, 126, 130–2, 147–51,
    157, 158
Worsley, Peter 17
Wuthnow, Robert 11

Yao, Xinzhong 138, 148
Yoder, Don 42
yoga 23, 52–3, 84, 87, 89, 96, 118, 139
York, Michael 83
Yoruba 57, 62, 129–31, 133

Zoroastrianism 3, 34, 80, 142
Zygmunt, Joseph F. 99